Bodily Sensibility

Series in Affective Science

Series Editors
Richard J. Davidson
Paul Ekman
Klaus Scherer

Bodily Sensibility: Intelligent Action

Jay Schulkin

UNIVERSITY PRESS

2004

OXFORD
UNIVERSITY PRESS

Oxford   New York
Auckland Bangkok Buenos Aires Cape Town Chennai
Dar es Salaam Delhi Hong Kong Istanbul Karachi Kolkata
Kuala Lumpur Madrid Melbourne Mexico City Mumbai Nairobi
São Paulo Shanghai Taipei Tokyo Toronto

Copyright © 2004 by Oxford University Press, Inc.

Published by Oxford University Press, Inc.
198 Madison Avenue, New York, New York 10016

www.oup.com

Oxford is a registered trademark of Oxford University Press

Library of Congress Cataloging-in-Publication Data
Schulkin, Jay
  Bodily sensibility : intelligent action / Jay Schulkin.
      p. cm.—(Series in affective science)
   Includes bibliographical references and index.
   ISBN 0-19-514994-7
     1. Mind and body.   2. Cognition.   3. Human information processing.
   I. Title. II. Series.
   BF161 .S3512 2003
   150—dc21   2002011554

9 8 7 6 5 4 3 2 1

Printed in the United States of America
on acid-free paper

Dedicated to three friends:

Patrick Heelan

Nora Peck

Alan Questel

Preface

On occasion (and sometimes often) in this book I disagree with friends and colleagues; I hope the tone is respectful. I certainly mean it that way. To disagree is not to disrespect, and there are conceptual issues where I do disagree with a number of my friends and colleagues. For those not acknowledged in the work, I apologize in advance.

I am indebted to my colleagues. The lifeblood of the mind and its enjoyment are in the bonds that are formed, the engaged conversations, the experiments and the help extended. I thank my family, particularly my wife, April Oliver, my mother, Rosalind Schulkin, my children, Danielle and Nick, and my friends for their constant support and encouragement. I also want to thank my colleagues for providing me with the most excellent intellectual community.

Contents

Bodily Sensibility

Introduction

Some intellectual traditions have rendered the body as dumb and inert, or as the seducer of reason and temperance. Others have elevated it beyond reason. A middle ground is surely more reflective of our current understanding of the mind-body interplay, a mind integrated within a body, adapting in concert to changing circumstances, directing the organism to approach or avoid the objects and people around it. Information-processing systems are pervasive in the central nervous system and are inherently part of the body's sensibility. This seems such obvious, common sense. Yet what lingers still is an insidious separation of cognition from the bodily sensibilities, often so ingrained that it goes unnoticed or trivialized.

This text reflects my philosophical orientation (pragmatism), my orientation to the cognitive sciences, and my scientific investigations and interests (psychobiology). Some of us have inhabited intellectual traditions in which the mind was not separate from the body, in which diverse dualisms were not embraced, and where cognition was not separate from basic bodily action.

The early classical pragmatists—Peirce, James, Dewey, Mead—imbued with a biological perspective emphasized behavioral/cognitive adaptation. Whereas James exaggerated and mistakenly identified the emotions with bodily consciousness, the emphasis is on engagement with the world in problem solving. Cognitive systems are at the root of problem solving.

Cognitive systems can appear perfunctory or intimate, calculating a sum or selecting a mate. It is this latter category of function, in particular, where bodily sensibility and visceral information processing are vital for successful problem solving . Many of the examples provided in this text reflect the tradition of regulatory physiology and psychobiology (gustatory hedonics;

appetites and aversions to fluids, minerals, and food sources; the regulation of the internal milieu; approach and avoidance of people and other species; pleasure; behavioral adaptation). These are all bodily events in which visceral and emotional representations are vital to the organization of action. The brain is by its nature a cognitive device.

In chapter 1, I suggest that the body as opposed to the mind has too often been rendered inert, dumb, and fixed, and mind has been elevated in rationalistic space. The tradition in which behavior serves in the regulation of the internal milieu emphasizes the role of visceral information, for example, as essential for successful problem solving, whether to approach or avoid an object (eat something or not). There is no Cartesian seduction or separation of mind from body. Adaptation and information processing are part of the evolutionary arms race. The anatomical revolution demonstrated that visceral information traverses the neural axis. Cortical and brainstem sites revealed that direct anatomical and functional connectivity and visceral information processing is vital for adaptive behaviors. Moreover, recent work in human cognitive neuroscience reveals the extent to which the visceral/autonomic systems are vital for successful problem solving, and cognitive systems traverse the range of central neural function. Cognition is not just confined to *cortical* function.

In chapter 2, I defend the view that demythologizing the emotions is placing them in a biological context of problem solving—*good enough* adaptive systems.[1] Rather than viewing the emotions as a bodily burden to be borne, the emotions are great sources of information and information processing. In my view, all emotions are cognitive, but not all cognitive systems are emotional. There are core emotions that underlie our adaptive responses. One rich source of information is the facial response to events. The facial taxonomic responses emitted reflect whether the organism is going to ingest or reject a food source. Underlying these approach and avoidance behavioral responses are biological needs and a social or ecological context. A core visceral/autonomic nervous system underlies facial/emotional expression and processing of information.

In chapter 3, I suggest that underlying the experience of aesthetics in at least some instances is the interplay between expectation and disappointment from its infraction. Syntactical expectations, for example, contribute to musical sensibility (Meyer, 1973). Regions of the brain that underlie syntax in language, in addition to other regions of the brain, also underlie musical syntactical expectations and their violation (Broca's area). Probabilistic reasoning, linked to expectation, learning, or information processing, is fundamental to several regions of the brain. One major neurotransmitter linked to expectations and their violations and the rewarding value of events is dopamine, a neurotransmitter that underlies the structure of action and the structure of thought.

In chapter 4, I suggest that repulsion and attraction to the cries and joys of others underlies moral responsiveness. The approach and avoidance behavioral mechanisms that underlie moral delight and revulsion may have bootstrapped on some elementary mechanisms (the gustatory system, described in chapter 2) of approach and avoidance linked to, for example, gustatory disgust (revulsion) and attraction (e.g., the innate protective mechanisms of olfactory/gustatory disgust to putrefied meat have been usurped or borrowed for moral sensibility; Rozin, 1999). Recognizing the states of others, or disregarding them, using them to our advantage or not, is a feature that stands out about us humans, but perhaps is not unique to us. Moral approach or revulsion, rapid moral judgments, may reflect the activation of sets of neurons in the neocortex, in addition to other regions of the brain (amygdala, striatum).

In chapter 5, I discuss some key features in the organization of drive and motivation and its representation in the brain. Curiosity has often been construed as a drive state (e.g., James, 1890/1952). Indeed, curiosity often arises when expectations are noted and the search for a solution emerges as a perceived information need (Loewenstein, 1994). But we also come prepared to recognize a wide variety of objects despite the fact that there is no need or particular drive state (e.g., what is associated with sodium, distinguishing animate from inanimate objects) in the context of cognitive devices that provide coherence in the organization of action.

In the conclusion, I reiterate the fact that bodily sensibility is intertwined with problem solving of a type that is close up and dominant. The alternative view is that of inert bodies, of disembodied minds, of noncognitive emotions, aesthetics, and morals construed in the context of bodily responses. Cephalic organization of bodily sensibility in the organization of action, as selected by evolution, reflects fast appraisal systems that are fundamental for successful problem solving. Key features of this are found in emotional appraisals, aesthetic judgment, moral sensibility, and our drive and the satisfaction that we derive from our explanations of events. The brain is a cognitive organ, and regions of the brain that traverse brainstem and cortical sites are embodied by bodily sensibility.

All of the above claims are taken in the spirit of their being understood in a historical context, hypothetical and not dogmatic in scope, and building on the important insights of many other investigators. There is a rich tradition in psychobiology that stretches back to James and Dewey and reaches into Richter, Rozin, and Stellar in which the mind and body were never separate—no Cartesian fallacy.

1

Bodily Representations, Behavior, and the Brain

Introduction

The great biological revolution beginning in the 19th century demythologized the body and placed it in nature: Adaptive, diverse, majestic in shape, these are all appropriate descriptions of the phenomenal body in nature. Intelligence could only mean, from Darwin's perspective, adaptation. According to Darwin, intelligence takes on many forms and shapes, including that of the body serving as a vessel for problem solving. All those millennia and generations of evolving produced animals with internal as well as external adaptations to their environment that promote their survival.

The Darwinian revolution rendered bodies beautiful and ugly and utterly adaptive and oriented to problem solving. Bodies are intelligent, not inert dumb brutes. Of course, the range of adaptation in the body reflects an evolutionary order, but then bodies could only go so far. Running fast, having big teeth, camouflage—as these physical features evolve, so does another piece of the puzzle: the brain.

Darwin understood that point. What he did not know is that neural innervations of the peripheral organs are the rule, not the exception (see below). The body is an active entity adapting to its surroundings. It may be limited, and it may not survive, but it is not passive in the struggle to survive. The Darwinian revolution concerns the multitude of ways in which bodies, including their brains—the head ganglia of the body—adapt to and in some cases (ours) expand our horizons.

In this chapter, I examine several information-processing systems that serve the animal (visceral mechanisms linked to approach and avoidance of objects that they encounter). These visceral information-processing sys-

7

tems are sources of cognitive physiology. Moreover, as this chapter argues, bodily sensibility is well represented in the brain; the cortex is linked to the brainstem in one synapse, and this fast-acting input figures in problem solving.

Bodily Representations and the Brain

The study of the brain, and other end organ systems, is the study of biological function. The cognitive mechanisms that permeate neural function are a cardinal piece of biological function and biological adaptation. Cognitive mechanisms cut across the wide range of behavioral expressions that we emit, that we experience, and for which we strive. There are different kinds of information-processing systems (quite a number of them), but there are no systems in the brain, or systems informing the brain, that are not a part of the cognitive architecture. In other words, all aspects of brain involvement require cognitive processing.

When we are referring to information-processing systems as they reflect the actions of the brain, we start to refer to cognitive systems. The problem for some is this: What is not cognitive? I am not talking about the kidney or the heart or the liver or the skin in isolation. I am talking about the information processing that takes place in the brain. In other words, bodily sensibility is cephalic in origin. One feature of cephalic involvement is its prominence in the regulation of visceral and autonomic physiology (Schulkin, 2003; Sterling & Eyer, 1988).

Bodily sensibility reflects the myriad ways in which the brain is involved in information processing: emotional, aesthetic, and moral. I want to emphasize the fact that cognitive systems are pervasive to who we are. There are many kinds of cognitive systems; there is no one canonical exemplar that captures the plethora of cognitive systems. Thus, cognitive systems are construed here in a broad sense; they underlie the anticipation and interpretation of events, memory, and specific and general problem solving (e.g., Goldman, 1979; Parrott & Schulkin, 1993).[1]

Not all of us are prone to Descartes' error, a mind divorced from a body—one variant of which is representations in the mind/brain divorced from visceral/autonomic input (Damasio, 1994, 1999). Perhaps another characterization would be "Descartes' tear"—leaving out bodily expression (figure 1.1). Cognitive science needed to include visceral/bodily sensibility. In fact, the tradition of psychobiology (e.g., Moran & Schulkin, 2000; Richter, 1942–1943, 1976) did not commit Descartes' Error; other errors were committed to be sure, but not that one. Within this tradition, visceral/autonomic input is an important source of information and essential in problem solving (Dewey, 1934/1968; Garcia, Hankins, & Rusiniak, 1974; Richter, 1976; Rozin, 1976a). The recognition of illness, the detection of desired substances, and gustatory hedonics were all part of the problem-solving arsenal.

Fig. 1.1. Descartes' tear (Yansen & Schulkin, 2002).

These issues are not abstract and distant. Representations of the heart, for example, in a number of functional contexts are computed throughout the neural axis. The concept of representation, like intelligence, cognition, mind, body, or theory, does not have one unequivocal meaning.

The integration of the cognitive revolution with that of the biological finally puts to rest the separation of mind and body; it does not denigrate the emotions as secondhand or as poor mechanisms in a coherent attempt to make sense of one's body's surroundings or to communicate to others. This is a major theme of this book. There is no reification of bodily sensibility, emotional, aesthetic, moral, or otherwise, or any other vehicle that serves successful adaptation.

Again, I do not believe that there is one definition of cognitive that captures the rich problem-solving abilities of the nervous system (cf. Gazzaniga, 2000; Parrott & Schulkin, 1993; Posner, 1990; Sternberg, 1999). The experimental orientation is to break down distinctions that tend to undercut inquiry and do a disservice to the body and to our conceptions of the mind. Bodily sensibility is about appraisal systems endemic to problem solving.

In the past, we have traditionally elevated cognition and denigrated the body. Cognition was rarified and the body vilified. We have now begun to demythologize cognition and place it, rightfully, in problem solving and adaptation, amid rough heuristics that subserve these events (Gigerenzer, 2000).

What is the alternative? The alternative has been detached mental representations, what Damasio alluded to in his *Descartes' Error*, namely, a science of the mind that construed the mind as representations divorced from bodily input and construing bodily representations as noncognitive reflexes. And there are investigators that still adhere to that view. But cognitive systems, I suggest, can indeed look very reflex-like in their speed and rigidity.

Cephalic Adaptative Systems

In the past fifty years, an important step toward understanding ourselves has been taken in the computational or cognitive sciences (Newell, 1990; Peirce, 1868a, 1868b; Simon, 1982; Turing,1950; Von Neuman, 1958/2000). Diverse forms of information processing are portrayed (Gazzaniga, 2000; Kosslyn, 1994; McClelland & Rumelhart, 1986; Posner, 1990) and are endemic to bodily functions.[2] As we have come to understand, the brain, in part, is a cognitive organ. It deciphers information and organizes behavioral responses, projecting future possibilities and expressing a wide variety of behavioral options, all varying with the species and the environmental context (Newel, 1990). From bug detectors in the brainstem (McCulloch, 1965/1988) to semantic networks linked to the neocortex (Martin & Caramazza, 2003), the brain is in the business of processing, utilizing, and organizing behavioral responses (Gazzaniga, 2000; Kosslyn, 1994; Posner, 1996).

But just as fixed action patterns should not exclusively define behavioral adaptations organized by the brain (e.g., Tinbergen, 1951/1969), they are nonetheless a common feature in behavioral adaptation. Both the behavioral adaptations and the mechanisms are diverse, not narrow. They are rich in expression (Allen & Bekoff, 1997; Hauser, 2000; Marler, 2000a).

One classical view that dominates but is mistaken and regurgitates reflexively is the following: Bodily pangs are an undifferentiated bit of matter to which the mind gives meaning, structure, and coherence. This view is old; the body is not just a stomachache. Even so, a stomachache is detected by mechanisms originating in the stomach (e.g., volume and stretch receptors) that convey signals to and from the vagus nerve, which then innervates brainstem structures (e.g., solitary nucleus parabrachial nuclei) and forebrain structures (amygdala, bed nucleus of the stria terminalis, insular cortex), which organize the behavioral responses (Norgren, 1995; Powley et al., 2001). Cephalic innervation of diverse peripheral systems is the rule, not the exception, in the organization of behavioral and physiological adaptation.

In fact, we now know that the central nervous system helps regulate peripheral organs (Schulkin, 2003; Sterling & Eyer, 1988). Earlier thinking in the field identified thought with the cortex,[3] with cognition or thought being something nonreflexive. But cognition can surely be reflexive (syntax, spatial perception, probability judgment), as can bodily responses. Moreover, the brain is essentially involved in both lower-level and higher-level appraisal and information-processing systems (e.g., Gazzaniga, 2000; Swanson, 2000a, 2003).

Identifying cognition with the cortex is the traditional trapping of the mind/body split. Structures on the bottom (to speak metaphorically) of the brain are low level, reflexive, and brute; structures on the top of the brain are free and nonreflexive. The mistake inherent in this approach lies in the dominant view of bodily sensibility as dumb and inert. This error is perhaps best expressed in the context of the emotions. Emotions are often characterized as only bodily changes.

This misleading and mistaken view held for James (see Cannon, 1927), and was expanded by a number of investigators (Mandler, 1990; S. Schacter, 1975; S. Schacter & Singer, 1962). James, it is well-known, asserted, "My heart beats fast; thus I know I am afraid." This bodily state must be interpreted: The bear is perceived and my body acts in a coordinated fashion to ensure, under most conditions, that I can stay out of harm's way. I either stay immobilized or run fast.

In reality, a variety of bodily reactions can appear when I see a bear. True, I am afraid, but I can be afraid of something and have an overt bodily reaction or not. The fear represents a central state of the brain: Peripheral input informs and sustains the central state of the brain. But the mechanisms that help generate the emotional response, the central brain state, are unconscious (e.g., LeDoux, 1996; Rosen & Schulkin, 1998). Moreover, a wide range of bodily sensibilities, such as those linked to preferences, reflect information processing in noncortical regions of the brain, including the nucleus accumbens and the parabrachial region (e.g., Berridge, 2000; Damasio, 1996, 1999). These reflect unconscious mechanisms that influence choices that are made. They are probably pervasive in reasoning. That is not to say that neocortical sites are not important in bodily sensibility, only that a wide range of information processing takes place without my conscious awareness of it. Freud was at least right about that (Kihlstrom, 1987; Kihlstrom, Mulvaney, Tobias, & Tobis, 2000).

Cognition, mistakenly, was placed on the mantle of the brain. In a beautiful, anatomically rich vision of the neural organization of basic behavioral functions, cognition is associated with the cortex (Saper, 1996; Swanson, 2000a, 2003).[4] This is shorthand; cognition is also often treated as synonymous with consciousness. The conscious mind is a corticalized human. Of course, the figure (figure 1.2) nicely depicts the inputs and outputs that are essentially related to the central state of thirst (Denton et al., 1996, 1999; Denton, McKinley, & Wessinger, 1996; Fitzsimons, 1979, 1998; Swanson, 2000a). I want to draw your attention to the cortex associated with cognition. The routine assumption is that consciousness, cortex, and cognition are

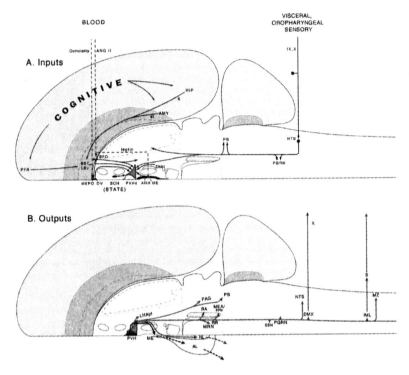

Fig. 1.2. It is the all too frequent assumption that the cortex depicted in the figure is the cognitive part of the brain (adapted from Swanson, 2000).

knotted together. But the thirst that generates a conscious cognitive problem-solving orientation is driven more from regions below the cortex (Denton et al., 1996, 1999), and many of the routine appraisal systems (where water is located, what time of day it might appear, what the water is associated with, in addition to the detection of water needs) are below the cortex (figure 1.2).

Even the bodily detection of thirst and the search for water to satisfy water demands are composed of multiple appraisal systems;[5] devices in the body are designed to detect, determine, and organize the behavioral and physiological responses in order to repair, maintain, and predict future water sources (Fitzsimons, 1998; Mistlberger, 1992). The important point concerning bodily sensibility is that both the low- and high-level appraisal systems work together toward survival. One has to recognize the need for water, recall where water might be found, generate search strategies to find water, and avoid predators and competitors.

As I elaborate throughout this book, cognitive systems are often not knotted to consciousness and the neocortex (see critiques by Berridge, 2000; LeDoux, 1996; Rosen & Schulkin, 1998). For example, appraisal systems in the brain that allow detection of signals (snake, harm, smiling faces, safety) are not necessarily accessible to consciousness. The systems linked to emotional appraisal are represented not just outside the neocortex (see chapter 2), just as the mechanisms that mediate traditional conceptions of cognition are not just neocortical. Moreover, a detection system can be incredibly low grade, recognizing one taste over another (salt or sweet), this facial expression over that (happy or sad), and so on. The mechanisms may or may not be conscious, are mediated by brainstem structures, and they certainly can be reflexive.

Cognitive systems reflect an orientation to events. They can be reflexive, as with face detection and imitation in neonates (Meltzoff & Moore, 1997). One feature of evolution and successful adaptation is the panoply of information processing in the brain, the various lenses that we have for seeing the object (Gigerenzer, 2000; Hanson, 1958; Popper, 1959). Thus, information-processing system networks, whether naturally or culturally derived, are richly coded in frameworks that allow inferences to be made easily (Lane & Nadel, 2000; G. I. Murphy, 2000, 2003). Reflexes do not render something noncognitive; this is the old pernicious split appearing between the mind free and distant and the body reflexive and obligatory (figure 1.3).

An orientation to events is rarely neutral (cf. Bruner, 1973; Hanson, 1958; Peirce, 1868, 1898/1992b; Wittgenstein, 1953). As one important thinker expressed with regard to perception, "Visual perception involves concep-

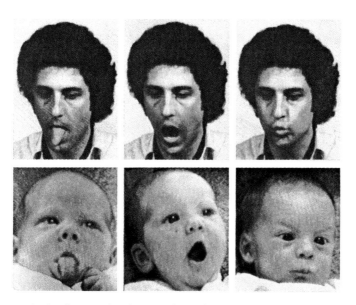

Fig. 1.3. Imitation is natural to humans from birth. Low-level appraisal systems underlie the imitative response to others. Meltzoff and Moore (1977) think that imitation helps infants make social contact with other humans. They argue that early imitation provides a very primitive foundation for later social cognition.

tual representation" (Sellars, 1968, p. 12). Information-processing systems are embedded in action and are not removed from discerning events in real time.

The remnants of the detached reasoner are to be traced back to Aristotle; the unmoved mover was the highest form of thought, and movement was a privation. These privations were linked to bodily sensibility, or to the passions. Inferences within appraisal systems, fast or slow, are not means of becoming detached and separating from others and the world. Quite the contrary, they are important information-processing systems by which we engage each other and the world (Dewey, 1925/1989).

Cephalic representations of events are anchored to perceptions that orient one in the world to which one is trying to adapt. Perception, while not identical to action, is obviously linked to action (Berthoz, 2000; Gibson, 1979; Kornblith, 1993; Reid, 1785/1969). One is oriented to objects and comes to an understanding of how to respond to them.

Behavioral systems are organized for approach and exploration and to avoid and reject objects. These systems are linked to bodily experiences, some good, some bad, and some neutral (Berridge, 2000; Maier & Schneirla, 1935/1964; Stellar & Stellar, 1985). Appraisal mechanisms are endemic to these behavioral systems (Scherer, Schorr, & Johnstone, 2001). Regulatory events impinge on ancient circuitry to generate behavioral options toward the world (Herrick, 1905, 1929; Richter, 1976) mediated by information-processing systems that range from maps of environments (Tolman, 1949) to the prediction of events in time (Gallistel, 1992), and their associations with events (Rescorla, 1990). Notably, cognitive processing is not something detached from bodily function, but is an essential part of reasoning processes in the brain.

We know enough to be able to envision the functional organization of autonomic, visceral, and somatic activity in the brain (Gallistel, 2000; W. R. Hess, 1957; Petrovich, Canteras, & Swanson, 2001; Swanson, 2000a). For example, columns of motor programs are designed to translate different kinds of behavioral states. The traditional motor systems beneath the neocortex (striatum) are linked to a variety of behavioral events (e.g., Graybiel, Aosaki, Flaherty, & Kimura, 1994; Linas, 2001; Nauta & Domesick, 1982; Saper, 1996), including the functional organization of the emotions (Berridge, 1996, 2003; Calder, Lawrence, & Young, 2001).

Bodily Responses and the Regulation of the Internal Milieu

When most animals eat, if they get visceral sickness, represented in the brain, they recall the resource and avoid the substance (Garcia et al., 1974). The learning is profound and phylogenetically ancient (Rozin, 1976b). A wide variety of species learn to associate a food they've eaten with subsequent sickness readily and over long time delays; the essential association is between the ingestion of a food source with particular gustatory characteristics and gastrointestinal milieu and discomfort (Garcia et al. 1974; Rozin, 1976b; figure 1.4). In fact, one prepared heuristic that many species display is a wariness of new food sources, or "bait shyness," as Curt Richter (1976; Rzoska, 1953) called this adaptive behavior. This specific adaptation is useful for distinguishing safe from unsafe food sources. This learning was dependent on visceral information reaching the brain and playing a fundamental role in the organization of action.

A variety of animals are prepared to draw causal links between events, to map causal relations (Dickinson, 1980; Gallistel, 2000).[6] Even within learning theory itself, an analysis of learning of associations has not been construed in terms of causal inference and has reached intellectual respectability within that community (Dickinson, 1980). The valuation of a food source is tied to appraisal systems and to motivational central states. Brainstem sites such as the parabrachial region are vital for the integration of visceral malaise following the ingestion of a food source (Flynn, Grill, Schulkin, & Norgren, 1991; Spector, Norgren, & Grill, 1992).[7]

Importantly, there are also constraints on specific learning systems: All stimuli are not equal (Rozin, 1976a, 1976b, 1998; Shettleworth, 1998). A wide variety of animals are prepared to associate visceral distress with food ingestion. For a rat, learning an association between food ingestion and illness is special and requires, at minimum, both taste and olfaction (Garcia et al., 1974). The learning of food source is rapid and long lasting.

Physiological regulation is replete with behavioral and physiological mechanisms that strive to maintain balance amid changing external conditions (Bernard, 1859; Cannon, 1916/1929; Richter, 1976). Both broad-based and local mechanisms work in unison to maintain internal stability; the mechanisms are anything but bestial (Denton et al, 1996; Fitzsimons, 1998).

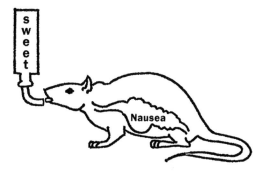

Fig. 1.4. The effects of pairing a gustatory cue with internal illness (adapted from Garcia et al., 1974).

There are a variety of cephalic mechanisms to minimize disturbances (Siegel & Allan, 1998; Woods, 1991) by both behavioral and physiological means. One mechanism of balance comprises the bodily enjoyments and aversions that figure in the orientation to objects. Nature holds that some bodily objects attract and some repulse; a large number are replete with both. Food sources are a good example (Rozin & Fallon, 1987). At one extreme are feces, which typically repulse, although not always. At the other extreme is the sight of ripe fruit, which consistently generates approach behaviors (figure 1.5). Being attracted to objects of nurturance and avoidant of harmful objects is a basic adaptation to the biological environment (see chapter 2).

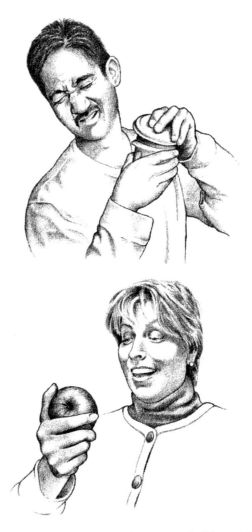

Fig. 1.5. Rejection and acceptance of food (Yansen & Schulkin, 2002).

At low to mid-levels of stimulation, objects can be attractive. At higher levels of sensory stimulation (sensory overload), they tend to be aversive (Berridge, 1996; Fox & Davidson, 1989; Schneirla, 1959; P. T. Young, 1959). Objects that provoke attraction or revulsion through bodily contact are mediated by cephalic systems (see table 1.1).

Schneirla's (1959) theoretical framework is a good example of the primacy of bodily sensibility in adaptation/regulation. Although I do not believe the data necessitated that there be one system for approach and one system for avoidance (see Cacioppo & Bernston, 1999; R. J. Davidson, Ekman, Saron, Senulis, & Friesen, 1990; R. J. Davidson, Putnam, & Larson, 2000; Stellar & Stellar, 1985), I do believe there are many systems that may be involved in approach or avoidance behavior; this is perhaps analogous to the idea that there is not one attention or learning system, but many. Despite this caveat, think about the rich source of bodily information that informs the adaptive responses of the ant; imagine simulating this ability. Bodily information marks out the world into coherent pockets of sanity. Bodily responses are rich in adaptation; no mere passive organ, the body is the vehicle by which we navigate the world, inform our decision making, and make accurate predictions. Included in this elegant package are the underlying behavioral mechanisms for approaching and avoiding objects (e.g., detection and prediction of danger; N. E. Miller, 1959). Even the ant, rich in peripheral ganglia but small in central control, generates a wide array of adaptive responses to changing circumstances. These ganglia are rich sources for information-processing systems designed to detect sensory stimuli, find food, avoid predators, find mates, and on and on.

Table 1.1 Approach-Withdrawal Adjustments

Intense Stimuli	Weak Stimuli
Reaction:	Reaction:
More vigorous	Less vigorous
More generalized flexion	More localized extension
"Interruptive" visceral condition	"Vegetative" visceral condition
Withdrawal	Approach

Particular qualities of objects, situations, experiences	
Negative Valences	Positive Valences
Escape	Approach
Refusal	Tolerance
Aggression	Acquisition

Adapted from Schneirla, 1959.

Cephalic Organization of Action

The organization of action—to reach for this cup for a sip of coffee, to type on this computer, to listen to you on the telephone—is replete with cognitive design (Gallistel, 2000). John Dewey (1896) early on understood that simple sensorimotor reflexes are rich in cognitive function. In other words, rudimentary reflexes, such as startle responses to fearful objects, have an organization and are replete with cognitive processing (e.g., typing on the computer is not a rudimentary reflex, but an action built up from more rudimentary, automatic responses). This organization reflects building blocks, chunks of organized action, which are replete with cognitive structure and processes (e.g., Graybiel et al., 1994; Knowlton, Mangels, & Squire, 1996; Lashley, 1951; P. Lieberman, 2000; M. T. Ullman et al., 1997).

Dewey (1896), in other words, at the turn of the 20th century, attempted to modify the idea of the reflex arc inherited from Descartes by building cognitive systems right into the reflex responses. This was a prescient orientation, for we have recognized that elementary motor control is embedded in cognitive systems that organize the structure of action (Gallistel, 1992).

Karl Lashley (1951), following Dewey (1896), understood that a simple passive reflex theory would never account for the organization of action. Lashley recognized that the idea that the brain is asleep, passive, and waiting to be acted on was a misguided notion, though deeply held. The problem of "serial order," as Lashley understood it, involves recognizing the brain as an active organ that modifies stimuli as they come in; the brain is no mere passive receptor. Lashley alluded to syntactic structure, an active processing of incoming information, and he extended this as a metaphor to a wide variety of domains. He understood that the cognitive mechanisms that render information processing possible are unconscious (Lashley, 1951).

The organization of action is perhaps best expressed in terms of preparatory and consummatory behaviors that are organized in the brain (see also Craig, 1918). Konorski (1967), in the middle of the twentieth century, concurrently developed rich behavioral and neural theories to account for the organization of behavior.[8] Perceptual organization dominates the endless depiction of reflexes in Konorski's work; these reflexes prepare us for action, to perceive faces, and to put perceptual space together (Rescorla, 1988). The perception of faces is a primary cognitive system (A. W. Young, 1998).

Looking at a face activates regions of the brain that are prepared to play a fundamental role in the organization of action (basal ganglia). Perceptions and actions do not occur in isolation from each other. For example, even the most rudimentary reflexes reflect cognitive structure and the activation of basal ganglia neural structure. These structural habits have been linked to learned processes, echoing the distinction between procedural and episodic memory (Eichenbaum & Cohen, 2001; Squire, Knowlton, & Musen, 1993). Moreover, we now know that the head ganglia of motor control and the organization of movement and habit—the basal ganglia—is linked to a wide array of cognitive functions. They include language production, the paradigmatic example of a cognitive system (P. Lieberman, 2000; Pinker, 1994, 1997). For example, syntax production for regular verbs (Ullman et al., 1997), the prediction of a probabilistic event (Knowlton et al., 1996), the organization of specific movements (Graybiel et al., 1994), and the *appraisal of rewards* (Berridge, 2000; Calder et al., 2001; Schultz, 2002) all involve the basal ganglia.

Conceptual organization coevolved with the organization of action (M. Johnson, 1990; Varela, Thompson, & Rosch, 1991). Basic categories such as pushing, pulling, throwing, lifting, giving, and taking are what Lakoff and Johnson (1999) have characterized as core-level categories pervasive in human action (see also Boroditsky & Ramscar, 2002). Thus, underlying this exploration of the world is a cognitively mediated sense of the structure of objects by categorical features (cf. Carey, 1985, 1995; Lakoff & Johnson, 1999; Piaget, 1932, 1952). A pervasive cognitive unconscious underlies the behavioral performance that one witnesses in everyday life (Rozin, 1976a). Table 1.2 lists some of the ways we characterize knowing and bodily action.

Visceral/Bodily Representations and the Central Nervous System

It has been known for some time that visceral representations reach the forebrain. The special senses (smell and taste) have long been linked to the visceral system in the brain (Herrick, 1905). Consider the classic work of C. Judson Herrick (1905, 1929, 1948). Working with several species—catfish, tiger salamander, among other animals—and using classical anatomical methods, Herrick mapped out projections from the solitary nucleus to the amygdala that provide the animal with information about taste as well as more general information about the viscera (Norgren, 1995). The amygdala was thought, at that time, to be a primary area for olfaction; indeed, regions of the amygdala receive direct projections from the olfactory bulb. What Herrick was right to emphasize is the important role of the amygdala as part of the gustatory/visceral neural network.

The amygdala also receives input from the solitary nucleus and the parabrachial nucleus (Norgren, 1976). The important point here is that a broad range of information from the first-order visceral systems in the brainstem is en route to forebrain sites. Conversely, there is direct input from the amygdala to these brainstem sites (e.g., Norgren, 1995). More generally, a number of direct connections were uncovered that project from the forebrain and hypothalamus to lower brainstem sites that are essential for basic visceral/motor function (Saper, 1996; Saper, Loewy, & Cowan, 1976). Depicted in figure 1.6 is gustatory/visceral connectivity in the rat and the modern emphasis on projections from the brainstem (Norgren, 1995).

Table 1.2 Ideas about Events
_____

Thinking is perceiving
Ideas are things perceived
Knowing is seeing
Communicating is showing
Attempting to gain knowledge is searching
Becoming aware is noticing
Being able to know is being able to see
Being ignorant is being unable to see
Impediments to knowledge are impediments to vision
Knowing from a "perspective" is seeing from a point of view
Explaining is drawing a picture
Directing attention is pointing
Paying attention is looking at
Being receptive is hearing
Taking seriously is listening
Sensing is smelling
_____

Adapted from Lakoff & Johnson, 1999.

The amygdala, a region now understood in the context of fear (LeDoux, 1996), was first thought of in terms of bodily information being transported to paleocortical sites (Norgren, 1995; Swanson, 2000a, 2000b). The amygdala, in fact, plays an integrative role in a broad array of visceral processing: Cardiovascular, gastrointestinal, gustatory, and olfactory information is routed through the amygdala (Norgren, 1995; Petrovich et al., 2001; Swanson & Petrovich, 1998). Modern neuroscientists have referred to the amygdala as a "sensory gateway" (e.g., both the chemical and other sensory systems such as vision; Aggleton, 2000; Swanson, 2000a, 2000b, 2003). The fact that a wide array of sensory information goes through the amygdala indicates that the amygdala plays an important role in the appraisal systems processing information (Calder et al., 2001) in addition to its relaying the information to other sites in the brain (Aggleton, 2000). The important points are that the amygdala is a major target from the brainstem and is essential for bodily sensibility.

The neuroscientific "track tracing" revolution of the 1970s and 1980s resulted in discerning numerous instances of anatomical connectivity (see Swanson, 1999, for a discussion of the hypothalamus; see also Nauta & Feirtag, 1986; Nauta & Haymaker, 1969). In the late 1960s there were seven known pathways in and out of the amygdala. There are now two orders of magnitude more than that (Swanson, 2002, personal communication), and reason to believe that there are still more. The amygdala and other forebrain sites are directly connected to viscerally related organs in the periphery and

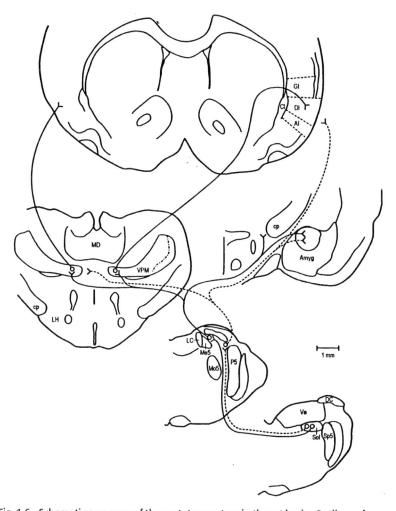

Fig. 1.6. Schematic summary of the gustatory system in the rat brain. Outlines of coronal sections through the rostral medulla (lower right), pons, diencephalon, hypothalamus and amygdala, and cerebral cortex covering a rostrocaudal distance of about 122 mm. The solid lines connecting the panels represent axons known to convey gustatory information; dashed lines represent axons associated with the taste system, but without documented sensory function. None of the lines follow actual pathways, nor do the bifurcations necessarily imply collateral projections. Abbreviations: AI, agranular insular cortex; Amyg, amygdala; Cl, claustrum; cp, cerebral peduncle; DC, dorsal cochlear nucleus; DI, dysgranular insular cortex; GI, granular insular cortex; LC, locus coeruleus; LH, lateral hypothalamus; MD, mediodorsal nucleus; Me5, mesencephalic trigeminal nucleus; Mo5, motor trigeminal nucleus; P5, principal sensory trigeminal nucleus; Sp5, spinal trigeminal nucleus; Sol, nucleus of the solitary tract; Ve, vestibular nuclei; VPM, ventral posteromedial nucleus (Norgren, 1995).

the brainstem (Kapp, Schwaber, & Driscoll, 1985; Norgren, 1995; Saper, 1996; Schwaber, Kapp, Higgins, & Rapp, 1982; though there are species differences in these brainstem forebrain projections; see Pritchard, Hamilton, & Norgren, 2000).

Neural tracking studies revealed that various sites in the gastrointestinal tract activate cortical sites. In other words, not only would regions of the solitary nucleus or other brainstem sites close to first-order afferents from the gut become active, but so would the forebrain. The connectivity between sites in the gastrointestinal tract and the neocortex is also often bilateral. This means that the most evolved regions of the brain are directly connected to basic visceral information sites, allowing them to be informed about systemic physiological states and to influence them (Saper, 1982a, 1982b, 1995). The important visceral connections from the brainstem to cortical sites had been known earlier (Herrick, 1905, 1948), but now we understand something about bodily representations, and how far up the neural axis they traverse (figure 1.7).

The visceral nervous system comprises the autonomic and neuroendocrine systems (Swanson, 2000a, 2000b, 2003). Visceral representations in the brain are aided by chemical messengers. Both neuropeptides and neurotransmitters produced in the brain are importantly involved in all aspects of bodily sensibility (Herbert, 1993; Schulkin, 1999). For example, corticotropin releasing hormone (CRH) telegraphs danger to the body at various levels of the neural axis: At the level of the heart it is a signal about atrial myocardia; at the level of the placenta it is a trigger of preterm delivery when signals of danger impact pregnancy (e.g., infections, metabolic stress, psychosocial danger; Majzoub et al., 1999); at the level of extrahypothalamic sites in the brain it serves to signal danger, to sustain vigilance, to focus attention on environmental stimuli, and so on (Schulkin, 1999).[9] Chemical messengers such as CRH provide important signals about bodily information in the integration or organization of behavioral responses (Herbert, 1993). In other words, the same chemical that traverses the body informs about bodily function and serves to maintain stability.

A large class of "information molecules" is embedded within the visceral nervous system, in both the central and the peripheral systems (Herbert & Schulkin, 2002). At the level of the brain, the chemical that is released to avert bodily harm mobilizes the animal at a behavioral level. In other words, neurochemical messengers, in particular neuropeptides and neurotransmitters, code for behavioral responses (Carter, 1998; Herbert & Schulkin, 2002; Pfaff, 1999). They can be responsive to specific needs such as the recognition of a water deficit, to the behavioral search responses produced to ameliorate the need for water, to coding of the memory for the location of water, and to the ingestion of water. For example, angiotensin is a primary dipsogenic signal; when synthesized by peripheral organs deriving from the kidney, it acts in the mobilization of water retention and peripheral stability. When synthesized in the brain as a neuropeptide, it acts

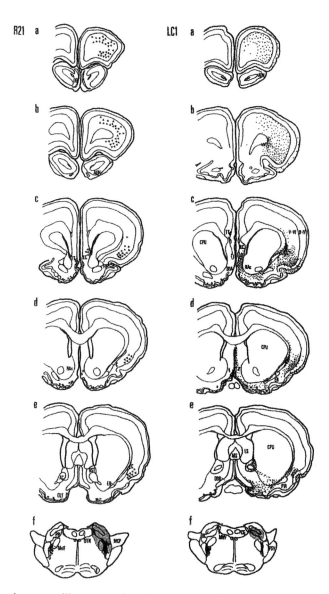

Fig. 1.7. Diagram to illustrate reciprocity of parabrachial-cortical connections follow-ing injection of a tract tracer into the parabrachial region (f). In column R21, triangles schematically represent the distribution of retrogradely labeled neurons seen follow-ing an injection of WGA-HRP into the parabrachial region. In column LC1, black dots schematically illustrate the pattern of autoradiographic axonal labeling seen after in-jecting PB with triitated amino acids. The shaded areas in R21f and LC1f show the ex-tent of the injection site in each experiment (after Saper, 1982).

via an elaborate circuit in the forebrain to elicit thirst and sodium inges-tion, which are essential for body fluid balance (Denton, 1982; A. N. Epstein, Fitzsimons, & Simons, 1968; Fitzsimons, 1998). These chemical messengers can work rapidly. Drinking can occur within seconds after angiotensin is infused in the brain. Multiple cephalic appraisal systems are operative, such as the detection of the need for water, where the water is located, and in what foods it can be obtained. In other words, the same peptide that acts in the peripheral systems to mobilize and regulate body fluid homeostasis also generates behavior as a neuropeptide in the brain; the behavior in turn serves regulatory physiology by maintaining body fluid stability. The peptide is localized and acts within the visceral neural axis in the central and periph-eral systems (see chapters 2 and 5). Figure 1.8 indicates, from a physiologi-cal and regulatory point of view, the wide range of both the peripheral and central functions of this one particular peptide in the body and one puta-tive representation of its actions in the brain.

These chemical messengers run through the visceral or autonomic nervous systems outlined by Papez (1937, following Broca, 1878) and then elaborated on by a number of investigators (MacLean, 1970, 1990; Nauta, 1971). An elabo-rate set of structures constitutes the limbic system, including the olfactory cortex, hippocampus, amygdala, septum, and regions of the hypothalamus and neocortex (Brodal, 1981; Gloor, 1978, 1997; Nauta & Feirtag, 1986; Swanson, 2003). Indeed, the limbic system traverses the whole of the central nervous system, extending from the gastrointestinal tract and cardiovascu-lar control to their representations at the level of the solitary nucleus, parabrachial nucleus, amygdala, and the bed nucleus of the stria terminalis to a wide array of cortical and neocortical regions (T. S. Gray, 1999; Swanson, 2003; Swanson, Sawchenko, Rivier, & Vale, 1983). Central broad-based chemical messengers, such as serotonin, norepinephrine, and dopamine, in addition to neuropeptides, are critical for bodily function and bodily sensi-bility. They are found in high levels in structures of the visceral system. I think, in fact, that one would be better served to refer to the visceral ner-vous system instead of the limbic system. In both chemical and functional terms, information processing in the visceral nervous system traverses all levels of the nervous system.

Visceral/Affective Impact on Decision Making

For the tradition that elevated the mind from the body in an attempt to keep cognition pure and untutored by bodily concerns, the new resurgence in the neurosciences of bodily sensibility and its importance to decision making must seem sacrilegious (Damasio, 1999). So many worked to keep mind pure, tracing back to the mind of Plato and to Aristotle's perfect reasoner, the unmoved mover, through the classical rationalists (Descartes, Spinoza), and culminating in Kant. For these philosophers, cognition needed to be divorced

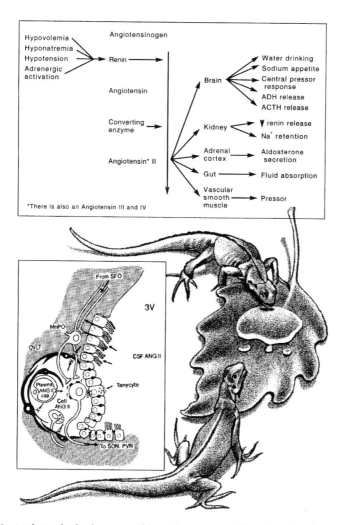

Fig. 1.8. Angiotensin, both as a peptide and a neuropeptide, plays a fundamental role in body fluid regulation, including the ingestion of water and sodium. The water ingestion of the iguana is depicted in the figure. Model of a circumventricular organ (CVO) with a glial barrier. In this case, model of OVLT that is separated from adjacent MnPO nucleus. Ependyma over OVLT has tight junctions, and substances can only move into OVLT from CSF by uptake at tanycytes. Plasma ANG II has access to OVLT receptors, but glial barrier prevents diffusion into MnPO nucleus (x at arrowhead). Cells containing endogenous brain ANG II have been found in OVLT (adapted from Fitzsimons, 1998).

from bodily sensibility to keep reason clear and formidable, correct and knowledgeable, pure. This view is so deeply ingrained that it pervades commonsense parlance and discourse. *Descartes' Error* (Damasio, 1994, 1996) is indeed a mistake. The body as a metaphor took on the form of the misleader of judgment. Sound judgment would be kept straight by the clear light of reason, reason unfettered by the pulls and pangs of the body, of the senses. But the notion of bodily sensibility includes feedback from and changes in the internal milieu and the visceral system, which I am emphasizing in this book (Bernard, 1859; Cannon, 1916/1929; Richter, 1976; see review by Moran & Schulkin, 2000), and proprioceptive feedback or musculoskeletal actuation, thereby informing and enhancing our decision-making abilities. But my emphasis is on the cephalic representations, on visceral representations within the central nervous system. The peripheral system, visceral input (e.g., gut, heat), contributes to the organization of action, whether to approach or avoid an object, but it is the vast network in the brain itself that produces and processes visceral/autonomic information processing that underlies the behaviors. The central visceral/autonomic representations are not the same as the peripheral visceral/autonomic. These really are separate. Functionally, in other words, dry mouth contributes to thirst, stomach contractions contribute to hunger, but one can drink and be thirsty or eat and be hungry without the peripheral visceral/autonomic input.

Of course, there is an obvious sense in which the narrowing of our interests can be overwhelmed by bodily needs. Decision making is hampered when the organism's focus becomes too narrow, but it can also be enhanced. Under diverse conditions, the range of focus narrows to the one desired object at the expense of all else, as is the case in addiction. In our evolutionary past, during bouts of food or water scarcity, focus narrowed to acquire these commodities at any or nearly any cost.

Diverse brain regions underlie a broad array of human reasoning and problem solving, for which the decisions are linked to visceral input that informs judgment (H. D. Critchley, Cortfield, Chandler, Mathias, & Dolan, 2000; Critchley, Mathias, & Dolan, 2001a, 2001b; Damasio, 1996). Damage to the ventral medial prefrontal cortex impairs anticipatory responses to a variety of contexts (Bechara, Damasio, Damasio, & Anderson,1994; Bechara, Damasio, Damasio, & Lee, 1999; Bechara, Damasio, Tranel, & Damasio, 1997). The celebrated Phineas Gage was unable to plan for the future following damage to the prefrontal cortex (Damasio, 1996; Harlow, 1868/1993; see also MacMillan, 2000).

The "somatic marker" hypothesis (Damasio, 1996) is an orientation toward discerning ways in which visceral or bodily sensibility informs and enhances decision making, acknowledging that autonomic information processing is an important ingredient in decision making about the present and the future. For example, in gambling experiments in which controls and patients with frontal lobe damage were compared, sensitivity to risk—the autonomic representation of risk—was correlated with correct decision making in a variety of experimental contexts (Bechara et al., 1997; figure 1.9). Normal subjects who generated risky strategies on these gambling tasks in the choice between advantageous and disadvantageous card decks revealed greater anticipatory skin conductance (SCR); frontal damage patients did not. The important observation from this study is that the autonomic measure of skin conduction is apparent before decision making in a number of these experimental paradigms in normal subjects, but not in those in which the visceral cortical representations have been damaged or destroyed and their judgment diminished or compromised (Bechara, Damasio, & Damasio, 2000; table 1.3; though see Manes et al., 2002). One still does not know if subjects without this peripheral input would be unable to perform, nor should one exaggerate the importance of this peripheral measure. And one should not, again, confuse peripheral visceral/autonomic input from cephalic representations—the central nervous system's own visceral/autonomic architecture.

Consider an interesting set of experiments monitoring the link among a sense of uncertainty, arousal, and autonomic activity by another group of investigators (H. D. Critchley, Mathias, & Dolan, 2001a). Subjects were placed in a context in which there was a delay between a reward and a decision (playing cards) that they would make. Varying conditions of uncertainty and arousal were created (H. D. Critchey, Cortfield, et al., 2000; H. D. Critchley et al., 2001a). Subjects' degree of anticipatory autonomic arousal was associated with activation of the right anterior cingulate and insula cortex (figure 1.10).

Other studies have provided a wide variety of examples that demonstrate relationships between reasoning about probability and activation of a wide network of structures in the brain (Knowlton et al., 1996). Representations of future monetary rewards, for example, activate regions of the orbitofrontal cortex (O'Doherty, Kringelbach, Rolls, Hornak, & Andrews, 2001). Anticipatory autonomic activity affects the neural systems in normal decision making under uncertainty and arousal. In fact, as one would expect, a wide

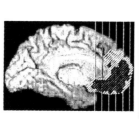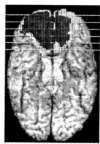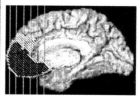

Fig. 1.9. Overlap of lesion (dark area) in ventral medial patients (adapted from Bechara et al., 2000).

Table 1.3 Changes in Skin Conductance (SCR) in Patients and Controls

	Control	VM Patient
Disadvantageous	SCR increases	No SCR change
Advantageous	No SCR change	No SCR change

Adapted from Bechara et al., 2000.

array of neural sites are linked to the organization of anticipated rewards (e.g., Berridge, 1996; Breiter, Aharon, Kahneman, Dale, & Shizgal, 2001; Elliott, Friston, & Dolan, 2000; Rolls, 1999; Schultz, 2002; Stellar & Stellar, 1985). These sites extend from the neocortex through the brainstem (e.g., orbitofrontal and cingulate cortex, parabrachial region, striatum; Graybiel, Aosaki, Flaherty, & Kimura, 1994; Saper, 1996).

Regions of the prefrontal cortex, orbitofrontal cortex, and cingulate cortex run the range of cognitive functions (e.g., executive functions, memory functions, and general problem-solving functions; Duncan & Owen, 2000; Fuster, 2001; Goldberg, 2001; Goldman-Rakic, 1996; Nauta, 1971). The frontal/orbital cortex also possesses important sensory functions, such as olfaction and gustation (E. T. Rolls, 1996, 2000). This same prefrontal cortical region (almost a third of the brain in humans) is also tied to the organization of somatic-visceral integration in the context of action. At each level of the neural axis there are visceral appraisal systems that are integral in the organization of action. Cognition is not one side of a divide and viscera the other, with action merely a reflexive outcome. Research over the past fifty years, especially since the 1970s, has demonstrated that the brain is not carved up into structures functioning in isolation. Appraisal systems reside at every level of the nervous system.

Conclusion

Bodily representations traverse the whole of the brain, which is understandable, as they provide vital sources of information for every facet of an animal's behavior, and such direct neural connectivity of visceral input throughout the nervous system demonstrates just how linked cognitive systems are to bodily representations. First-order visceral afferents contain detectors, specific sensors. In many instances, cognition may be primitive, but it is not detached. There is no divide between cognition and bodily functions once the brain is involved.

The evolution of neural structure resulted in greater accessibility of specific functions for greater use (Rozin, 1976a, 1998). The term "preadaptation" depicts a specific function that evolved for one purpose that now extends to other purposes (Darwin, 1871/1982; Mayr, 1960). Such adaptive

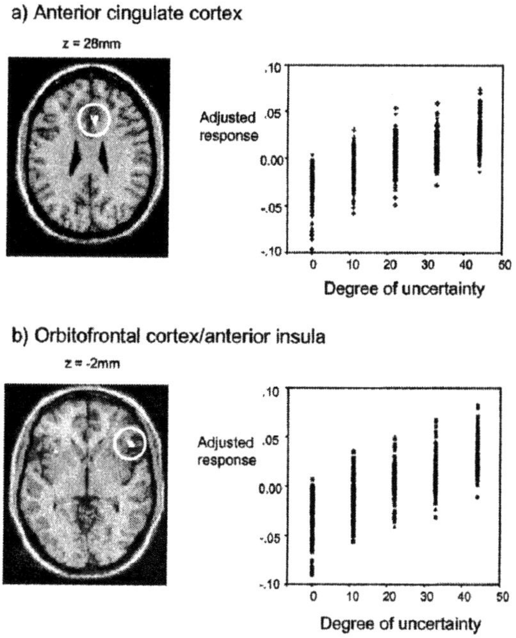

a) Anterior cingulate cortex

z = 28mm

b) Orbitofrontal cortex/anterior insula

z = -2mm

Fig. 1.10. Modulation of anticipatory delay period activity by risk: The figure illustrates (a) anterior cingulate cortex and (b) right anterior insula where activity during delay was modulated by decision uncertainty. Conjunction analysis across subjects was used to highlight activations common to all subjects. Spatial locations of group activity (p<0.001, uncorrected for illustration) are displayed on horizontal sections of a normalized template structural scan. Vertical distance from AC-PC line is given as Z coordinates above the sections. Adjacent to each section is a plot of how activity in this region was modulated by the degree of uncertainty. The adjusted response of the maximally activated voxel was extracted from time-series data. The mean response of the hrf-convolved boxcar representing delay period activity is plotted against the degree of uncertainty of outcome, a function of the face value of the cue card. Different symbols denote responses in the different subjects (H. D. Critchley et al., 2001).

specializations (Tinbergen, 1951/1969) are common. Disgust reactions were originally linked to gustatory stimulation; bad-tasting substances elicit withdrawal, as I described earlier, and good-tasting substances elicit approach. Other kinds of objects, through association with or contamination by an object, can elicit the same sort of reaction-contagion effects. We also become more morally repulsed, and perhaps the same basic disgust process that we utilize for food sources is utilized for affective reactions, for moral character (Rozin, 1999, chap. 4). Systems that perhaps evolved for one function (e.g., facial responses to gustatory stimuli for acceptance or rejection) are now activated by another set of stimuli (e.g., nongustatory stimulation, whether something is visually aesthetic, morally acceptable).

2

Demythologizing the Emotions

Introduction

The emotions are an integral part of who we are (Darwin, 1872/1965; Davidson, Sherer, & Goldsmith, 2003). Emotions are diverse (e.g., Darwin, 1872/1965; Ekman, 1972; Oehman, 1997), and they can be subtle (cf. Ben-Zeev, 2000; Kagan, 1998; Sabini & Silver, 1998; Solomon, 1980, 1990, 1999). Demythologizing the emotions, like demythologizing reason in general, is depicting them less as perfect systems and more as good enough problem-solving devices (Simon, 1956, 1967, 1979). They are rich in expression and essential for human health and well-being and represent beautiful forms of intelligence and adaptation (Nussbaum, 2001). The emotions evolved, in part, to solidify approach and avoidance behavioral responses. The emotions reflect visceral information processing in the central nervous system, the experiences that we have, the behavioral expressions. A partial list of the emotions is depicted in table 2.1. It represents a wide range of emotions, and no single definition of emotion can capture them all.

Darwin understood the emotions to be part of bodily expressions and information processing. The bodily response (figure 2.1) depicts a range of meanings (J. D. Smith, 1977). Bodily displays are prevalent in nature and impart essential meanings (Marler & Hamilton, 1966; J. D. Smith, 1977). They are fundamental for attachment and avoidance behaviors (cf. Bowlby, 1988; Gray, 1971/1987; N. E. Miller, 1959; Tinbergen, 1951/1969). Communicative competence and expression are at the very heart of animal life and development (Hauser & Konishi, 2000; Tomasello, 1999).

Communication by definition involves a transmitter and a receiver, both of which need to be adept interpreters of environmental/social events for

Table 2.1 Partial List of the Emotions

Joy (Elation)
Sadness
Anger
Fear
Disgust
Frustration
Satisfaction (Calm)
Embarrassment
Love
Aggression
Security
Guilt
Shame
Envy
Hatred

---

immediate and long-term survival. Appraisal systems function both to produce a reaction to an environmental stimulus (transmitter) and to interpret that reaction or emotion (receiver). Adaptation requires fast or slow appraisals of bodily expressions in the discernment of communicative understanding (Ekman, 1972, 1992; Lazarus, 1984, 1991a; Oatley & Jenkins, 1996; Ortony, Clore, & Collins, 1988). The appraisal can reflect a range of emotions, expressing both positive and negative reactions to a stimulus. Disgust and fear, for example, both reflect immediate reactions to objects.

An evolutionary perspective was very much at the heart of the work of Darwin's contemporary, William James. James linked emotions to adaptation, and envisioned the brain in the context of evolution. Similar to the great British neurologist Hughlings Jackson (1884/1958a, 1958b),[1] James held a view of the nervous system that incorporates evolutionary reasoning. Jackson asserted, "The organ of mind is nothing whatever else than the highest level of evolution, an organ representing all parts of the body" (1897/1958, p. 111).

As I have indicated, James overidentified the emotions with peripheral physiology and overt bodily acts. James was a peripheralist with regard to the recognition of one's emotional states, as Cannon (1916/1929) was a peripheralist with regard to motivational states (drinking and dry mouth; chap. 5). As I indicated in the previous chapter, emotional states are cephalic in nature; moreover, visceral representations are a vital part of diverse regions of the brain, in addition to cephalic innervation of diverse systemic systems that are vital to emotional regulation (e.g. heart, stomach).

Fig. 2.1. Cat interacting with a person (Darwin, 1872/1965).

This chapter begins by briefly outlining the history of the emotion-sensation split, primarily because of its similarity to the real focus of this chapter, namely, the split between emotion and cognition. After recounting the history of the split between emotion and cognition, I build a case for their reunification by demythologizing the emotions, analogous to demythologizing human reason (e.g. Dewey, 1925/1989; Gigerenzer, 2000; Simon, 1956, 1992). Emotional systems are not perfect, are rooted in biological adaptation, and are knotted to problem solving.

Sensations, Feelings, and the Emotions

The body in pain is typically an undeniable event (Scarry, 1985). Victims of torture are emotionally scarred. The pain of the event is not an emotion, but the fear, anger, and hopelessness engendered by pain are. Pain is a signal of external danger to warn us and prod us into action. It is a phylogenetically ancient sensation, coded in neural circuits that traverse the brain and the bodily extremities, motivating behavioral action (Herbert & Schulkin, 2002). The focus of one's attention narrows; the impact can be devastating and long-lasting. Even a toothache can have long-term effects. Pain, the physiological sensation, is not an emotion.

Through a long history of emotions being linked to sensations, pleasure and pain are seen as sensory events. But something can taste sweet (sensation) and not be liked (emotion; Berridge, 1996). A sensory impact is not the same as the emotional state of enjoyment. And diverse sensory information-processing systems are obviously an inherent part of the emotions. The hedonic pushes and pulls of the sort that Hobbes (1651/1958) envisioned as the major motivator of people are no doubt a real fact about us, particularly as humans. But to define emotion as a sensation or simply a hedonic attraction or aversion to events, and then lace it in utility functions, is too narrow a portrayal of the emotions. The emotions would then be too narrowly defined by the reaction to sensation, although this is not a trivial feature of the emotions.

Sensory information processing impacts the emotions whether or not we are aware of it. For example, we know that subliminal exposure to stimuli can alter affective decision making (Nisbett & Wilson, 1977; Zajonc, 1984, 2001). A wide variety of experimental findings demonstrates subliminal exposure effects on human and animal performance (Monahan, Murphy, & Zajonc, 2000). Subliminal exposure to other facial responses alters the aesthetic value of an object (e.g., Chinese ideogram). Preferences are altered regularly, presumably without awareness, while a vast array of events occurs unconsciously by mechanisms in the mind/brain. The affective subliminal experience shifts the response toward particular objects that are in keeping with the explicit affective nature of the subliminal stimuli. This is a real effect demonstrated in a wide array of contexts (Zajonc, 1964, 2000). For example, subjects who reported being mildly thirsty and were shown subliminal happy faces tended to rate the wanting of a particular drink and the pouring of a particular drink as a pleasant experience to a greater extent than thirsty subjects not shown the happy face (Berridge & Winkielman, 2003; Winkielman, Zajonc, & Schwartz, 1997).

These sorts of results lie at the heart of distinguishing feeling from thinking (Zajonc, 1980, 2000). Feeling, it was proposed, is not inferential; it just occurs along sensory pathways. Thinking, on the other hand, is inferential. But what does inference mean here? Is syntax production inferential? Is facial recognition (happy, sad) inferential? Suppose it is or not. Does that mean it's noncognitive? I would not think so, for in both cases, cephalic organization is prominent. Moreover, sensations exist in specific neural/cognitive systems. For instance, gustatory processing is information processing; appraisal systems detect saltiness, sweetness, bitterness, and so on (Bartoshuk,

1991). They are phylogenetically ancient and important to animals in determining what to eat and what to avoid.

The emotions, however, are not reduced to sensations (e.g., Solomon, 1980, 1990). Pain is not an emotion, as a toothache is not an emotion. But being pained by the loss of a girlfriend or spouse—the grief that emanates surely is an emotion. Even the anguish at the presence of the toothache pain is surely an emotion. And what pervades the emotion is bodily sensibility.

Unconscious cognitive mechanisms, as Helmholtz (1867/1963; see also Leibniz, 1765/1982) suggested, underlie basic sensory events (Gregory, 1973; Zeki, 1999) and underlie emotions (cf. Berridge, 2000; Clore, 1992; Kihlstrom, 1987; Oehman, 1997). Basic sensory events are always part of the information processing in the brain (Hebb, 1949). The real work is to determine the range of information processing that basic sensory systems can do, and how they link to emotional/cognitive events. And the real work is describing and explaining the diverse forms of emotional systems. They range from fear and joy to desire and repulsion; the emotional systems range across the motivational and sensory systems.

Cognition and the Emotions

Cognitive systems are embedded in the structure of action, the act of seeing, the perception of faces, and so on. Whether the emotions are fast acting or deliberate (Dewey, 1896; Ekman, 1992; Lazarus, 1991a, 1991b), appraisals predominate, as does the readiness under a number of conditions to behave in characteristic ways (cf. Ellsworth, 1994, 1995; Frijda, 1986; Johnson-Laird & Oatley, 1992; Lang, 1995; Ortony & Turner, 1990; Rosen & Schulkin, 1998; Scherer, 1988; Scherer et al., 2001; Wollheim, 1999).

There is no one definition of emotion, just as there is no one definition of cognition. The debates concerning cognition and emotion seem endless. I begin this section by exploring the historical context of this separation. The separation of cognition from emotion is not a necessary feature of our conceptual framework, but it certainly has had a great hold on us; it is something that we cannot give up. It is a reflexive intellectual response: Feel, don't think; think, don't feel; keep separate, like milk and meat products in a kosher house. Defense of either position goes on endlessly (e.g., Elster, 1999; Lazarus, 1984; LeDoux, 2001; Leventhal, 1982; Metcalf & Mischel, 1999; Panksepp, 1982, 1990; Parrott & Sabini, 1989; Parrott & Schulkin, 1993; Zajonc, 2000).

I suggest that even rudimentary, bare bodily responses, as soon as they are cephalic in origin, are coded in cognitive systems. The question is not whether they are cognitive or not, but cognitive to what degree, at what level of complexity.[2] Feelings are part of our computational sensory systems (Damasio, 1999).

Those who study regulatory systems have always envisioned an important role for the emotions in the context of whole body regulation and maintenance (Hebb, 1949; Stellar, 1974). Emotions are importantly linked to motivational systems, approach and avoidance systems, arousal systems, and quiescence systems. For example, one recognizes with whom to play and whom not. The activation of motor systems in play requires extensive cognitive/bodily impact. It is not cognition detached from bodily expression—that is the vital piece. Appraisal systems are embedded in these broad-based regulatory systems. Recognition of sodium hunger, thirst, or other regulatory components essential for maintaining stability presupposes appraisal systems for recognizing what is required, or further, that something is required at all (Schulkin, 1991). It is a low-level cognitive device, but a cognitive device nonetheless (Lane & Nadel, 2000).

Although most neuroscientists refer to both the affective and cognitive regions of the brain (e.g., LeDoux, 1996; Swanson, 2003), perhaps a better, less misleading way to characterize their functions is to refer to different kinds of information processing. For example, insisting on referring to the amygdala as the affective computational system and the hippocampus as the cognitive system (cf. LeDoux, 1993; Parrott & Schulkin, 1993) creates a flawed division, as both are within the cognitive domain. Again, there are a number of information-processing systems in the brain, some of which are about emotional stimuli and some of which are about getting through doors, arriving at an engagement on time, avoiding people that might be harmful, or getting to a place in anticipation of a loved one.[3]

Emotional systems evolved to organize behavior into coherent adaptive action (e.g., Clore et al., 2001; Ekman, 1972, 1992; Frijda, 1986; Izard, 1971, 1993; Johnson-Laird & Oatley, 1992; Lazarus, 1984; Tomkins, 1962, 1963). They are universal features of a species; the appraisal systems can be either automatic or deliberative (Ekman, 1972, 1992). Emotions are importantly tied to social interactions. Facial responses, for example, evolved largely in social contexts (Fridlund, 1994).

Arguments against the Emotions Being Adaptive

The link between the emotions and the body is ancient in evolution and in our understanding. As Spinoza stated several centuries ago, "By emotion, I mean the modification of the body" (1668/1955, p. 130). Emotion as a privation is a typical view. Spinoza asserted, "Emotion, which is called a passivity of the soul, is a confused idea" (p. 185). Emotion on this traditional view compromises thought and action.

Even in contemporary thought, not all accept the view that the emotions are adaptive or that they evolved to facilitate problem solving (cf. Berridge, 2003; Loewenstein, 1996, 2003; Metcalf & Mischel, 1999; Sabini & Silver, 1998). In the modern vernacular, emotions render one less adaptive. This, I submit, is false. Emotion certainly is not any more fallible than most forms of information processing. The emotions are often a clear signal of whole bodily reaction (P. Fisher, 2002).

Emotions are said to emerge in just those cases in which we are unable to act. In cases in which we can perform, these actions are construed as motivational: the motivation to avoid danger, to seek comfort, and so on. Motivation takes on the property of effective action, whereas emotion is ineffective action or, rather, inaction (Sabini & Silver, 1998). Of course, this disinclination echoes a familiar theme: Emotions are perhaps necessary but not helpful, and they are degrading in terms of long-term performance. After all, sitting there as a frustrated junior faculty afraid to speak (a Sabini and Silver example) is an example of rather hapless impotence; emotion's naysayers would suggest that where the emotions do exist they are ineffectual or, even worse, debilitating.

Others liken the emotions to addiction; they are placed in the context of the loss of control (Elster, 1999). Emotions are construed as "events" and not actions (passive reactions). They give the sense of the addict with a narrow focus, of obsessiveness (Elster, 1999; Loewenstein, 1996). Moreover, some research has shown that people are not particularly good at predicting hedonic states. For example, we hold an inconsistent view about happiness that we may derive from future events (Loewenstein & Schkade, 1999). But this aspect of uncertainty is not unique to the emotions; people are not great predictors of a number of events, as the decision sciences have demonstrated (Kahneman, Diener, & Schwarz, 1999). A number of sources contribute to errors in reasoning, such as limited perspective or theories and the salience of a factor. Human reasoning is fallible. That is why the 19th-early-20th-century philosopher/scientist C. S. Peirce (1878) embraced probabilistic reasoning, self-corrective inquiry or "falliblism," and this is no less true for our own emotional predictions.

Expected emotions can be distinguished from immediate emotions. Immediate emotions can enhance decision making, such as fear of a snake or detection of a friendly face (Mellers et al., 2001; Oatley & Jenkins, 1996; Simon, 1967). Expected or anticipatory emotions from being in a certain place run the consistent risk of limiting resources in the cognitive practice comprising decisions (e.g., expected utility functions). People distort small probabilities, they often miss mid-level probabilities, and they undervalue moderate to high probabilities (Kanheman & Tversky, 1982, 1984, 1996). Recent investigations in the decision sciences suggest that our less than stellar ability to predict emotional reactions, and our distortion of the probabilities of experiencing certain emotional states, placed emotional appraisals in terms of other forms of mistakes that we are vulnerable to. The emotions are no different from other imperfect problem-solving abilities.

Although the study of the emotions has gained more respectability as a focus of neurological and biological inquiry over the past ten years in the psychological sciences in general (e.g., Davidson et al., 2000, 2003), hedonic states still appear ominous. In other words, many cognitive scientists still view hedonic states as maladaptive. They would say that hedonic states need to be reduced in terms of their impact; hedonic adaptation is the process of modulating the impact of events on internal physiology (Frederick & Loewenstein, 1999). There is still a tendency in the sciences of human decision making to link emotions to pathology; emotions are couched in terms of addictions (Elster, 1999) and homeostatic imbalances. More recently, emphasis has been placed on both the adaptive and the nonadaptive features in emotional decision making (Loewenstein & Lerner, 2003).

Visceral factors have been characterized as undermining decision making by minimizing factors that are essential for maintaining self-interest in decision making. Loewenstein (1996) talks of being "out of control." Visceral factors undermine the sense of being in control. In this view, visceral factors tend to be negative and have a disruptive effect on this perception of control. Addictions are—again—likened to emotions (Elster, 1999). Of course, this is the traditional view of the emotions: Emotions cloud thought, undermine decision making, render one out of control and impulsive. Certain emotions, and contexts, can undermine adaptive problem solving. Moreover, the underestimation of future emotional reactions is quite congruent with erroneous judgments about a number of events.

There is little doubt from human experience, and now from the context of behavioral and neural science laboratories, that organisms may act to obtain what they do not like and is not good for them. I can want the food that past experience has shown me will not sit well with me. Of course, the addict's life is replete with this. Wanting grows as expectations and salience of associations grow (see Berridge, 1996). Irrational wanting comes in degrees, as does rational wanting. Diverse emotions and motivations compete for expression.

Nevertheless, emotional appraisal, though often fast and, importantly, essentially so, can be quite accurate. The essential point is that demythologizing reason from its perfect pedestal resulted in a conception of reason that seemed balanced and accurate. Human reason is rich with a set of heuristics (Baron, 1988/2000; Kahneman & Tversky, 1982, 1984, 1996) or biases that limit and aid human reason (including reproductive conflicts; Buss, 2001). Recognizing faces or avoiding toxic material is often fast and accurate and with somewhat limited resources informing the judgment. Moreover, heuristic is not a bad word; less than perfect reason can still be informed reason (Gigerenzer, 1991, 2000). Recognizing a taste or a face may be fast and accurate, or fast and less accurate, providing one of the mechanisms for organizing adaptive behavioral responses. The capacity for such rapid responding surely stems from the greater importance of recognizing potential dangers than the milder consequences from initially rejecting what may turn out to be harmless substances or strangers.

Let's turn to an example of the extension of adaptive functions tied to emotions, the gustatory system. Gustation is both rule-governed and sensory. Gustatory sensibility is also hedonic, tied to motivational changes, and serves adaptive functions. Moreover, the study of facial expression as linked to gustation has been a fruitful area of inquiry into the emotions.

The Emotions as Adaptive

The emotions serve adaptive functions and are importantly tied to motivational systems. Let's turn to several examples, focusing on facial expressions.

Gustatory Facial Expressions: Good and Bad Tastes

The gustatory system provides an example of low-level appraisal and reveals species-specific rule-governed facial responses. Simple rules underlie the basic behavioral responses. Intraoral infusions of salty or bitter tastes elicit negative oral facial responses, and sweet tastes elicit positive responses (Berridge & Grill, 1983; Grill & Norgren, 1978a, 1978b; Nowlis, 1977). Negative responses are characterized, for example, by the opening of the mouth (gaping), depression of the jaw, and extension of the tongue out of the mouth to permit chin rubbing (figure 2.2).

These facial responses have been noted in a number of mammals, including the chimpanzee, gorilla, orangutan, and a variety of old world monkeys (Steiner, Glaser, Hawilo, & Berridge, 2001). Human neonates also produce

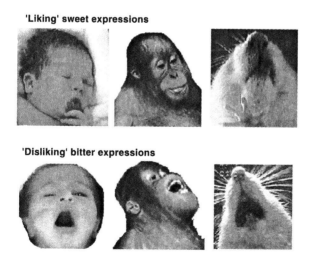

Fig. 2.2. Positive and negative responses to sweet and bitter tastes in several species (Berridge, 2000; Steiner et al., 2001).

comparable responses to gustatory stimulation (Rosenstein & Oster, 1988; Steiner, 1973, 1974; Steiner et al., 2001). Bitter gustatory stimulation elicits facial responses of distaste, which promotes rejection of the aversive substance, whereas a positive taste elicits facial responses conducive to ingestion (i.e., not just expressive, but functional for ingestion). These facial responses are produced in the context of other behavioral responses that are characterized by approach or avoidance to affordable objects (Gibson, 1966). Positive emotions are associated with the approach or ingestion of various objects of ingestion; negative emotions are associated with avoidance of various objects of ingestion.

Similarities among various species in hedonic and aversive responses to certain stimuli suggest an evolutionarily adaptive role for these responses. In nature, sweet taste generally signals nutritious food, whereas bitter taste usually signals that the food may be dangerous. Furthermore, the mechanics of the reaction to sweet stimuli may serve to maximize acceptance of the food, whereas the reactions to bitter stimuli maximize rejection of bitter foods, which are likely to be poisonous or spoiled (Janzen, 1977; Steiner et al., 2001).

The value of a substance can be influenced by the state of the internal milieu, such that a usually desirable commodity may not elicit approach behavior, but instead may produce facial responses linked to either distaste or disgust (Rozin, 1999; Rozin & Schulkin, 1990). Disgust emerges from "bad taste" (P. Gilbert & Andrews, 1998). For example, when the stomach of a rat is loaded with a food substance via a catheter, the oral-facial responses to a sweet taste shift from a positive to a negative oral-facial profile (Cabanac & LaFrance, 1990). When the stomach is no longer full, the response is the reverse, and the positive oral-facial responses are apparent. The system is labile, adaptive to the current state of the organism. The hedonic responses can reflect regulatory needs, past experience, or saturation of gustatory receptors (Rolls, 1999; Stellar, 1954, 1974).

Rats made sick during a taste aversion procedure (ingestion of a particular food or taste temporally associated with visceral discomfort) will subsequently demonstrate profound shifts in their oral-facial responses to a previously palatable substance (Pelchat, Grill, Rozin, & Jacobs, 1983). Not only will rats come to avoid sweet sources when they have been rendered ill by ingestion of those foods, but (at a later time) they will emit characteristic aversive or disgust reactions to the sweet taste when it is orally infused or forced on them (figure 2.3). This class of learned gustatory aversion is well documented outside of the laboratory and is known to occur in a wide variety of contexts and species (Garcia et al., 1974).

The sensory changes, mediated by visceral or bodily input, reflect changes in appraisal of the stimulation as good, neutral, or bad for the organism (Pfaffmann, 1960; Troland, 1928). Sensory pleasure is linked to context, which is linked to past experience (Pfaffmann, 1960). If the sensory experience is too intense (as defined by the limits of the sensory receptors and by

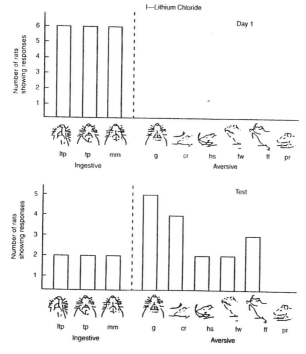

Fig. 2.3. Taste reactivity in taste aversion learning to lithium chloride on day 1 and at test. Graphs show the number of rats who display the indicated behavior. ltp=lateral tongue protrusions, tp=tongue protrusions, mm=mouth movements, g=gape, cr=chin rub, hs=head shaking, fw=face washing, ff=forelimb flailing, pr=paw rubbing. (Pelchat et al., 1983)

the internal milieu), it tends to be aversive (Schnierla, 1959). Consider the change when something is perceived as hedonically pleasing. Concentrated sodium chloride (seawater), when infused into the oral cavity, elicits mixed ingestive and aversive responses. Within seconds it becomes mostly aversive (Berridge, Flynn, Schulkin, & Grill, 1984; Grill & Norgren, 1978b). But when the bodily need for sodium is great, there is a shift in the oral-facial profile from a mixed/aversive responsive to a now purely ingestive response. The sodium is ingested as if it were sucrose (figure 2.4).

Moreover, nonpreferential foods that the sodium was associated with in a presodium hunger state are also now ingested (Fudim, 1978; Rescorla, 1981; Symonds, Hall, & Bailey, 2002). When a bitter taste, such as quinine, was experimentally mixed with sodium prior to the rats developing sodium hunger, it produced a strong aversive response. However, when the quinine, now sodium-free, was later offered during sodium hunger, not only was it ingested (Rescorla, 1981), but there was a shift in the hedonic perception of the quinine (Berridge & Schulkin, 1989). In the motivation to ingest something salty, incentive cues associated with sodium in the organization of

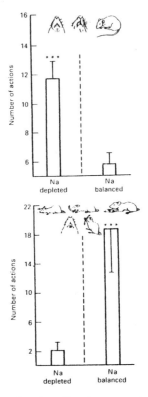

Fig. 2.4. Taste reactivity to sodium in sodium-hungry and sodium-replete rats (Berridge et al., 1984; Berridge & Schulkin, 1989).

behavior when sodium need arises. In other words, even prior to the motivation to ingest something salty, cues can become associated with sodium, prefiguring into the organization of behavior such that they become incentive cues when sodium need arises (Krieckhaus, 1970; Schulkin, 1991). Hedonic appraisals are just one factor among others in the organization of the behaviors that are expressed to restore sodium balance (Denton, 1982; Wolf, 1969).

Some facial expressions used in primate social communication (e.g., smile and disgust) may have evolved from an expanded use of the simple rule-governed gustatory facial responses. When a change in hedonic valence occurs, a palatability judgment is made. The shifts in reactions to stimuli resulting from regulatory changes or learning are adaptive because they promote wellness and, therefore, survival. Additionally, conspecifics can observe these facial responses and use the information gained from the observation to modify their own behavior and decisions. A communicative role of emotional facial expression is illustrated by animals learning what is safe to eat by observing conspecifics' reactions to food (Galef, 1986, 1996; Whiten

& Custance, 1996). In the laboratory, if a rat observes a conspecific become ill from eating a food, it will avoid that food source (Galef, 1986). Social observation in Norway rats was also shown to influence the amount of food ingested (Galef & Whiskin, 2000). This communicative and social role of facial expression is the result of extended use of basic survival responses. The oral-facial reaction is presumably originally a response to aid in the ingestion or rejection of a substance; this reaction can then be evaluated by others as a reflection of the substance's being pleasurable or offensive. This facial/emotional information can be used by others to modify their own behavior in determining what to ingest. The utility of this facial expressiveness was then expanded to valence judgments about other visceral, nongustatory reactions. This serves as one link to facial expressions and of the emotions in problem solving.

Communicative and Social Functions of Emotional Facial Expressions

One primary function of the emotions is to facilitate social bonds (Darwin, 1872/1965; Turner, 2000). The facial responses to sweet and bitter tastes observed in neonates may have functional origins and communicative value to the caregiver (Rosenstein & Oster, 1988). Though these expressions are basic responses to simple stimuli, they may serve as the building blocks of later emotional experience and development. The responses are adaptive because, in the case of human infants, they transmit information from the infant to the caregiver regarding experience of various environmental stimuli, and in the case of smiles, may serve as a reinforcer to the caregiver. Even some anencephalic neonates produce facial expressions suggesting a smile, and judged by impartial adult observers as a smile, in response to touching or slight pressure indicating enjoyment of the stimuli (Luyendijk & Treffers, 1992; Steiner, 1973).

The salience of facial expressions to conspecifics during early development is illustrated by the responses of both infant monkeys and humans to observing facial stimuli (Darwin, 1872/1965; Ekman, 1972). However, before one can use facial expressions to read emotional states in others, one must be able to distinguish and recognize different facial expressions. The ability to perceive and discriminate among facial expressions involves information-processing systems (Ekman, 1972, 1992). Within the first few days of life, human neonates can distinguish among expressions of happiness, sadness, and surprise (Field, Woodson, Greenberg, & Cohen, 1982). Four- to six-month-old human infants show preferences for facial expressions of happiness over neutral and angry expressions (LaBarbera, Izard, Vietze, & Parisi, 1976), and by 7 months they can distinguish among expressions of fear, anger, surprise, happiness, and sadness (Serrano, Iglesias, & Loeches, 1992; Soken & Pick, 1999). Preschool-age children can correctly label happy, sad, surprised, and angry faces, but they are more accurate with happy faces than with afraid and angry facial expressions (Walden & Field, 1982).

The abilities to distinguish and match facial expressions develop into the capacity to identify those expressions and make inferences about others' emotional states. The ability to recognize facial expressions is important for effective social interaction and for gathering information about the environment. By 12 to 14 months of age, infants can use adults' facial expressions as referents or indicators about objects in the environment, and can thus avoid objects toward which adults display negative facial reactions, such as disgust (Mumme, Fernald & Herrera, 1996; Repacholi, 1998). Preschoolers who can accurately recognize and interpret facial expressions also tend to engage in prosocial behaviors (Nowicki & Mitchell, 1998; Walden & Field, 1982), suggesting a relationship between facial expression recognition and the ability to regulate one's own emotions and behave in a socially appropriate manner. This association extends to production of facial expressions. More accurate facial expression production in preschool children is associated with greater peer acceptance (Walden & Field, 1982). Facial expression interpretation and production abilities are important for effective communication and, therefore, are a vital part of social interaction.

Thus, the processes of facial expression production and perception are both inherent and rule-governed. Facial expression can be reflective of emotions, as in the examples of rule-governed reflex-like expression observed in neonates, and communicate information to others. We identified several examples of the communicative nature of facial expressions. The evolution of pleasure/approach reactions and disgust/avoidance reactions to food are important for survival and may have evolved side by side with the ability to recognize facial expression in a context of nonverbal social communication, serving both the producer and the observer. Proficiency in facial expression identification and in other prosocial behaviors forms a cluster of related abilities that may be associated with evolutionary fitness. Social influences interact with production and interpretation of facial expression.

The species-specific topographies of facial displays are further modified by cultural and environmental influences. Though neonates produce characteristic facial responses when presented with simple stimuli, these responses are modified during the first year of life, possibly as a result of reinforcement within a cultural context, sometimes referred to as display rules (Ekman, Sorenson, & Friesen, 1969). These influences are described in cross-cultural studies of facial affective responses in Chinese, Japanese, and Caucasian infants (Camras et al., 1998; Kisilevsky et al., 1997). Mothers encourage or discourage their infants' emotional responses depending on cultural norms, and there are associated observable emotional displays or lack of displays in the infants (figure 2.5).

In various cultures, people behave differently when alone versus when in the presence of others, and these differences include facial expressions of emotion. An infant's smile when playing with a toy likely reflects the

Fig. 2.5. Social cues to ingest something (banana) as the infant watches the mother (Yansen & Schulkin, 2003).

emotional state of the child. However, joint attention with an adult leads to increased frequency in the infant's smiling, and in these cases the smiling is directed toward the adult, not the toy (Cossette, Pomerleau, Malcuit, & Kaczorowski, 1996; S. S. Jones & Raag, 1989). The infant is "sharing" his or her enjoyment with the adult and is communicating that enjoyment through socially directed facial expression. The social smiling can be viewed as being elicited reflexively by the presence of a social stimulus, the mother (Lane & Nadel, 2000), but this is an intentional social and communicative act.

Social context affects emotional responses in both adults and children (Wagner & Lee, 1999). Children are less likely to express sadness or anger in the presence of peers than when with a parent, and this tendency increases with age (Zeman & Garber, 1996). When alone, individuals' facial responses to various odors are not as pronounced as when other people are present (A. N. Gilbert, Fridlund, & Sabini, 1987). Similarly, when viewing films with another person, the relationship to the other person in the room affects facial responses. The expressions displayed are different when a friend is present than when a stranger is present (Buck, Loslow, Murphy, & Costanzo, 1992).

As figure 2.6 shows, imagined audiences also affect production of emotional expression, such as to an unpleasant odor, and people tend to behave as if others were in the room (Fridlund, Sabini, Hedlund, Schaut, & Knauer, 1990; A. N. Gilbert et al., 1987). Regulation of outward emotional displays and the ability to modulate emotional responses are associated with social status among children (Fabes et al., 1999). The child who can modulate outward expression of emotional states in the presence of others experiences greater social acceptance and, therefore, is rewarded for adhering to cultural rules of emotional display.

As human beings, we reconstruct and interpret the world around us into useful and understandable categories, and we predict and understand events in a meaningful way that is central to human survival and experience. Most of these interpretations reflect unconscious mechanisms that operate on what we see and what we experience. Situational factors influence adults' and children's judgment of others' facial expressions (Carroll & Russell, 1996; Ito, 1997). For example, when observing a person in a frightening situation, his or her facial expression is judged as fearful whether the actual expression shows fear or not. Reliance on situational cues to judge a person's emotion increases with age, whereas reliance on actual facial expression decreases with age (Hoffner & Badzinski, 1989). When interpreting facial expressions of others, we take into account the situational and social mi-

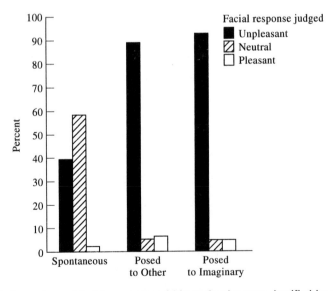

Fig. 2.6. Percentage of facial responses within each odor type classified by raters as unpleasant, neutral, or pleasant (adapted from A. N. Gilbert et al., 1987).

lieu in which the expression is being produced in an attempt to make sense of the observed situation.

The face is more than a means for communicating emotions; faces are also vehicles for communicating intentions to conspecifics (Darwin, 1872/ 1965; Ekman, 1972; Hinde, 1980; A. W. Young, 1998). Inferring the intentions and desires of others is a natural ability that we employ in everyday situations. People often infer social situations or intentions from still photographs of people producing facial expressions (Frijda, Kulpers, & ter Schure, 1989; A. W. Young, 1998). For example, a photograph of a smiling woman might elicit a comment about how the woman is watching a child play, whereas an angry facial expression might elicit a supposition about the intent of the person in the photograph. Social situations occur in association with facial expression production; when facial expressions are viewed in everyday life, they rarely occur in isolation.

Eye gaze and processing of facial and other biologically relevant movement all contribute to the evaluation of intent in others. Research with children supports the link between competent identification of emotions and the ability to infer the intentions of others (Cassidy, Parke, Butkovsky, & Braungart, 1992; Gnepp & Hess, 1986). The ability to identify and understand deceptive facial displays of emotion in which the facial emotion and intention are incongruous also develops during childhood.

Sensitivity to eye gaze is found across primate species, and mutual eye gaze can influence facial expressions and facilitate social communication (Bruner, 1973; Hinde, 1980; Tomasello & Call, 1997). Monkeys communicate threat and submission through facial displays as part of a complex social system. Eye gaze can initiate or terminate aggressive behavior among nonhuman and human primates, though the meaning of eye contact may differ depending on the species. Infants use eye gaze direction, along with facial expression, to gather information about the environment by the end of the first year of life (Baldwin & Moses, 1994). The ability to make connections about likes and dislikes through directional gaze develops later than mutual gaze perception, which develops by 2 to 3 months of age (Caron, Caron, Roberts, & Brooks, 1997). At 3 to 6 months of age, infants smile more when an adult's eye gaze is fixed on them (mutual/dyadic eye gaze) than when the gaze is averted (Haines & Muir, 1996). By 4 years of age, children can infer desires of others through direction of gaze (Gopnik & Meltzoff, 1997; Lee, Eskritt, Symons, & Muir, 1998). This ability continues to develop, and 6-year-olds are more likely than 4-year-olds to judge prolonged looking at an object as a more important cue to a person's desire than a brief glance (Montgomery, Bach, & Moran, 1998).

Movement is important for recognizing facial expressions and for attributing intentions and goals to others (Bassili, 1979; Heider & Simmel, 1944). When presented with films of two balls interacting in either an apparently random manner or an intentional manner, 5-year-old children show more interest in the intentional condition, illustrating the connection between movement and intention (Dasser, Ulbaek, & Premack, 1989). Postural cues in still pictures imply movement to both children and adults (S. L. Friedman & Stevenson, 1975), and emotion can be implied through bodily movement (Darwin, 1872/1965). Facial expressions in everyday life are not static but are constructed by movement of the eyes, mouth, and other face elements. Mouth movements (opening and baring teeth) are components of threat or fear in nonhuman primates (Chevalier-Skolnikoff, 1973). Observation of facial movement facilitates recognition of emotion (Bassili, 1979; Harwood, Hall, & Shinkfield, 1999). Three-month-old infants show equal preference for static and moving emotional faces (Biringen, 1987), but neuropsychological evidence supports the dissociation of facial expression recognition from static and moving faces (Humphreys, Donnelly, & Riddoch, 1993).

People can distinguish a smile of enjoyment from a fabricated social smile (Ekman, 1992). However, detecting deceit can be difficult, and people are generally able to detect deceit in the faces of others at only chance levels, even though behavioral cues give indications of deception to the observer (Porter, Woodworth. & Birt, 2000). For example, when giving deceptive responses, eye movement and facial expressions decrease (Pennebaker & Chew, 1985), and the ability to detect these cues is enhanced with training (Porter et al., 2000). Being able to detect deceit can also enhance one's ability to deceive. The ability to make judgments about people based on their actions rather than their facial expression develops markedly between the ages of 3 and 5 (Flavell, Lindberg, Green, & Flavell, 1992). Facial displays and vigilance for facial displays probably coevolved (Ekman, 1972, 1992; Fridlund, 1991). In evolutionary terms, the ability to deceive another using facial expression and to show expressions inconsistent with emotions can be advantageous. For example, displaying one's emotions and intentions in the face of possible resistance is counterproductive; it may be to one's advantage to conceal intention and therefore gain an advantage over another. Also, interpreting facial expressions in the presence of possible deceit requires more problem-solving and cognitive resources. The individual who can identify deceit from facial and other behavioral displays in others has an advantage.

Neuroscientific Considerations: Affective and Communicative Facial Expressions

I have suggested that taste reactivity is an example of rule-governed facial responses. Decerebrated rats (Grill & Norgren, 1978b) and human anencephalic neonates (Steiner, 1974) show taste reactivity, and in some cases produce facial responses to tactile stimuli, suggesting that the brainstem is sufficient for basic hedonic and aversive reactions. In these anencephalic rats and neonates, the parabrachial nucleus, solitary nucleus, and locus ceruleus are intact. Gustatory information travels from the taste receptors of the mouth along the seventh, ninth, and tenth cranial nerves to the brainstem solitary nucleus (Pfaffmann, 1960). Gustatory information from the solitary nucleus moves along two different pathways (Norgren, 1995). One pathway projects to the taste area in the ventral posterior thalamus and on to the cortical taste area in forebrain insular cortex (Norgren & Wolf, 1975). The other pathway projects to the hypothalamus and then to the central nucleus of the amygdala and the bed nucleus of the stria terminalis (Norgren, 1976). These pathways are both afferent and efferent, and efferent activity of the forebrain alters the responsiveness of the brainstem sites (Lundy & Norgren, 2001). The involvement of the amygdala in gustatory behavior suggests that gustation and motivation are linked neuroanatomically (Pfaffmann, Norgren, & Grill, 1977; Schulkin, 1991; Spector, 1995). Many of these same regions within the gustatory/visceral pathways are rich storehouses of chemical (angiotensin, CRH) information-processing systems in the brain (Herbert & Schulkin, 2002; Pfaff, 1999; Schulkin, 1999; figure 2.7).

Recognition of the facial expression of disgust is tied to a neural circuit that includes the basal ganglia and insular cortex (Sprengelmeyer, Rausch, Eysel, & Przuntek, 1998; Phillips et al., 1997) and the amygdala can respond to both fearful and uncertain events (Breiter et al., 1996; Morris et al., 1996; Phillips et al., 1999) and happy facial expressions (L. Liu, Ioannides, & Streit, 1999). There is differential expression of neural activation in the brain to different kinds of emotions (Davidson et al., 2000, 2003) and higher-order states such as sadness and happiness (Lane, Chau & Dolan, 1999). Interestingly, damage to the insular cortex interferes with disgust more profoundly than other emotions (Adolphs, Tranel, & Damasio, 2001; E. T. Rolls, 2000). A large set of neural structures, both cortical and subcortical, underlies a wide range of emotions (figure 2.8). They include many cortical structures: the cingulate and insular cortex, frontal cortex, the amygdala, and ventral striatum.[4] We know that many of these regions are not separate from visceral processing and appraisal systems fundamental in the organization of emotional experience (see Thayer & Lane, 2000).

Although the brainstem is sufficient for producing facial expressions in response to various simple and vegetative-function-related stimuli, forebrain areas interact with brainstem nuclei to produce responses in the intact animal (Travers, Urbanek, & Grill, 1999). In fact, as indicated above, the brainstem in both human and other mammals is sufficient to generate the basic oral-facial responses of "likes" and "dislikes" to gustatory stimulation (Berridge, 1996; Grill & Norgen, 1978b; Nowlis, 1977; Steiner, 1977). Forebrain regions buttress the basic responses (Berridge, 1996).

A large body of data also indicates differential right and left hemisphere mediation of emotional experience and production (Davidson et al., 1990, 2000). EEG, PET, and MRI have revealed this differential expression of the cortex to pleasant and unpleasant emotions—and that is not just reflected at the level of the frontal cortex (Lane et al., 1999; Lane, Reiman, Ahern, Schwartz, & Davidson, 1997; Lane, Reiman, Bradley, et al., 1997). Recording of electrical cortical responses to various taste stimuli in newborns shows greater activation of the left frontal and parietal regions during sucrose pre-

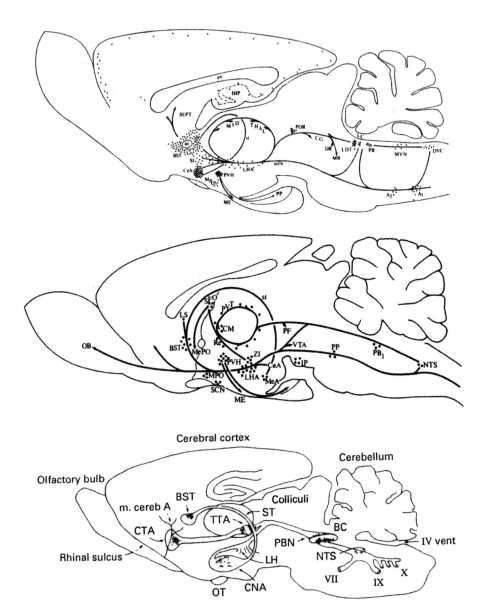

Fig. 2.7. The top panel depicts corticotropin releasing hormone in the brain (Swanson et al., 1983), the middle depicts angiotensin sites in the brain (Lind et al., 1983), and the bottom depicts the central gustatory neural axis (Norgren, 1995). The point one should note is that many of the peptide sites overlap with gustatory sites in the brain.

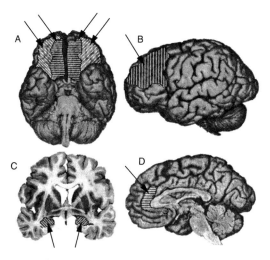

Fig. 2.8. Key structures in the circuitry underlying emotion regulation. A. Orbital prefrontal cortex (diagonal lines) and the ventral medial prefrontal cortex (horizontal lines). B. Dorsalateral prefrontal cortex (vertical lines). C. Amygdala (diagonal lines). D. Anterior cingulate cortex (horizontal lines) (adapted from Davidson et al., 2000).

sentation, and greater right hemisphere activation paired with a facial expression of disgust during presentation of water (Fox & Davidson, 1986). Production of posed (voluntary) facial expressions tends to be symmetrical when comparing expressivity of the left and right sides of the face (Weddell, Miller, & Trevarthen, 1990). However, the right anterior cortical areas may be more involved during production of spontaneous emotional facial expressions than is the left hemisphere (Blonder, Burns, Bowers, Moore, & Heilman, 1993; Hauser, 1993; Weddell, Miller, & Trevarthen, 1990; Wylie & Goodale, 1988). For example, production of facial expressions during complex social interactions is decreased in right hemisphere-lesioned patients (Blonder et al., 1993).

Regions of the temporal lobe and amygdalar areas in nonhuman primates selectively respond to eye gaze and eye movement, illustrating the importance of these facial stimuli (Perrett et al., 1985). The amygdala (Kawashima et al., 1999) and parietal areas (Wicker, Michel, Henaff, & Decety, 1998) also play a role in gaze monitoring (Emery, 2000; Perrett et al., 1984, 1985, 1989; Perrett & Mistlin, 1990). The amygdala, in other words, is part of a circuitry linked to the perception of others, what others are looking at and are interested in (Baron-Cohen, 1995; Brothers, 1997; Canli et al., 2002; Emery & Amaral, 2000; Schulkin, 2000; figure 2.9).[5]

The amygdala is also involved in generating the motivation to approach a novel food source after witnessing a conspecific eat and enjoy it, and perhaps noting the oral-facial and other bodily responses of the conspecific

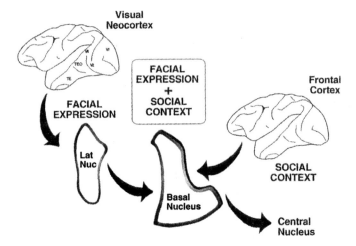

Fig. 2.9. The hypothesis of amygdala function in primate social cognition suggests that social stimuli, such as facial expressions, enter the lateral nucleus of the amygdala from visual neocortex. Facial expressions are usually communicated within a particular social context (i.e., during an aggressive encounter by a particular individual). The basal nucleus receives a projection from the lateral nucleus (expression) and projections from the orbitofrontal cortex. Information concerning social context (based on stored social knowledge of group members) is conveyed to the basal nucleus from the orbitofrontal cortex, where an appropriate response (physiological and behavioral) is evaluated. The appropriate response is then initiated via basal nuclei projections back to the neocortex and via central nucleus projections to effector structures, such as the brainstem and hypothalamus (with permission from Emery & Amaral, 1999).

recruited in this region of the brain (E. T. Rolls, 1999). For example, lesions of the amygdala have long been known to disrupt the normal perception of external objects, as in the inappropriate ingestion of nonfood objects or an increase in exploration of objects that may not be safe (Aggleton, 1995, 2000; Kluver & Bucy, 1939). The amygdala is broadly involved in the perception of external events (Emery et al., 2001; Kling & Cornell, 1971), specifically, the detection of uncertain and fear-provoking events (e.g., Davis & Whalen, 2001; LeDoux, 1996; M. Gallagher & Holland, 1994; Rosen & Schulkin, 1998). The amygdala can also be activated by positive emotions (Canli et al., 2002; Hamann, Ely, Hoffman, & Kilts, 2002) and is vital in the integration of internal needs with external circumstances (Schulkin, 1991).

In human and nonhuman primates, specialized neurons in the temporal (Hasselmo, Rolls, & Baylis, 1989; Heywood & Cowey, 1992; Perrett et al., 1984; Yamane, Kaji, & Kawano, 1988) and prefrontal (O'Scalaidhe, Wilson, & Goldman-Rakic, 1997) cortex respond to faces, including selectivity for affective facial stimuli (Hasselmo et al., 1989; Haxby et al., 2001; E. T. Rolls,

1999). Eye gaze following is an important feature in primate evolution, and a window into the experiences of others (Baron-Cohen, 1995; Baron-Cohen, Flusberg, & Cohen, 2000). An important adaptation is to see what another is looking at. These facial responses are notable pieces of information and seem to involve the superior temporal sulcus, amygdala, and orbitofrontal cortex (Emery, 2000).

Brain-imaging studies of normal human adults and studies of patients with brain lesions that investigate facial expression recognition ability implicate a number of brain sites, including amygdala (Breiter et al., 1996; Morris, Friston, et al., 1998), basal ganglia (Cancelliere & Kertesz, 1990), temporal lobe (Blair, Morris, Frith, Perrett, & Dolan, 2000), parietal lobe (Devinsky, Morrell, & Vogt, 1995; Phillips, Young, et al., 1998), and prefrontal cortex (Nakamura et al., 1999). For example, the perception of sad and fearful faces is associated with amygdala (left side) and temporal lobe activation (right side; Blair, Morris, Perrett, & Dolan, 1999; Lane et al., 1998, 1999; Morris, Friston, et al., 1998; Morris, Ohman, & Dolan, 1998; Morris, Ohman, & Dolan, 1999; Morris, Scott, & Dolan, 1999). Interestingly, fMRI studies suggest that fast-acting appraisal requires amygdala function, whereas more sustained, long-acting appraisal necessitates the use of the prefrontal cortex (Wright et al., 2001). In other words, many brain regions contribute to normal recognition of facial affective information.

Human brain imaging shows activation in the superior temporal sulcus during observation of mouth and eye movements (Puce, Allison, Bentin, Gore, & McCarthy, 1998). The cortical area primarily involved in processing facial movements appears to be the superior temporal sulcus, but this area is also involved in other related motion-detecting operations (Allison, Puce, & McCarthy, 2000; Puce et al., 1998). Monkeys and humans can distinguish between intentional and random movement (Hietanen & Perrett, 1996), and the cortical regions involved in processing the two types of movements may be different, according to imaging studies. Neurons in temporal regions are apparently involved in cognitive processing of meaningful "intentional" movement and bodily motion, as well as face and eye movement, illustrating a wide range of function within a cortical area, as well as the selectivity of response within specific neurons. Although neurons respond selectively to certain stimuli (e.g., faces), the neurons also respond to related stimuli (e.g., animals; Chao, Martin, & Haxby, 1999; L. Liu, Ioannides, & Streit, 1999). This suggests an evolutionary recruitment of areas for face and emotion processing from areas originally mediating other related cognitive operations (see also chapter 4).

Flexibility and Emotional Adaptations

Rule-governed facial responses to simple stimuli are tied to such systems as gustation, and high-order processing of facial stimuli is subsumed by the neurocognitive systems involved in object recognition and motion detection. Even structures that appear linked to a specific emotion, such as the amygdala, are also associated with a greater range of appraisal processes, such as recognizing happy, sad, or fearful faces of conspecifics, interpreting social scenes, and recognizing a variety of objects (Adolphs, 1999; Fonberg, 1974; Rolls, 1999; Weiskrantz, 1956, 1997). But looking at a fearful face does not mean that I am fearful when I look at it; it just means that the appraisal mechanisms are activated (but perhaps more primed to be fearful). Moreover, regions of the amygdala are activated whether one looks at something, imagines it, or is shown sentences that depict fearful events.

The amygdala is not only responsive to fear (e.g., Phillips, Bullmore, et al., 1998), though it does appear to be consistently activated in response to fearful events. Perhaps the amygdala, as an appraisal device, is a region of the brain critical for the detection of a variety of discrepant or attentional events (Davis & Whalen, 2001; M. Gallagher & Holland, 1994; Rosen & Schulkin, 1998). The detection of discrepancy is a fundamental behavioral adaptation orchestrated by the brain (Hebb, 1946, 1949; Kagan, 2002) that is important in learning (Rescorla, 1988) and attention (MacIntosh, 1975). This detection of discrepancy is a common theme, both within the emotions and aesthetics, and perhaps in some forms of curiosity (see chapters 3, 4, and 5). We are highly motivated and geared toward perceiving disruptions of expectations in order to evaluate and understand our status and safety in relation to this new, discrepant state of the world.

Although the amygdala may be responsive to a wide range of *discrepant* events, this region of the brain underlies basic gustatory responses (Herrick, 1926/1963, 1948; Norgren, 1995; Rolls, 1999). Areas involved in higher-order production, identification, and interpretation of emotional expression are probably the result of expanded use of previously existing functional areas.

More than the amygdala is recruited in the determination of discrepancy. The frontal cortex, that massive assortment of tissue, is also involved in this appraisal (Mesulam, 1998, 1999), adding more content to the assessment of events. Regions of the frontal cortex are involved in determination of approach and avoidance, of the positive and negative valence of events (Adolphs, Tranel, Damasio, & Damasio, 1994; Davidson et al., 2000, 2003; Paus, 2001). EEGs, PET, and functional brain-imaging studies have been useful in showing that positive or negative emotions differentially activate the hemispheres of the frontal cortical regions (Davidson et al., 1990, 2000; Fox & Davidson, 1989).

Conclusion

Emotional expression and perception are an integral part of human interaction. At one level, emotional expressions are governed by rules and can be elicited by simple stimuli, as in the example of disgust in the presence of bitter tastes. However, humans and other animals also use facial expressions to communicate various types of information to members of their own species and to others. The expression of fear, disgust, threat, or pleasure is meaningful to the observer.

As a neonate matures, simple rule-governed facial responses are modified through interactions with others, and the infant learns to regulate emotional response (Meltzoff & Moore, 1997, 1999). But the emotions are more than fixed-action pattern expressions, in the same way that thirst is more than a dry mouth. The labile nature of specific facial response topographies suggests a recruitment of simple facial actions during evolution to facilitate communication and social interaction among human beings. Presumably, the ability to express and interpret facial displays led to increased fitness and survivability (Adolphs, 1999; Dolan, 2000; A. W. Young, 1998).

The abilities to accurately interpret and express emotions through facial actions develop during infancy and childhood. As children mature, they learn to modify their emotional expression in socially appropriate ways. Detection of intentions and deceit also improves during childhood; conveying and concealing intentions through nonverbal means are parts of human interaction, and probably evolved in concert. The development of deception and the parallel development of the detection of deception is sometimes referred to as the evolutionary arms race (Byrne & Whiten, 1988; De Waal, 1982, 1991). The ability to convey and conceal intentions is advantageous, as is the ability to comprehend intentions and detect deceit in others.

I suggest that no special emotion center exists over and above cognitive systems in the brain, and that emotion should not be considered divorced from cognition (e.g., Dewey, 1925/1989; Lane & Nadel, 2000). One argument against studying emotion in the framework of cognitive science is the historical separation of cognition from visceral processes. Merging cognitive science and affective science would rule out the study of a disembodied mind, a calculating mind uninformed by the viscera. Many areas of research and theory contribute to the study of emotion, including cognitive, evolutionary, developmental, comparative, and social psychology, as well as the neurosciences. Emotions are studied using each of these methodologies, and each discipline contributes valuable information and new hypotheses regarding the emotions. From a neuroscience perspective, the neural systems engaged during various cognitive processes are also engaged while processing various emotional stimuli. And although cognitivists, and the representational theory of information processing, have viewed the emotions as "rather like digestion or respiration" (Rey, 1980, p. 189), this orientation is now changing.

In some instances, emotional information processing, one form of bodily sensibility, can predict social well-being and social performance, as well as predict who is at risk for behavioral abnormalities (Izard et al., 2001). A wide variety of information-processing systems figure importantly in everyday life, in getting things right. Bodily sensibility (cephalic in origin) in the context of the emotions highlights the fast appraisal systems that underlie emotional judgment and the brain mechanisms involved in getting the "gist of things" (Adolphs, Denburg, & Tranel, 2001). The fact that valence or coloring is another way, in emotional terms, of talking about heuristics or biases or orientation does not make it less cognitive than the other.

Visceral/autonomic information processing occurs at virtually every level of the neural axis, and what distinguishes emotional cognition from nonemotional cognition is the imposition of the visceral nervous system in decision making. This is a point about drinking, it is a point about fear, it is a point about joy of attachment, and it also occurs for our attraction and revulsion to works of art and people (see chapters 3 and 4).

3

Aesthetic Judgment, Discrepancy, and Inquiry

Introduction

We are clearly and profoundly a species that is responsive to wondrous beauty. We marvel at the smallest of objects to the greatest, we are in tune to diverse sounds, we create and admire objects as representations of ourselves, of others, and of our experiences. Information- processing systems pervade aesthetic judgment; our representational capacity, the play and flexibility of cognitive systems, the detection of discrepancy—all are reflective of our aesthetic judgments.

I think it is mistaken to suggest that "the main value of art is emotional. More accurately, perhaps, whereas the value of a work of art can be exclusively emotional, it cannot be exclusively cognitive" (Elster, 2000b, p. 205). As I indicated in the previous chapter, this is the very distinction that I believe is misleading. There is no separation, on my view, as should be clear, between the cognitive and the emotional; there are, however, different kinds of information-processing systems that subserve different functions.

In this chapter, I begin with a consideration of the biology of aesthetic experience and cognitive play with some speculation about the origins of aesthetics in song and movement. The chapter then switches to a discussion of musical syntax, discrepancy from expectations, and behavioral and neural responses. One neurotransmitter, dopamine, is linked to the organization of cognitive systems and the organization of action, and may underlie the behavioral responses to musical syntax and reward. Why dopamine? Because dopamine has long been linked to reward processes, and more recently has been linked to violations of expected reward. In other words, expectations of reward are tied to dopamine activation. The chapter ends with some general remarks about the neural mechanisms involved in the detection of novel and discrepant events. Aesthetic experience is pervasive across human experience, and the detection of discrepancy is one mechanism, but certainly not the only one, that underlies aesthetic experience.

Everyday Aesthetics

Aesthetic judgment is ultimately a profound part of our life. We value a person's character as a work of beauty, a beautiful soul; we view a masterfully rendered painting with awe; a majestic mountain just come into view renders us speechless. Aesthetics is pervasive in everyday life. It is not just for the museum, parlor, or theater. Aesthetic judgments draw one close, eliciting approach behaviors, but they also can repulse and make us withdraw from objects. John Dewey, in his book *Art as Experience* (1934/1958), stated romantically, "Because experience is the fulfillment of an organism in its struggles and achievements in a world of things, it is art in germ. Even in its rudimentary forms, it contains the promise of that delightful perception which is esthetic experience" (p. 18).

Art is thus the stuff of everyday life. Aesthetics is a profound part of our experience. It heightens and deepens our experience.[1] It is not something that closes us off, but expands us beyond ourselves and toward others. Art is a vital source of communication, and, therefore, it is perhaps not surprising that rudimentary forms of aesthetic appreciation may be expressed in a variety of species that, for example, sing (Geissmann, 2000; Marler, 2000b). Functional units that facilitate successful behavioral and reproductive strategies are recruited from a number of information-processing systems, aesthetic and otherwise. They serve diverse purposes.

Representations of objects are ancient, and we come prepared to understand objects in our environments. Cave art is but one example of this phenomenon that we find across cultures (Mithen, 1988). The desire to represent and understand the objects in our world is a fundamental motivation. N. K. Humphrey's (1976) work on rhyme, for example, suggests that aesthetic sensibility evolved because elegant classificatory cognitive systems are adaptive. We come prepared with a variety of cognitive systems, information processing, inferential mechanisms, and representational capacities for depicting and making sense of the objects that we are likely to encounter (Pinker, 1994, 1997; table 3.1; chapter 5; see also Cosmides & Tooby, 1994; Rozin, 1976a, 1998). These systems pervade our experiences, help determine how we interpret and predict events. And they underlie our problem-solving proclivities that reach into aesthetic judgment.

Such a predilection is wired in our mind/brains (Ramachandran & Hirstein, 1999; Zeki, 1999, 2001). Aesthetic judgment is part of our appraisal of ourselves and others, and is about both what is attractive and what we are trying to understand. It represents the objects we eat, copy, capture, and try to control (Mithen, 1996).

Table 3.1 Ideas about Events

Ideas about living objects
Ideas about objects and mechanics
Ideas about language
Ideas about probability
Ideas about food sources (avoidance and approach)
Ideas about kinship relations
Ideas about fairness

Adapted from Pinker, 1994, 1997.

Kant (1792/1951) tied aesthetic judgment, a "free play of the imagination," of cognitive capacities and faculties, to the perception of beauty or the sublime. Aesthetic judgment is intimately tied to bodily sensibility (see Croce's 1909/1983 masterful history of aesthetics in the classical and premodern period). In Suzanne Langer's view,[2] information-processing systems are continuous with bodily representation, and they reach their zenith in aesthetic sensibility or perception. As Langer stated, "All works of art create forms to express the life of feeling" (1957, p. 80). And like many other investigators, I would add that "feelings" are part of the perceptual apparatus that underlies information processing.

The sense of aesthetics is a feature of the way we come prepared to interpret the world (Gadamer, 1986). Such aesthetics are historically variable but universal, and are historically rich when the ecological conditions are suitable (N. K. Humphrey, 1973, 1999; Mithen, 1988, 1996). Aesthetic judgment reflects our cognitive flexibility and extension and use of specific cognitive mechanisms to wider domains of human expression (Mithen, 1988, 1996; Rozin, 1976a, 1998; figure 3.1).

Song and Movement: Biological Considerations of Aesthetics

Two lines of investigation suggest that aesthetics is not just the domain of the human species. The first line of investigation involves bird song, and the other concerns the perception of movement. Both are suggestive; there is no knockdown argument for the attribution of aesthetics in other species (though see P. M. Gray, Krauss, Atema, Payne, Krumhanst, & Baptista, 2001; Wallin, Merkre, & Brown, 2000). I do not want to unnecessarily distract the reader from the strong sense of the importance of aesthetics in us. I do suggest that aesthetic sensibility evolved in the context of information-processing systems and adaptive responses to the world in which we were trying to make sense, to survive and thrive (see also, for the evolution of musical sensibility and the functional role that is plays in our adaptation to our surroundings, Cross, 2001; Huron, 2001; Peretz & Zattore, 2003).

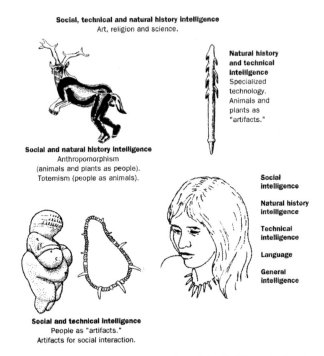

Social, technical and natural history intelligence
Art, religion and science.

**Natural history
and technical
intelligence**
Specialized
technology.
Animals and
plants as
"artifacts."

Social and natural history intelligence
Anthropomorphism
(animals and plants as people).
Totemism (people as animals).

**Social
intelligence**

**Natural history
intelligence**

**Technical
intelligence**

Language

**General
intelligence**

Social and technical intelligence
People as "artifacts."
Artifacts for social interaction.

Fig. 3.1. Cultural explosion as a consequence of cognitive fluidity (adapted from Mithen, 1996).

Experiments with bird song demonstrate that song production in song-birds is intricate (Marler, 2000b; Thorpe, 1974). Experiments show that song production and full song expression reveal several properties of importance: (1) There are critical stages in which the hearing of song is important for the later expression of song production; (2) song production reveals a form of syntax, of creative variation; (3) song is essential for successful reproduc-tion in songbirds; and (4) song syntax systems are lateralized to the left side of the bird brain, analogous to syntax and language lateralized to the left side of the human brain (e.g., Whaling, 2000). The point relevant for this chapter is that song production and song perception presuppose a rich cog-nitive system in the brain of these birds that serves diverse functional roles (e.g., territory, mate attraction; figure 3.2). And as Darwin noted, "With birds the voice serves to express various emotions" (1872/1965, p. 363).

In other words, bird song presupposes an innate template of possible syntax structure over which semantic content is conveyed to conspecifics (Gurney & Konishi, 1980; Marler, Peters, Ball, Duffy, & Wingfield, 1988). But song appears aesthetic to us; is it to birds? We do not know. It certainly can be aesthetically pleasing to our ears. We do know that communicative func-tion, the full form of expression, incurs biologically greater increases for successful reproduction. Song is part of the communicative interactions

Fig. 3.2. In (a), the female zebra finch on the right was treated with estrogen as a chick and then with testosterone as an adult. When courting a Bengalese finch (left), she approached it in a behavioral sequence that closely resembled the courtship behavior of a normal male. In (b), an example of the stereotyped male song developed by this female after 28 days of continued exposure to testosterone (with permission from Gurney & Konishi, 1980).

between living things that sing and understand the song, using the information in functional contexts (approach, avoid, find, etc.). The unique phonological combination from a syntactical template suggests a possible precursor for song production in humans (Marler, 2000a, 2000b; Hauser & McDermott, 2003).

Experiments with Sarah, a chimpanzee with extensive communication training, have suggested that, when shown movement by humans that we would judge as graceful and aesthetically pleasing in comparison to more awkward movement, the chimpanzee tended to look longer at the better form (Premack, 1982, personal communication). Form mattered, perhaps to the visual systems of the chimpanzee. But these effects in Sarah are modest when compared to the aesthetic judgment about movement in a 5-year-old (Premack & Premack, 2003). Nonetheless, the extent to which the chimpanzee's gaze favored the better form is a fascinating phenomenon.

Sexual selection, as Darwin first asserted, takes on a wondrous form, an alluring bodily sensibility. Bodily form, its appreciation and reach for excellence, clearly serves biological functions (e.g., health, indication of good genes, of being able to master physical challenges). Aesthetic enjoyment of bodily shape reaches across cultures (Delza, 1996; Devi, 1962; D. Humphrey, 1959). In fact, bodily form, in human play, development, the arts, and martial disciplines, is expressed cross-culturally. It has long been known to be essential for human well-being. Positive bodily sensibility emerges quite naturally in the diverse learning of bodily disciplines, physical mastery, and enjoyment. The sheer delight occurs amid the drudgery of bodily discipline, with the mind couched in the body in the learning of a particular movement sequence (figure 3.3).

There is nothing abstract here; having myself studied Tai Chi Chuan with someone who had been a modern dancer earlier in her career (Delza, 1996), I was very impressed with the role played by cognitive systems in the learning of new movements. There is an emphasis on the cognitive within the bodily, both as the "mental discipline" necessary to produce the masterful bodily movement and the cognitive appreciation of the beauty of the form. Information processing was endemic to the initial learning and then to the perfection of this bodily expression. It is part art, part martial expression, and all about aesthetic appreciation of bodily form. An utterly rigorous discipline, Tai Chi Chuan combines bodily excellence and peacefulness of mind in alertness while reaching toward critical goals.

Underlying the perceptual or bodily sensibility is a framework, unconsciously expressed, for responding to some kinds of stimuli (Graybiel et al., 1994; Lakoff & Johnson, 1999) over others (e.g., responding preferentially to the more elegant). Regions of the brain (frontal cortex, striatum) that orchestrate the organization of action in addition to complicated thought (language, etc.) underlie, no doubt, the actual expression of Tai Chi. And as we know now, these same regions are active when we watch someone perform an action, which might further explain why we appreciate graceful movement (Gallese, 2001; Jeannerod, 1997, 1999).

Fig. 3.3. Photograph of my deceased Tai Chi Chuan teacher, Sophia Delza.

Musical Expectations, Discrepancy, and Aesthetic Judgment

Cognition is often construed as detached, and because the emotions are anything but detached, they are considered noncognitive. Aesthetic experience is surely up close and personal; therefore, one can understand why many investigators construe aesthetic experience as not "exclusively cognitive" (Elster, 2000b, p. 205; Elster, 2000a). But I don't know what part of aesthetics is not linked to information-processing systems in the brain. In other words, aesthetic appreciation is replete with information processing; it is not as if one side of us is doing the thinking and another is appreciating.

Our attention becomes focused when encountering something that stands out as discrepant from the usual. Our curiosity is piqued; beholding an aesthetically pleasing or offensive object, our interest is raised or offended (Hebb, 1946, 1949). Expectancy in information processing in the brain permeates what Lashley (1951) called "the serial order of behavior." Lashley, among others, suggested that "input is never into a quiescent or static system, but always into a system which is already actively excited and organized." And "only when we can state the general characteristics of this background of excitation, can we understand the effects of a given input" (p. 506). We know something about the central control of motor or syntax programs (Fentress, 1984, 1999; Graybiel et al., 1994; Linas, 2001). The serial organization of appetitive and consummatory behaviors reflects the central organization of the brain. They no doubt underlie some of our aesthetic judgments.

John Dewey (1934/1968) also held the view of neural preparedness and is closely associated with theories in which behavior toward aesthetic objects reveals both appetitive and consummatory experiences and in which stability is sought while precariousness is restrained. All of us in the search for stable, secure relationships experience both the appetitive (the search mode) and the consummatory (found some relief) components (see Craig, 1918). Emotion, in this view, becomes salient only when a habit, a way of behaving that has been successful, is no longer effective. Of course, this renders emotions only in the context of conflict, and I suggest that emotions are not just about conflict and their expressions and resolutions. For Dewey, often emotions look a bit like hunger, and behavior serves to reduce them, eradicate them. What is valuable in Dewey for the present discussion are the diverse ways he reveals how bodily sensibility and visceral input figure in adapting to an environment, including aesthetics (see also Gombrich, 1963/1978).

Dewey's (1925/1989) view of learning, whether aesthetic or otherwise, is one in which the failure of an expectation initiates the process of learning, a cognitive behaviorism (Tolman, 1949). This view of aesthetics is explicated, for example, in Leonard Meyer's 1956 book, *Emotion and Meaning in Music*, in which the discrepancy model of learning figures throughout, as well as in the conflict theory of the emotions (see also Meyer, 1967, 1973). The breakdown of an expectation results in the search for a solution, as seen in musical expectations and the fulfillment of an expectation. The orientation of an expert, to be sure, is to the syntax or the form of music, and is usually couched in terms of tonality of musical composition (M. R. Jones, 1981, 1982; Langer, 1957; Weber, 1931).

In some experimental contexts, syntactic forms take precedence over emotional imagery, as is suggested in Meyer's model. I would not suggest that syntax predominates over other forms of information processing that permeate our musical experiences. But for experts, particularly extreme experts, that is a different matter. For example, in experimental studies, musical experts tend to prefer syntactical understanding compared with novices in their expectations of form and play (J. D. Smith, 1997; table 3.2).

It has been suggested that nonsyntactical experiences of music tend to be devalued by musical experts; on the other hand, high experts tend to enjoy the atypical in musical composition (J. D. Smith, 1997). But even novices are sensitive to syntactic atypicality (J. D. Smith & Melara, 1990). The search for something new, original, can evoke cognitive pleasure that permeates bodily sensibility. Again, the emphasis on syntactic structure and music does not mean that the other forms of music experience are not within information-processing systems; surely they are, as information processing extends to images (e.g., Farah, 1984; Kosslyn, 1994; Shepard, 1984, 1994; table 3.3).

Feelings of pleasure are, in many contexts, linked to familiarity. We enjoy the familiar; it is reassuring; we come back to what is familiar during times of crisis for reassurance. A trade-off between what is familiar and what is novel pervades much of human and, no doubt, animal experience (Rozin, 1976a, 1976b). Exposure tends to evoke enhanced preference for that to which one has been exposed or with which one is already familiar (e.g., music, food, or a person; Zajonc, 1964). A feeling of "warmth" and "intimacy" predominates the familiar (Titchner, 1910). But again, one does not have to set this up in terms of cognition versus visceral preference.

Preferences are coded in representations in the brain, a highly important form of information processing that serves us well. Desires presuppose information processing about objects that are preferred. Bodily feelings are important sources of information, which is why so many investigators (Can-

Table 3.2 Aesthetic Profile

Aesthetic Dimension	Rating
Syntactic	1.41
Referential	0.06
Sensual	0.47
Emotional	0.76

Adapted from J. D. Smith, 1997.

Table 3.3   Atypicality: Transformation, Unusualness, Complexity

Novices	Experts	High Experts
Prefer harmonic prototypes	Indifferent	Prefer atypicality

Adapted from J. D. Smith, 1997.

non, 1927; James, 1890/1952) have emphasized them. It is important to gain insight into whether a piece of music elicits chills or calmness, and how different phenomenological experiences vary with an underlying physiology of the bodily experience (Panksepp, 1993).

Perhaps this way of couching events in music is somewhat similar to that of couching cognition and the emotions. When cognition is centered squarely within syntactic structure, those unable to appreciate the fine syntactic form still enjoy the great works in music. We may presuppose an innate musical proclivity perhaps (Sloboda, 2000), but what matters in the emotional integration in music is much greater than simply the syntactical part, albeit that is a very important part in the cultural evolution of music (Wallin et al., 2000). The same sort of issue permeates the discussion of the aesthetics of music as it does the emotions; the cognitive, in this case the syntactical play, takes precedence over all else. But again, other forms of aesthetics—the sensual, the emotional—are all part of the information processing and aesthetic sensibility of music (J. D. Smith, 1997).

With regard to an aesthetic appreciation of music, bodily sensibility cuts through the distinction between images and syntax, as both are part of the information-processing systems that underlie bodily sensibility. "Music is the great link between the sensuous and the intellect" (Sullivan, 1955, p. 4),[3] and the expansion of what we can experience occurs through musical composition. Like the telescope or microscope, the horizons for seeing, hearing, and sensing are expanded; it is a mind in a body.

Musicians come with different musical strengths. If one does not have a feel for the music one is never going to be a really good musician; similarly, if one does not have a feel for a phenomenon as a scientist, one is never going to do good research on that phenomenon. Nothing takes the place of this feel for something. It is certainly basic to the human knower experiencing the world. Although expectations linked to probability judgments are only part of the story for musical aesthetic appreciation, they still seem to be elements of the feel for the phenomena, which requires a number of information-processing systems.

Musical Syntax, Discrepancy, and Activation

I do not focus on all aesthetic experiences, and the example I do use here is for the purpose of making a small point, namely, that regions of the brain that may underlie musical syntax, probability judgments, responses to novelty, also underlie aesthetic experiences (Falk, 2000; Patel, 2003). I do not think there is an extra area of the brain that evolved exclusively for aesthetic judgment. Thus, for example, Broca's area is known for its involvement in the processing of the formal aspects of language, and there are obviously formal cognitive aspects in musical structure (e.g., Lerdahl & Jackendoff, 1999; Raffmann, 1993; Sloboda, 1985, 2000), and interestingly, a variety of brain-imaging studies have linked the activation of Broca's area to musical syntax (Koelsch, Gunter, Friederici, & Schröeger, 2000; Koelsch, Gunter, Cramon, Zysset, Lohmann, & Friederici, 2002; Koelsch, Schroger, & Gunter, 2002; Maess, Koelsch, Gunter, & Friederici, 2001; Patel, 2003; Patel, Gibson, Ratner, Besson, & Holcomb, 1998; Sergent, 1993).

In one brain activation study (using magnetoencephalography), unexpected or discrepant musical syntactical structure elicited greater activation of Broca's area (and the homologous right side) than a musical composition that was reported as syntactically predicted (Maess et al., 2001; figure 3.4). This region of the brain is generally responsive to syntactical musical expression. The authors suggested that the left (pars opercularis) region is more involved in the processing of language, and the right (pars opercularis) side in the processing of musical syntax.

In other related studies, syntactical discrepancy has been linked to event-related brain potentials for both music and language recognition. The P600 event-related potential was initially linked to language syntax, but it has now been demonstrated that the P600 evoked potential is linked to a broader class of syntactical organization in the brain (e.g., music; Patel, Gibson, Ratner, Besson, & Holcomb, 1998). The neural mechanisms for the organization of musical judgment are not identical to those of human language expression, but there are interesting overlaps, and one appears to be in the context of Broca's area.

The detection of discrepancy is one component that figures in aesthetic appreciation (Krumhansl, 2002; Meyer, 1973, 2001), but surely not the only factor (J. D. Smith, 1987). The brain is oriented to detect and respond to discrepancy (e.g., Opitz, Mecklinger, Friederici, & von Cramon, 1999). And, indeed, although there is no specific music center in the brain, it is important to note that a wide variety of both neocortical and paleocortical sites have been linked to musical sight reading, hearing, and performance (e.g., Falk, 2000; Koelsch, Schroger, & Gunter, 2002; Parsons, 2001; Peretz, 2001, 2002; Petr et al., 2002; Rauschecker, 2001; Sergent, Zuck, Terriah, & MacDonald, 1992; figure 3.5).

Probability, Expectations, and Learning

Probability judgments to assess the condition of uncertainty are at the heart of human reasoning, and while it is a mistake to exaggerate their role in aesthetic judgment, one can assume that in some contexts, such as the one

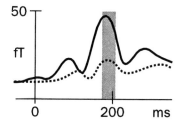

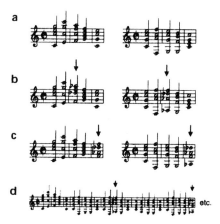

Fig. 3.4. Neuronal activation (top) in discrepant (shaded region) and nondiscrepant musical conditions and examples (bottom) of chord sequences. (a) Cadences consisting exclusively of in-key chords. (b) Chord sequences containing a Neapolitan sixth chord at the third position. (c) Chord sequences containing a Neapolitan at the fifth position; Neapolitan chords are indicated by arrows. (d) Examples of directly succeeding chord sequences as presented in the experiment (adapted from Maess et al., 2001).

depicted above, they do play a role. Uncertainty is a basic feature of our existence. And we have evolved a wide variety of resources to cope with uncertainty. Moreover, as one noted musicologist has remarked, "Uncertainty is anathema to humankind," and "we devise ways of reducing uncertainty both in the out-there world and in our personal lives." But "in the arts and other playful activities such as sports, games and gambling we actually relish and cultivate a considerable amount of uncertainty" (Meyer, 2001, p. 353; see also Krumhansl, 2002).

Probability and detection of discrepancies are a definitive part of problem solving and are one part of aesthetic judgment. Many issues related to probability have been couched in terms of expectations. Indeed, syntactic

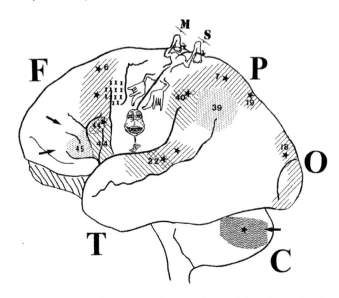

Fig. 3.5. Left hemisphere of the human brain. Lobes are labeled at their edges: F, frontal; T, temporal; P, parietal; and O, occipital. C indicates the cerebellum. The homun-
culus is a simplification of the approximate organization of primary somatosensory (S)
and primary motor (M) cortices. Representations of the tongue (illustrated) and larynx
are located below the face regions. Numbers represent Brodmann's areas that provide
foci for specific linguistic and musical processes. The Xs indicate an area that subserves
writing; 44 and 45 form Broca's speech area, and 22 and 39 form Wernicke's area.
Auditory areas 41 and 42 are not illustrated because they are buried deep within the
sylvian fissure (above area 22), as is also the case for the planum temporale. Arrows
indicate areas of prefrontal cortex and neocerebellum that recently were shown to
participate in linguistic and musical processing. Stars represent areas activated on one
or both sides as musicians sight-read, listened to, and played a Bach partita with their
right hand (Sergent et al., 1992). It should be noted that processing of language and
music entails activation of more widely distributed networks than indicated here, and
that each uses both hemispheres to some extent (with permission from Falk, 2000).

predictions may have their base in general issues about probability and
human reasoning.

Clearly, we embody diverse cognitive mechanisms for appraising probabilistic relations. The history of understanding human reasoning has high-
lighted this ability,imperfect and replete with biases as it is. Human beings
use probabilities to assess the likelihood of events, but never, or hardly ever,
perfectly (cf. Brunswik, 1943, 1955; Gigerenzer, 2000; Kahneman & Snell,
1992; Peirce, 1898/1992b).

"Statistics" initially meant keeping records, for the state, of deaths, births,
plagues, and so on (Hacking, 1965/1979). The goal of statistics was to com-
pute likelihoods so that danger could be anticipated and the state could be

better organized. Keeping records was the primary role of statisticians, along with determining probabilities with logical and statistical tools (R. A. Fisher, 1956). A number of axiomatic approaches and tools emerged from this early stage of statistics (e.g., ANOVAS), and the logic of statistical inference to aid reasoning was developed (Gigerenzer, 1991; Hacking, 1965/1979). A critical issue of the logic of statistical reasoning is what constitutes support for a hypothesis. A vast array of ratios and likelihoods is required (Hacking, 1965/1979). Bayes' theorem is one formal tool to scrutinize how frequency information is related to probability judgments (Baron, 1988/2000; Gigerenzer, 1991) in attempting to link relative frequencies and sample size. Bayes' theorem penalizes, among other things, unnecessary model parameters, and thus encourages simplicity.

Probability reasoning reflects, perhaps, a specific mechanism in the cognitive arsenal for understanding the world with which one is trying to cope. It is a mechanism that evolved to detect danger and to promote reproductive success and underlies our appraisals about diverse events, including affective ones, and has been extended to ever novel domains, including evolved aesthetic ones.

A legitimate question concerns the process by which and the extent to which mechanisms designed to predict predators and prey, food sources, and sexual success might have became linked to aesthetics (Dewey, 1934/1968; Meyer, 1956, 1967, 1973). Prediction for one set of circumstances extends to new domains in our evolutionary ascent; our cognitive apparatus extends and expands and now can underlie aesthetic judgments.

Within learning theory (N. E. Miller, 1959; Rescorla, 1988), prediction was coupled to expectancies and their breakdown. When expectations are thwarted, a broad array of learning occurs through new problem-solving search principles. This is close in scope to Peirce's (1878) view of inquiry and the development of new solutions to problems. Of course, inquiry is more than this. An important discovery was that not only is there a set of learning equations that is not coupled to contingencies, but time of occurrence is not an axiomatic factor in learning per se, but rather for predicting events (Rescorla & Wagner, 1972). In the hands of Dickinson (1980), causal inference linked to prediction was a feature in perhaps a wide array of animals. This view of inquiry and learning was prescient, for the variants of this view would capture learning theory through what became known as the Rescorla-Wagner equation:

$$\Delta V = \alpha\beta \, (\lambda - V)$$

The Rescorla-Wagner model depicts the associative strengths of stimuli and how discrepancies from expectations are resolved. An association, and thereby learning, occurs by the strength of the predictions that are being developed. The model becomes then not simply a mathematical approach to neural science, but also incorporates a cognitive point of view. In the equation, V represents the current associative strength of the stimulus, and λ shows the maximum associative strength of the primary motivating event. The salience of conditioned and unconditioned stimuli is represented by α and β, respectively. The predictability of the primary motivating event is shown in the $(\lambda-V)$ term. When the current and maximum associative strengths of the stimulus are equal, the conditioned stimulus fully predicts the reinforcer. However, when the term is positive (λ is greater than V), the associative strength increases and the conditioned stimulus does not fully predict the reinforcer—there is room for learning to occur. With increased associative strength, learning occurs, and in fact occurs only when the conditioned stimulus does not entirely predict the reinforcer. In contrast, a negative $(\lambda-V)$ term occurs when there is a loss of associative strength and the predicted reinforcer has failed (extinction). General informational search and discrepancy mechanisms, such as the one outlined above, may play a role in those aesthetic judgments that reflect a response to violations of expectations. One neurotransmitter, tied to expectations of reward or pleasure, is dopamine, to which we now turn.

Dopamine, Discrepancy, and the Prediction of Reward

It's been known for a long time that neurotransmitters in the brain play an important role in learning and reward. There is no univocal conception of reward, and I use it in a commonsense manner: something desired, something labored for, something attained. Dopamine provides an excellent example of the role of the body in the prediction of rewarding events (Schultz, 2002), and may underlie aesthetic judgment. Dopamine is an important neurotransmitter involved in a wide range of functions. But one overriding theme of research findings involving dopamine is the organization of action and the organization of thought. Dopamine is involved in both action and thought, and, as such, is a necessary chemical information molecule for us in maintaining a coherent world in which to function (Kelley, 1999). Some key areas of dopamine expression in the brain are depicted in figure 3.6.

The dopamine pathways in the brain underlie a number of behavioral functions that range from syntax production (Ullman, 2001) and probability reasoning, to activation of specific motor programs and the learning of motor programs (Graybiel et al., 1994). For example, Parkinson's patients (who have depleted dopamine levels in the brain) have trouble with ordinary syntax, as they do with motor control (Marsden, 1984). An interesting set of studies on dopamine neurons in the brains of macaques has suggested that one function of this neurotransmitter in specific regions of the brain is the prediction of rewarding events; dopamine neurons tend to fire more in anticipation of rewarding events. The mechanisms for generating action are not separate from the mechanisms for thought; the serial order of behavior (Lashley, 1951) is organized by a number of regions of the brain, including

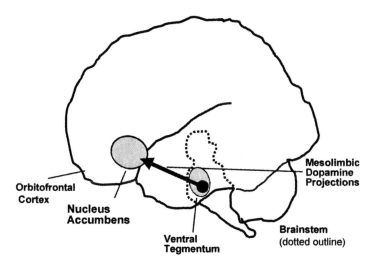

Fig. 3.6. Regions of the brain tied to dopamine.

the basal ganglia, in which dopamine is a primary neurotransmitter in the organization of behavior.

Dopamine has long been linked to issues of reward and the liking of and approaching toward objects (Kelley, 1999). But the concept of reward has a long and thorny history (Thorndike, 1911; Wise, 2002). Dopamine is not simply a neurotransmitter underlying the brain mechanisms linked to reward. It is much more complex; even when dopamine is blocked, animals can still like things (e.g., sucrose; Berridge, 2000). But importantly, dopamine is essential not only for the organization of drive, wanting something, but also for the salience of events (Berridge, 1996). In other words, dopamine expression is essential for incentive motivation: the range of associations that is generated in terms of objects to approach and objects to avoid (Spanagel & Weiss, 1999). The induction of dopamine in regions of the brain underlying the organization of action increases the propensity to perform a number of psychological functions. Some forms of aesthetic experiences would also be included.

The amines serotonin, norepinephrine, and dopamine are represented in specific neuronal sites in the brainstem and forebrain. From small clusters of cell bodies a diverse array of fiber pathways connects to a large part of the brain (e.g., dopamine; Groenewegen et al., 1991; Spanagel & Weiss, 1999). Dopaminergic pathways from the substantia nigra innervate the putamen and caudate nucleus of the striatum (Holt, Graybiel, & Saper, 1997). This is the nigrostriatal system involved in subcortical motor control. Dysfunction of this system is associated with certain movement disorders such as Parkinson's disease and tardive dyskinesia. The initiation of movement and the organization of thought are important functions of the nigrostriatal system and are illustrated by the characteristics of Parkinson's disease (Marsden, 1984).

The mesocorticolimbic dopamine system includes the brain systems important for water, food and salt ingestion, and drug use (Hajnal & Norgren, 2001; Hollerman, Tremblay, & Schultz, 1998; Kelley, 1999; Spanagel & Weiss, 1999). This system can be subdivided into two systems: the mesolimbic system and the mesocortical system. The mesolimbic system consists of dopaminergic projections from the midbrain ventral tegmental area to limbic forebrain areas, including the nucleus accumbens, stria terminalis, lateral septal nuclei, amygdala, and limbic areas of the striatum (Spanagel & Weiss, 1999; Swanson, 2003). In the mesocortical dopamine system, the dopamine cell bodies are also located in the ventral tegmental area. Subsets of dopaminergic projections terminate in the prefrontal cortex, anterior cingulate, and entorhinal cortex (Byne et al., 1999; Groenewegen et al., 1991).

The dopamine system does not function in isolation. Dopamine is colocalized with a number of neurotransmitters and neuropeptides in a variety of sites in the brain (Kelley, 1999). Neurons in the nucleus accumbens receive input from the hippocampus, as well as from brainstem serotonin neurons, and glutamate neurons from the cortex and thalamus. Neurons within the nucleus accumbens contain receptors for many other neurotransmitters (Kelley, 1999).

But dopamine neurons are linked to the learning phase in a number of paradigms and in response to novel events (Schultz, 2000, 2002). Dopamine neurons in the frontal cortex and striatum are active in anticipation of the events (e.g., gustatory and visual rewards; Hollerman, Tremblay, & Schultz, 1998; Schultz, 2000; Tremblay, Hollerman, & Schultz, 1998). In electrophysiological studies in macaques, before a reward becomes fully predictable, dopamine neurons are activated each time the reward is given. However, once the reward is predictable (i.e., always occurring without failure), dopamine no longer is activated to the same degree. Furthermore, if the predicted reward does not occur as expected, dopamine release is again activated (figure 3.7).

The unpredictable feature of the stimulus is importantly tied to dopaminergic activation and reinforces the Rescorla-Wagner model of predictability being a primary feature in expectancy, attention, and learning (Schultz, 2002). In further studies, representations of reward predictability or uncertainty were correlated in populations of dopaminergic neurons; the greater the uncertainty of reward occurrence, the greater activation of the dopamine neuronal population (Fiorillo, Tobler, & Schutz, 2003). Two sets of neuronal populations are responsive to these events: One set changes to reward probability, and another changes to reward uncertainty.

In other words, the important point is that this is a model of expectancy and learning, and the model of dopamine release should have some application to aesthetic appreciation. What is expected and easily predicted creates less of a reaction than something that is novel and unique. The same may hold perhaps for the perception of beauty or aesthetics (Juslin & Sloboda,

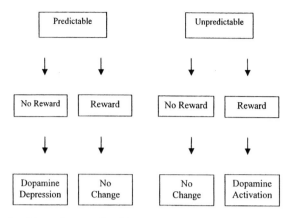

Fig. 3.7. Predictable and unpredictable events and expression of dopamine neurons (adapted from Schultz, 1998).

2001), which creates a definitive reaction in the brain, seen through the dopamine neurons.

Dopamine is just one neurotransmitter among others in the context of the organization of action. What is interesting is that this one neurotransmitter, so essential in the organization of movement, is also essential in the organization of thought—namely, the prediction of events. The prediction of events is one cognitive component that underlies a wide variety of our activities, including aesthetic judgments. One mechanism underlying aesthetic judgment of music may require (and this is speculative) dopamine neurons in rule-governed expectations that underlie grammar and syntax (Pinker, 1994, 1997; Ullman, 2001). Cognition is not on one side, and bodily sensibility to the music, the painting, the ballet, the sonnet on the other; they run together. Discrepancy is just one mechanism, but an important one, in the organization of action toward events in the world, including that of rewarding events.

Further Considerations of the Neural Regions Responsive to Novel and Unusual Events

Discrepancy detectors, for which there must be many variants (see Schultz, 2002), as I have indicated, reflect different systems in the brain and perhaps underlie some forms of aesthetic judgment (Meyer, 1973). The recognition of a discrepant event is a broad-based heuristic that pervades the organization of decisions and action. Moreover, syntactical processing and detection of discrepant syntactic events are detected early on by regions of the brain that include frontal and temporal cortex (Friederici, Wang, Hermann, Maess, & Oertel, 2000; Opitz et al., 1999).

One region of the brain, the amygdala, is linked to the detection of a number of discrepant events, and possibly to facial discrepant events as well (P. C. Holland, Chik, & Zhang, 2001; chapter 2); it also underlies a number of positive and negative responses (LeDoux, 1996, 2000; Parkinson et al., 2001). Interestingly, our understanding of amygdala function has evolved from taste, olfaction, and visceral regulation (Herrick, 1905, 1948) to social interpretation and perception (Kluver & Bucy, 1939), the magnification of events (McGaugh, Cahill, & Rozzendaal, 1996), reproductive and attachment behaviors (Ferguson, Aldag, Insel, & Young, 2001), fear-related systems (LeDoux, 1996), the regulation of mineral appetites (Schulkin, 1991), and uncertainty, expectancy, and attentional responses to events. Nonetheless, one core characteristic associated with amygdala function includes the detection of discrepant events and the readiness to perceive an event regardless of whether the event is dangerous or not. Dopaminergic neurons in the amygdala are elevated during problem solving (Fried et al., 2001), and they may also underlie the perception of reward and the detection of novelty.

In patients with dorsal lateral prefrontal damage, one feature stands out, namely, their impairment in responding to novel and unusual events (Daffner, Mesulam, Holcomb, et al., 2000; Daffner, Mesulam, Scinto, et al., 2000). Decrements in responsiveness to the world in part reflect sensory neglect, reduced attentional abilities, and a lack of orientation to novel events (Mesulam, 1999; Sokolov, 1963). Regions of the brain such as the cingulate cortex, a massive and complex structure that can include (with much confusion; see Swanson, 2000a, 2000b) the amygdala and the frontal cortex, are involved in both attentional and emotional mechanisms (Lane et al., 1998; Lane, Reiman, Ahern, Schwartz, & Davidson, 1997; Lane, Reiman, Bradley, et al., 1997) and responding to errors.

Uncertainty follows from the recognition of a discrepancy. And when expectations begin to falter, what formerly could be relied on no longer has the same weighted value. A search for a new solution emerges. In human experiments, as I alluded to in an earlier chapter, the anterior cingulate and lateral orbitofrontal cortex are activated by uncertainty. When subjects are playing cards and monetary awards are at stake, autonomic output is reflected in cortical activation (H. D. Critchley, Mathias, & Dolan, 2001a; Elliott, Newman, Longe, & Deakin, 2003). The cortical regions, in addition to regions of the basal ganglia, are linked to a wide range of discrepant events and underlie the organization of action: to approach or avoid objects.

The anticipation of monetary gains and losses and its effect on brain activation (Breiter et al., 2001; Elliott et al., 2003) has been associated with the activation of the nucleus accumbens (in addition to other areas of the brain). These results may reflect the activation of dopamine innervation from the brainstem ventral tegmental dopamine neurons. The activation of this system (dopamine) may reflect in part a prediction error, a difference between expectation and outcome. With regard to dopaminergic neurons, we know now, as I indicated, that they play a functional role in syntactical competence in humans (Ullman et al., 1997). They should also underlie the syntactical organization and the response to discrepancy for musical composition, and more generally for aesthetic judgment. In the context of listening to a piece of music, diverse regions that underlie dopamine activation should be activated to musical/syntactical discrepancy (figure 3. 8).

Conclusion

Aesthetic appreciation, in its myriad forms, is an essential part of the human condition and is inextricably linked to a sense of well-being (Nussbaum, 2001). The evocation of broad-based emotions is tied to aesthetics. Human aesthetic pleasure requires essential information processing and problem solving (Dissanyake, 2000). The organization or structure of music has long been linked to information-processing systems (Coons & Kraechenbuchl, 1958; Schwartz, Howe, & Purves, 2003), and these systems in the brain are oriented to discrepancies in musical syntax or form (Narmour, 1991).

The history of aesthetics is rich and wondrous, the diverse expressiveness of humans both in the appetitive and consummatory experiences; the

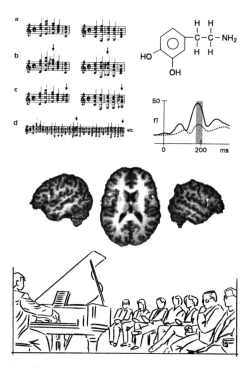

Fig. 3.8. Hypothetical link among dopamine expression, musical composition, and music listening (Yansen & Schulkin, 2000).

creative and constructive side is vastly rich in expression, as we all know. Aesthetic experiences pervade human life; my orientation is to music and dance. Demythologizing aesthetics is recognizing the pervasiveness of aesthetic sensibility, the cognitive resources that are allocated to it, and the common cognitive and neural systems that underlie aesthetic sensibility.

Evolution favored increased accessibility of core cognitive systems, allowing them to be extended in diverse domains of human expression; aesthetic appraisal gained its adaptive significance, perhaps, by extending from our exploration of novel and discrepant events involving those around us and the world in which we are trying to adapt, to carve out a meaningful existence. Aesthetic judgment exists amid the information-processing systems in the brain that underlie perception. Indeed, mechanisms that are oriented to novelty, familiarity, and syntax underlie aesthetic judgment (at least some forms).

Discrepancy (or novelty) detection underlies the brain processing in both musicians and nonmusicians (Koelsch et al., 2000). The recognition of musical discrepancy is expressed early on in development (Pick et al., 1994). Expectancy effects permeate the organization of the brain (Opitz et al., 1999) and are linked to appraisal systems for gains and losses (Breiter et al., 2001; Shidara & Richmond, 2002). But discrepancy detectors are only one system; aesthetic sensibility is much broader than simply the detection of discrepancy and the appreciation of filling in the information that is needed, sensing the syntactical and informational content of the aesthetic object.

Novelty detectors are operative across the human experience and in a number of regions of the human brain (Mecklinger, Opitz, & Friederici, 1997; Mesulman, 1998, 1999). Several areas of the brain, including the amygdala, basal ganglia, regions of the prefrontal cortex, and Broca's area and its analogue in the right hemisphere, are importantly involved in some forms of aesthetic judgment. Moreover, activation of the left prefrontal cortex is linked to music that generates feelings of joy and happiness, and activation of the right prefrontal cortex is linked to music that generates feelings of fear or sadness (Schmidt & Trainor, 2001; Zatorre & Krumbansl, 2002). Not surprisingly, in one PET study a number of brain regions that are linked to emotional appraisals were activated by music; they include the ventral striatum, the amygdala, and the orbitofrontal and ventromedial prefrontal cortices (Blood & Zatorre, 2001; Blood, Zatorre, Bermudez, & Evans, 1999). These findings are consistent with a large body of evidence in which laterality of frontal cortical expression is linked to positive and negative emotions (Davidson et al., 2000, 2003), and many of these same regions underlie detection of novelty and discrepancy and whether to approach or avoid objects (Small, Zatorre, Dagher, Evans, & Gotman, 2001).

An interesting question is: Why, from an evolutionary point of view, should we have aesthetic appreciation? I suggest the obvious: to mobilize approach and avoidance of objects that we like or loathe (see also Cardinal, Parkinson, Hall, & Everitt, 2002 for roughly the same suggestion for the origins of the *emotions*). The mechanisms for aesthetic appreciation utilize preexisting neural and behavioral systems in the organization of behavior. Therefore, it is not surprising that dopamine, one very important neurotransmitter in the organization of action and cognition, may also underlie aesthetic judgment. The activation of dopaminergic mechanisms under uncertainty is linked to the reward mechanisms in the brain; predictability of a stimulus has a direct impact on the human brain reward systems under a variety of experimental conditions (Berns, McClure, Pagnoni, & Montague, 2001). Thus again, the person who wins in the lottery goes out and buys a car, a house, and other objects of enjoyment, however pedestrian or mundane they seem; aesthetic sensibility is pervasive. Aesthetic experiences are pervasive, tied in part to problem solving and nicely depicted in Dewey's (1934/1968) classic work *Art as Experience*.

4

Moral Sensibility and Social Cohesion

Introduction

I watch a stranger cringe in pain, and I react to help. The cognitive/behavioral mechanisms are built into the brain. The origins are ancient. Underlying the response are rules for detection, detecting discomfort in another. The bodily sensibility is not on one side and the rules of engagement on the other.[1] Fast appraisal of these events generates approach or avoidance. The representations in the brain are rich in information processing and reflect bodily engagement. Bodily representations are inherent in what has been traditionally called the "moral sentiments" (A. Smith, 1759/1976; table 4.1).

Darwin (1871/1982) repeatedly referred to the "moral sense." He asserted, "Any animal whatever, endowed with a well-marked social instinct, the parental and filial affections being here included, would inevitably acquire a moral sense of conscience, as soon as its intellectual power had become as well or nearly as well developed as in man" (p. 95). The use of such social abilities is not necessarily solely oriented toward doing no harm or helping conspecifics.

In this chapter, I provide a brief historical context for the moral sentiments, then suggest that the separation of intuition from reason (Haidt, 2001) is another variant of the emotion-cognition separation that figured in the previous chapters. I then discuss the biological link between gustatory sensibility and morality (e.g., disgust or revulsion at a person's gluttony; Rozin, 1999), followed by a discussion of empathy and the brain. Moreover, I suggest that empathy is a fast appraisal system, and that the neural mechanisms operative in both first- and third-person perspective taking (Schulkin, 2000) contribute to moral sensibility (Preston & De Waal, 2002).

Table 4.1 A Partial List of
Moral Sentiments

Sympathy/empathy
Fairness
Self-regulation
Discipline
Duty
Loyalty

At the onset, one should know that I do not believe that there evolved a special moral neural system, but what did evolve were diverse problem-solving mechanisms that were recruited for moral judgment.[2] But I do believe that we come prepared to ascertain the experiences of others, whether to approach or avoid them (whether they are repulsive and to withdraw). In other words, rudimentary approach/avoidance mechanisms instantiated in the brain underlie moral sentiments.

Background

The emotions evolved (though not exclusively) to facilitate social interactions. They are intimately linked to behavioral mechanisms of approach and avoidance, and, as Adam Smith noted in 1759 (1976), emotions come to bear on easily and importantly elicited moral sentiments. In wonderful detail, Smith described the wide variety of moral sentiments, moral bodily sentiments (e.g., sympathy, empathy; see Hoffman, 2002; Hume, 1739/1984; Goldman, 1992; Scheler, 1992; Stein, 1964; E. Thompson, 2001). Many believe that the moral sentiments are fundamental for social cohesion and the evolution of human development (e.g., J. S. Wilson, 1993). As J. S. Wilson, a modern proponent of moral sensibility, has suggested, "Mankind's moral sense is not a strong beacon of light. . . . It is rather a small candle flame" (1995, p. 208). The possession of a brain that could detect the *experiences* of others probably was a major factor in our evolutionary history.

Adam Smith, as did many other classical empiricists (e.g., Hume, 1739/1984), tied the emotions to bodily hedonic states and more generally to a calculus of predicted pleasure or pain and broad-based utility functions (Hobbes, 1651/1958; Kahneman et al., 1999; Mill, 1861; Sidgwick, 1981). Smith suggested that, "as we sympathize with the joy of our companions when in prosperity, so we join with them in the complacency and satisfaction with which they naturally regard whatever is the cause of their good fortune" (p. 70). Well, sometimes we do. Of course, modern empiricists are also experimentalists; Smith was not. Smith's emphasis was that a wide variety of natural inclinations (both attractive and not) were implicated in tying us to each other (see J. S. Wilson, 1993), and they are a mixed assortment, some more easily thought of in terms of bodily sensibility than others.

Moral sentiments pervade decision making (R. H. Frank, 1988), and because they blend with cognitive information-processing systems so naturally and extensively, it has led some moral theorists to suggest that they are carried out by the same processes (e.g., Greenspan, 1995; G. E. Moore 1903/ 1968). They are importantly involved with our responses to one another. Moral sensibility reflects information processing—finding something attractive or repulsive—and there is a long tradition of linking moral appraisal to the emotions (e.g., classical Stoics; Sabini & Silver, 1982; Solomon, 1980). Moral sentiments, at least some of them, have long been thought to move one beyond narrow self-interest (R. H. Frank, 1988; Hoffman, 2000) to a broad array of human motivation (Blackbun, 1998; Hume, 1739/1984; A. Smith, 1759/1976).

Emotion and Moral Appraisals

Morality has been understood as being either rule-generated or emotive. When couched in terms of the emotions, morality was relegated to an inferior status and considered to lack cognitive structure (Stevenson, 1944). This was unfortunate. Something does not have to be true (or not) to be cognitive, obligatory or contingent.[3] Castigating morality as merely emotions did a disservice to both. When morality was dismissed in this manner, it became bodily, barren, and devoid of real content.

As I suggested in Chapter 2, the experience of a particular emotion may or may not be helpful, depending on the context, the emotions, and the person. Depiction of the emotions as the seducers in the excess of human behavior has long been apparent; the "deadly sins" are not ephemeral, but real and substantial (Solomon, 1999).

When couched in terms of abstract rules that were divorced and distant, morality was seen as the perfect judge: detached and dispassionate. Objectivity was put on a pedestal. But we are imperfect problem-solvers, whether smart or not, whether contemplating physics or morality. We rely on a number of heuristics that guide decision making (Gigerenzer, 2000). This does not deflate reason, but rather puts reason in perspective.[4] Now we can do the same for bodily sensibility that underlies our empathetic responses toward others: not a perfect system, just one important source of information processing among others. The same should be said for the emotions; they are not perfect systems, but very good ones that evolved to aid successful behavioral adaptation.

Emotivism (emotion without cognitive content) denied judgment to the emotions in part because judgment was linked to rational conscious considerations. If we relied on that sort of reasoning, we would be unable to put on our shoes. The vast array of cognitive events are not conscious, whether in the emotions, morally, or otherwise. It was a bogus choice. Cognition could permeate both, or not. The fact that issues are not weighed consciously simply reveals that moral sensibility is like most other sensibilities.

Emotional information processing provides an orientation to events (Wolheim, 1999). It is better to understand problem-solving proclivities as heuristics that aid decision making and can allow one to get things right or not (Baron, 1988/2000; Dewey, 1925/1989). Moral sentiments bound to emotions are typically, as James liked to describe them, "lively experiences," bodily in nature. The visceral expression is not divided into moral appraisal or cognitive functions. Imagination and metaphorical reasoning within bodily sensibility pervade moral reasoning (Johnson, 1993; on revulsion and attraction, see Bentham, 1789/1948; Hobbes, 1651/1958; Mill, 1861).

Intuition versus Reason: Back to Emotion versus Cognition

Just as emotion need not be contrasted with cognition, intuition need not be contrasted with rationality (Haidt, 2001; see Baron's 1998 critique of intuitionism and moral reasoning). Most of what is depicted in table 4.2 is more about how fast the information-processing system is than about intuition (fast) versus reason. This is why the divide depicted in this manner

Table 4.2 General Features of the Two Systems

The Intuitive System	The Reasoning System
Fast and effortless	Slow and effortful
Process is unintentional and runs automatically	Process is intentional and controllable
Process is inaccessible; only results enter awareness	Process is consciously accessible and viewable
Does not demand attentional resources	Demands attentional resources, which are limited
Parallel distributed processing	Serial processing
Pattern matching; thought is metaphorical, holistic	Symbol manipulation; thought is truth preserving, analytical
Common to all mammals	Unique to humans over age 2, and perhaps some language-trained apes
Context-dependent	Context-independent
Platform-dependent (depends on the brain and body that houses it)	Platform-independent (the process can be transported to any rule-following organism or machine)

Adapted from Haidt, 2001.

is misleading and is reminiscent of the cognition-emotion distinction. The divide between the two does not negate the broad-based information-processing systems that make what we call intuition possible. We can perhaps give endless reasons and still be mistaken, or give few and be right when it comes to how one ought to treat another. That is not to say that all of our decision making about others is fast, outside of consciousness. Ethical reasoning is not a second-rate form of reasoning (McGinn, 1999), but, like other forms of reasoning, it is not perfect.[5]

Intuition (sometimes described as implicit reason, or unconscious reason) means the judgment reflects a fast response. The judgment can be right or not, just as forms of reasoning can be right or not. The larger point about moral reasoning, demythologized from the heights of perfection, may not always be explicit in terms of everyday behavior, but it can be, and it can perhaps be self-reflective and self-corrective (Dewey, 1908/1960).

Intuitions about morality are no safeguard against acting mistakenly with ill-fated consequences. Why would we think otherwise (see Baron, 1998)? In fact, consequences ought to be part of one's purview in decision making (Baron, 1988; 1988/2000). One can still hold onto the outdated conception of the perfect reasoner, and then, of course, its demise, or one can demythologize the event and accept that reason is imperfect, whether tied to the *emotions* or not. It is imperfect but still rational. Heuristics for problem solving are not the descent into nonrationality (Baron, 1990; Gigerenzer, 2000; Kahneman et al., 1999). Makeshift fast appraisals may be inconsistent at times, but they aid adaptation and they do, indeed, serve functions.

I have no quibble with the use of the concept of intuition or with instinct. I just don't think intuition should be contrasted with reason. I think the better term is "problem solving"—the fast and slower kinds. Moreover, setting apart intuition by contrasting it with reason is, I think, posing the wrong contrast (Haidt, 2001; M. D. Lieberman, 2000; see Pizarro & Bloom, 2002).

Moral Decisions, Bodily Contact, and Emotional Conflict

Moral dilemmas abound—consider the "trolley car" dilemma. A train out of control is heading for five people. The five people can be saved by changing the course of the train toward one person (Kamm, 1996; J. Thompson 1976). The choice entails pressing a button to save five people by sacrificing one person. Another dilemma, called the "footbridge dilemma," requires bodily contact. This context requires that one push the individual to save five others, sacrificing one for the other five. In the abstract, the two dilemmas are the same, but in the concrete they are very different. One aspect of this decision is clearly different: the physical contact with another human. It is easier to choose to eliminate the person if doing so requires pressing a button from a distance. No physical contact is necessary. But when it requires having to push a person onto the tracks (footbridge dilemma), those subjects who said yes in this experiment, which could elicit an incongruent response, had longer reaction times than those who said no (moral inappropriate). There is less bodily/moral conflict, as the authors of this study note, in the trolley dilemma, and therefore less interference in decision making. The authors broke their experiment into three basic groups: the moral personal (problems that reflected the footbridge dilemma), the moral impersonal (variants of the trolley car dilemma, keeping money that one found from a wallet), and nonmoral tasks (memory tasks). Figure 4.1 depicts just the reaction times on the moral personal task for the individuals who said it was appropriate or inappropriate. In fact, there was a longer reaction time for those who said it was appropriate. Should one be surprised? Conflict from the emotions was the way the authors, probably rightfully, explained their results, and it was their prediction (Greene, Sommerville, Nystrom, Darley, & Cohen, 2001).

But I wonder whether this is an issue associated with the emotions in too narrow a sense.[6] Of course, the intellectual reflex is to identify the conflict situation with the emotions, the emotions traditionally associated with disruption and the impairment of judgment. Suppose it was an emotion, like the joy of seeing someone who is worthy and you are excited to be with; there might be little conflict, and one would be less likely to do something harmful. But again, for many investigators, conflict is associated with the

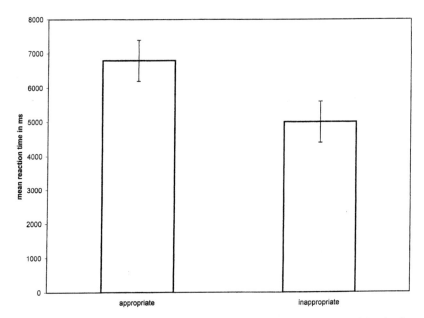

Fig. 4.1. The greater the conflict, and perhaps the more scenarios to consider, in the so-called appropriate condition, the longer the reaction time (adapted from Greene et al., 2001).

emotions—and with bodily contact, in this context. The interesting thing in this fMRI study is that there were differences in neural activation to the different scenarios that were associated with a wide range of emotions and that were activated to a greater degree in the moral personal condition (Greene et al., 2001). These regions, which are linked to conflicted emotions, include medial frontal gyrus (Brodmann's areas 9 and 10), posterior cingulate gyrus, and angular gyrus (Brodmann's area 39; see also Davidson et al., 2000).

The problem is that moral sensibility in this example is up front and personal and evokes more conflict when having to engage physically with the sacrificed individual; when one is physically detached and more distant, it is easier to make the choice. Emotions on one view are about conflict, not about adaptation. Emotions as they impact moral judgment can be about conflict, or obviously not about conflict.

Gustatory/Visceral Activation and Moral Disgust

The Nazis (and many kinds of zealot religious fanatics) clung to a theory that legitimated their actions; they understood their victims as viruses to the state, a germ to the rest of the human condition, and so to be eradicated. It was easy to kill, to obey orders, when the victims were seen as base, as not quite human. We rob them of their bodily dignity and take what makes them repulsive as bodily objects. In other words, to view their victims as amoral, as unfeeling, as irrational, was to rob them of their bodily dignity, thus making them repulsive, a pestilent nuisance that couldn't be overlooked (Arendt, 1963; Sabini & Silver, 1982). They became repulsive, vermin-like. It became easier to kill, to exterminate. Empathy (see below) perhaps can inhibit the transgression against others.[7] Nazi propaganda was focused on the idea of getting rid of cancers, of vermin that cause disease. They were bodily metaphors, and in that context the bestial expression of extermination was institutionalized, with what was thought was grounded reason. They rendered other individuals morally repulsive. What mechanisms could account for this?

One very interesting example that connects bodily sensibility with moral sentiments is the putative link between gustatory processing and the origins of attraction to and repulsion from people (Rozin, 1999). Darwin described the revulsion and the rejection of food sources (figure 4.2); this was elaborated by a number of investigators (Angyal, 1941) and most notably demonstrated by Paul Rozin and his colleagues (Rozin & Fallon, 1987; Rozin, Haidt, & McCauley, 1993).

One suggestion is that this basic emotion of disgust extended to moral revulsion is functionally linked to the rejection of food sources, and evolved in culture to become a powerful motivating property in the regulation of behavior. It is an important mechanism for avoidance of objects perceived

Fig. 4.2. Disgust reactions (from Darwin, 1872/1965).

as potentially harmful, a mechanism to constrain behavior. The avoidance response can be immediate, a fast appraisal, or linked to a more elaborate semantic network linked to other events. Disgust, as I suggested in Chapter 2, also plays a communicative role (see also W. I. Miller, 1997) and is a fundamental emotion (cf. Darwin, 1872/1965; Ekman, 1992; Royzman & Sabini, 2001; Rozin, 1999).

As I indicated in the previous chapter, disgust—a primordial response— may have evolved from the rejection/revulsion of a food source (Rozin & Fallon, 1987). It provides a way to deal with harm, to ensure rejection, and is a primary event of bodily contact. The strong link between gustation and visceral discomfort provides a strong mechanism in the organization of behavior: to approach or avoid someone. The bodily reaction is a metaphorical depiction when it is placed in the context of moral revulsion.[8] One becomes what one consumes, what one brushes up against, and is thus contaminated. Through cultural and evolutionary events, this one basic emotion, disgust, was expanded in use (Angyal, 1941; Rozin, 1999; figure 4.3) or perhaps played a key role in the evolution of moral judgment. As Hume writes in a disparaging note, "Fools disgust" (cited in W. I. Miller, 1997, p. 182).

We have thus extended disgust beyond its initial link to two sensory systems (gustation and olfaction). Sensory systems aid importantly in the organization of behavior. Moral sensibility is linked to bodily experiences.

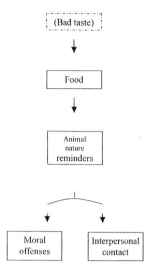

Fig. 4.3. The cultural evolution of disgust (adapted from Rozin, 1998).

This is not to say that moral revulsion or disgust is synonymous with gusta-tory disgust—surely it is not. But an essential link between the primary emotion of disgust, with its phylogenetic roots in gustatory-visceral sensa-tion, has been expanded. In other words, the simple suggestion that a pre-existing structure designed to remove from the body an object and to perceive it as offensive and off-putting has been bootstrapped to a more complex cognitive system, and that moral disgust is linked in a meaningful way to basic visceral-related gustatory/nausea disgust. Thus, one would not pre-dict that the nausea regions of the brainstem (area postrema) would neces-sarily be active during moral revulsion, but certainly one would predict that regions of the amygdala and frontal cortex would be. The amygdala's im-portant role in gustatory/visceral appraisals (Rolls, 2000) and in fast appraisal when getting the "gist" of certain kinds of events (Adolphs, Denburg, & Tranel, 2001) renders this region ideally suited to integrate internal and external events (Rosen & Schulkin, 1998). In addition, the range of lexical entries that are associatively linked (and thereby contaminated) by meta-phor and creative impulse is an expression of our cognitive competence (Royzman & Sabini, 2001). After all, there is a fundamental link between eating bad foods and getting sick. Perhaps, as Paul Rozin (1999) suggested, we extend emotions and preferences so that we have a wide range of value and moral notions. But whether disgust is a primary emotion or not is irrele-vant; what we do know is that when we are put off morally by a person, the gustatory/visceral axis is activated and plays a role in the organization of the behavioral response.

Visceral disgust has been linked to moral appraisals, with the moral aspect presumably being evolutionarily related to the original function of warning the organism about physical, bodily harm: A piece of meat covered in lesions indicates rot and must be avoided, shunned. Extending this function to moral appraisals, recruiting the visceral disgust response in a social context can be seen when we react with disgust to the glutton, at the sight of greedy insatiability. Why disgust? Of what real danger is the glutton to us? Perhaps the visceral response has been recruited here to act as a reminder of the importance of moderation, of temperance, both physiologically and socially. The disgust reaction generates the emotional/motivational wherewithal to remove, inhibit oneself from being like someone who lacks temperance. The disgust reaction underlies the organization of action.

It is interesting to note that regions of the brain that organize action have been tied to disgust reactions, such as the basal ganglia (Calder et al., 2001; Calder, Keane, Manes, Antoun, & Young, 2000; figure 4.4). For some anatomists the basal ganglia contains part of the extended amygdala (e.g., Alheid et al., 1996; McGinty, 1999), but for others it does not (Petrovich et al., 2001; Swanson & Petrovich, 1998). Nonetheless, this rather large region of the brain is linked to a wide variety of organized behavioral responses (e.g., probability judgments, syntax, statistical judgment, approach and avoid mechanisms).

In brain-imaging studies, when normal subjects are shown disgusting facial displays under various experimental conditions, basal ganglia, in

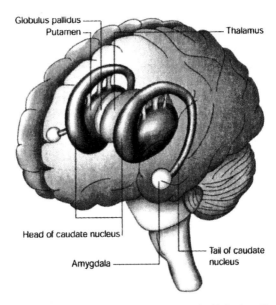

Fig. 4.4. The location of the amygdala and basal ganglia (linked to disgust appraisals) (adapted from Calder et al., 2001).

addition to a number of other brain regions (insula cortex, a gustatory region in the cortex), is activated under these conditions (Lane, Reiman, Ahern, et al., 1997; Lane, Reiman, Bradley, et al., 1997; Phillips et al., 1997; Phillips, Young, et al., 1998). In one fMRI study, viewing facial expressions activated regions of the basal ganglia and insula cortex, in addition to regions of the frontal and temporal cortex (Phillips, Young, et al., 1998). Subjects in this study were shown faces that were easily characterized as expressing either disgust or fear. What these investigators found was that there was preferential activation of the insular cortex to the faces that expressed disgust, and there was preferential activation in the amygdala to the face that expressed fear (Anderson, Christoff, Panitz, Rosa, & Gabriel, 2003; Phillips et al., 1997; figures 4.5, 4.6). Importantly, the cortical representation of the gustatory system is activated by visual facial displays of disgust.

In another study, the sight of spoiled food products evoked a pattern of neural activation similar to that of looking at individuals expressing disgust reactions (Phillips, Young, et al., 1998). Moreover, subjects with damage to this region perform perfectly well in recognizing a wide variety of emotions and in recalling the experience, but were impaired when it came to disgust (Calder et al., 2000).

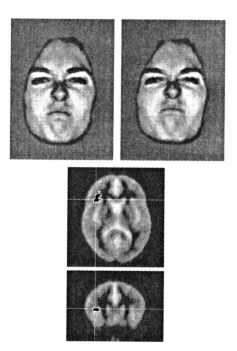

Fig. 4.5. Functional imaging studies of disgust reactions (insular cortex; adapted from Calder et al., 1997).

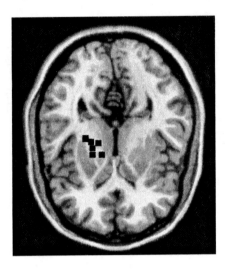

Fig. 4.6. Functional imaging studies of disgust reaction. Regions of the basal ganglia (black area) are more active at the sight of disgust pictures (adapted from Calder et al., 2001).

A number of neural regions underlie the organization of disgust. They include brainstem sites such as the solitary nucleus, area postrema, and parabrachial region, in addition to forebrain sites that include basal ganglia, hypothalamus, amygdala, insula, and frontal and temporal cortex (chapter 2). Regions of the brain that underlie alimentary functions (from the oral cavity to the anus constitutes the alimentary canal) are represented in the brain at all levels of the neural axis.

Empathy and Action Tendencies

I see you in distress or in discomfort, then I come (or not) to feel the same. The event motivates me into action. Of course, I suggest that one is not first perceiving the experience and then trying to make sense of it. We come prepared to understand other people's experience and to respond to them. The information processing and appraisal are not detached and distant, they are up front and immediate. The immediate response is like a broad range of capacities that figure in our responding to one another (e.g., infant imitation; S. Gallagher & Meltzoff, 1996; Meltzoff & Brooks, 2001; Meltzoff & Moore, 1977, 1997, 1999).

These events are bodily and are reflected in sensorimotor action. The embodied sensibility links one to others, quickly and without detachment. Inferences in appraisal systems need not, in other words, mean being detached from the other. Quite the contrary: My being open to you through a

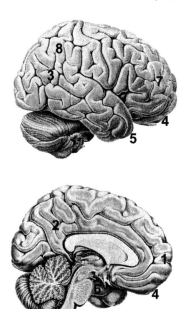

Fig. 4.11. Regions of the neocortex tied to moral appraisals (see reference for details on anatomy; reprinted from Greene et al., 2002, with permission of Elsevier).

Because reasoning can be rapid or slow, innervated by visceral impact to a greater or lesser degree, does not reduce moral sensibility into emotivism, emotions are seen as sensations and, therefore, in the older vernacular, noncognitive (Stevenson, 1944; see Urmson, 1968). If morality was a feeling, as Hume (1739/1984) and others suggested, then morality was not based on reason. Hume asserted, "Moral good and evil are certainly distinguished by our sentiments, not by reason" (p. 640), and though they may be flexible (A. C. Baier, 1991), they still are not based on reason. Because reason was understood in terms of necessary abstract and divorced reasoning, the conclusion was axiomatic. But it need not be once one demythologizes human reason from the stars and places reason in the context of probing and problem solving when confronted with problematic contexts (Gigerenzer, 1991, 1996, 2000; Simon, 1956, 1982, 1983). Moreover, once one places moral sentiments in moral theory, then "raw feeling" is bound by information processing. Feelings are not on one side and problem solving on the other. There is room, plenty of it, for the cognitive sciences to contribute to our understanding of moral behavior (Flanagan, 1991), but a contribution devoid of bodily sensibility would lose credibility because it would be disconnected from human experience.

Moral sensibility evolved in the context of our social ascent. It can be used for the good as well as the less than noble. Emotions permeate the valuation component of our judgments, moral and otherwise (e.g., Dewey,

1925/1989; Greenspan, 1995). Disgust appraisals elicit rejection and empathy appraisals elicit approach reactions to other individuals. Empathy is just one capacity that can orient our sense toward each other. Still, no safeguard exists against the ever-recurring theme of human moral transgressions. The depiction of contamination was one way that diverse groups legitimated their extermination policies; bad people, like bad cows, were to be eliminated so as not to contaminate the good Volk. But amid the stink of human excrement of ill expression there lingers the lure of what is humanly possible.

5

Drives and Explanations

Introduction

A fundamental feature of our condition is our curiosity, our exploration of events. We are driven, for a variety of reasons, to represent the world around us; representations lie at the heart of our evolution. But it is often not just representations divorced from action. The information-processing systems are up close and personal, not in the sense that the mechanisms are subject to introspection, but that visceral information predominates. As one cognitive scientist rightly has put it, "As visceral factors intensify, they focus attention and motivation" (Loewenstein, 1996, p. 273). The recognition of discrepant events, as I pointed out in previous chapters, is a heuristic that pervades information processing in the brain, including the organization of motivated behaviors. While the detection of discrepant events underlies the sense of the beautiful and the mundane, it also underlies the regulatory and the basic physiological behaviors (e.g., sodium cravings). Cognitive resources are required in trying to understand our surroundings and to forge a coherent world in which to move, in which to decide, and in which to act.

Our ability to represent the objects around us is fundamental. Depictions of objects in caves were early representations of events. The objects were linked to functional use, in adaptation. Driven to represent, and afforded the luxury to theorize, we started with the objects we encountered and with which we interacted, those with which we had bodily contact or would like to, or not. We are driven to explain the world around us, to control and master our surroundings. This is a core feature of us, though expressed differently in different cultures. One motive that underlies this search for knowledge is perceived informational needs; shortcomings are detected, new inquiry emerges (Peirce, 1877), new learning takes place (Rescorla, 1988). Of course, this is another version of discrepancy and expectations and their violation. And the knowing process is larger than this characterization. As Peirce put it, "The irritation of doubt causes a struggle to attain a state of belief. I shall term this struggle inquiry." But in closing the sentence, he says, ". . . though it must be admitted that this belief is sometimes not a very apt designation" (1877, p. 114).

We seek to explain our surroundings; we come prepared to categorize the world that we are adapting to. We are awed by our surroundings, wanting to get them under our control through representations and understanding. This is reflective of our cognitive/representational capacity, and our desire to seek information, to fill the gaps in what we know—to eradicate cognitive disequilibria.

My former professor and colleague Eliot Stellar, when commenting on the history of the hypothalamus and motivated behaviors and the endless controversies, would tell me, "Just live long enough and you see these controversies erupt and come back again." The concept of drive and motivation is one of those histories. Recently, it has made its way into the cognitive sciences, as in part having to do with visceral discomfort from an information gap in knowledge and the motivated behavior of curiosity. And drives are quintessential bodily events, bodily representations in the brain.

In this chapter, I begin with a brief description of general thoughts about the neural mechanisms underlying drives and a brief history of the concept. I then discuss the concept of a "curiosity" drive, as Loewenstein (1994) understands it in the context of curiosity in humans. Drive states and their satisfaction through successful problem solving reflects cephalic orchestration.

But curiosity is not simply a drive state, and the perception of an "information gap" does not constitute an aversive state. Tolman (1949) reminded us during the heyday of behaviorism that learning can take place with or without a particular drive. The ethologists always inferred this. I therefore discuss the issue of fast appraisal systems that reflect prepared learning (e.g., animals are prepared to recognize sodium rapidly and what it is associated with and how to find it when they are sodium hungry; young children are prepared to differentiate animate and inanimate early on in ontogeny).

The Brain Generates Drive States

Eliot Stellar (1954) formulated a view that has been held by a generation of investigators regarding the general mechanism that underlies motivational states. Stellar's view, put forward in the classic paper "The Physiology of Motivation," was that the hypothalamus plays a fundamental role in the regulation of excitatory and inhibitory central states (see also Hebb, 1949). Stellar's framework was one in which both internal physiological changes and sensory detection, mediated by central hypothalamic sites, result in behavioral adaptation. Although these central states were often construed as merely under hypothalamic control, Stellar understood that other regions of the brain are obviously involved in the expression of motivated behaviors (figure 5.1).

Experiments using electrical (Olds & Milner, 1954) and chemical self-stimulation of the hypothalamus and other forebrain sites (N. E. Miller, 1957) suggested specific systems in the brain that could elicit the expression of behavior. Indeed, a large body of research was focused on electrical and chemical stimulation of the brain and the resultant behaviors that were evoked. At the time, they were linked to theories of reinforcement and learning (e.g., N. E. Miller, 1959). Basic drives were being mapped onto the brain. It is not that this approach was wrong; it was just misleading. The language shifted away from brain centers to neural circuits, and these circuits could be used in a large number of contexts. Thus, for example, stimulation of a particular site in the hypothalamus could elicit a range of different behaviors depending on the context (Valenstein, 1973; Valenstein, Cox, & Kakolewski, 1970). The same stimulation in the same regions of the hypothalamus could elicit thirst, hunger, or sex drive depending on the context (Valenstein et al., 1970; Wise, 2002).[1] One reasonable explanation for the electrical self-stimulation effects on behavior is that the stimulation increases the salience of environmental stimuli (Berridge, 2000, 2003). Clearly, the expression of behavior by the activation of neural circuits depends on the context or eco-

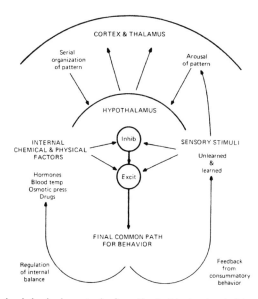

Fig. 5.1. The physiological control of motivated behavior (with permission from Stellar 1954).

logical conditions. Behavior does not exist in a vacuum. Both the incentives that are afforded in the environments that one is adapting to, along with the general orientation and organization of systems subserving arousal by the brain, are jointly integrated in ongoing behaviors. Moreover, there are, in fact, both general and specific mechanisms that underlie drive-related behaviors (Pfaff, 1999; Toates, 1986).

The general neural systems responsible for coordinated, adaptive motivated responses typically have the following features: (1) They are able to decode specific physiological and/or endocrine demand signals derived from the periphery; (2) they are able to relate this information to other information derived from the external environment; (3) they are able to organize (encode) a coordinated behavioral response, which has to include both endocrine and autonomic components; (4) they are able to prioritize an animal's response, so that the most immediate and urgent demands are dealt with over those that can wait or be subjugated until the principal challenge has either passed or been effectively dealt with; (5) they are able to assess the efficacy of the adaptive response; and (6) they take into account constraints from the animal's external environment, in particular those deriving from its social group. All these considerations suggest that the neural systems responsible will be both distributed (because each adaptive response has several components) and overlapping (because different adaptive responses nevertheless have common features, such as cardiovascular activation and adrenal corticoid secretion). Neurochemical coding within the limbic system is essentially involved in the integration and coordination of behavioral adaptation (Herbert, 1993; N. E. Miller, 1965; Schulkin, 1999); behavior is turned on, other behaviors are inhibited, priorities are established, conflict and partial resolution are endured. For example, oxytocin gene expression in the brain is linked to parental behavior and social attachments (Carter et al., 1999). Oxytocin gene expression in regions of the brain that underlie social recognition (amygdala) facilitates the adaptive behavioral responses for social attachment (Ferguson, Aldag, Insel, & Young, 2001).

The brain is an information-processing organ; motivation represented in neural circuits coded by neuropeptides or neurotransmitters is no different (Herbert & Schulkin, 2002; figure 5.2). We now know that a number of neuropeptides (e.g., CRH) and neurotransmitter systems (e.g., serotonin, dopamine) that project widely throughout the brain both arouse and placate neuronal systems that underlie central motive states. Some of the neurochemical coding systems that underlie motivated behaviors are depicted in table 5.1.

Recall the central gustatory/visceral system in the brain in which a wide variety of neuropeptides is synthesized. Angiotensin is one peptide involved in this system, and its receptor sites are localized in many of the regions of this visceral pathway in the brain (see Lind, Swanson, & Ganten, 1984a, 1984b). In addition, oxytocin, vasopressin, prolactin, neuropeptide Y, and CRH are also distributed along the central visceral axis. This axis includes

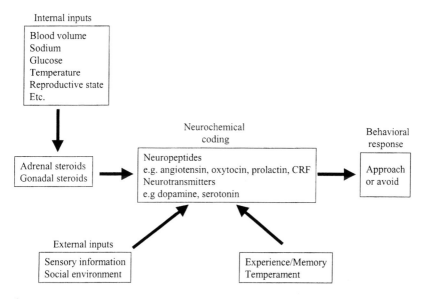

Fig. 5.2. Central states and chemical coding in the brain (adapted from Herbert & Schulkin, 2002).

the central nucleus of the amygdala, the bed nucleus of the stria terminalis, the paraventricular nucleus of the hypothalamus, and brainstem sites such as the parabrachial and solitary nuclei (Gray, 1999; Swanson et al., 1983). This is the same pathway that contributes to the organization of drives in general (Pfaffmann et al., 1977; Stellar & Stellar, 1985). It is part of the neural system—described by Herrick (1905, 1948) and expanded on by Nauta and Domesick (1982) and Norgren (1995)—that underlies central drive states of the brain (see Chapter 2).

The depiction of the limbic system, as I indicated, is itself evolving in our conceptual framework. The set of brain regions depicted by Papez (1937) and later elaborated by others was eventually called the limbic brain (MacLean, 1952). The original conception of the limbic brain did provide a map for which regions of the brain would be linked to the emotions. Again, more brain regions are now included than were in the original conception of the limbic system, and its separation from other systems in the brain appears untenable (LeDoux, 1996; Saper, 1996; Swanson, 2003). We now know that brainstem regions such as the solitary nucleus and parabrachial region, or locus coeruleus, are part of the limbic system, adding to the original anatomical depiction (Broca, 1878; MacLean, 1952; Papez, 1937). Bodily sensibility is found in a variety of neocortical regions in addition to what is considered old cortex (Damasio, 1999). What is and what is not included in the limbic systems is, in other words, much in dispute (see Herbert & Schulkin, 2002; Swanson, 2000a, 2000b), and some investigators have suggested dropping the concept (LeDoux, 1996). I suggest, as I indicated at the

Table 5.1 Diverse Chemical Codes in the Brain

Amino-acids	(Mono) amines	Peptides	Steroids
GABA	Serotonin	Vasopressin	Testosterone
Glutamate	Noradrenaline	CRF	Estradiol
Glycine	Adrenaline	β-endorphin	Progesterone
?Aspartate	Dopamine	Enkephalin	Cortisol
?Taurine	Acetylcholine	Dynorphin	Aldosterone
	Histamine	CCK	DHEA
	?Octopamine	Angiotensin	
		Bombesin	
		Somatostatin	
		VIP	
		PHI/GRF	
		Oxytocin	
		ANP	
		Substance P	
		Neurotensin	
		Galinin	
		GnRH	
		CGRP	
		aMSH	
		TRH	
		Endothelin	
		And many others	

Adapted from Herbert & Schulkin, 2002.

beginning of the book, that we choose to talk about the visceral nervous system instead of the limbic system. The visceral brain (which again includes the autonomic and neuroendocrine systems), from the brainstem to cortex, is involved with information processing that is critical for emotional judgment, good or bad.

Nauta (1971) noted that the concept of the limbic system should include motor regions of the basal ganglia (Mogenson, Jones, & Yim, 1980). The basal ganglia forms an essential link in translating motivational signals from the amygdala and hypothalamus into the organization of action (Kelley, 1999) via the activation of brainstem sites (e.g., Pfaff, 1999, female sexual motivation).

Regions of the basal ganglia do in fact seem to underlie a variety of motivated behaviors (e.g., addiction; Kelley, 1999), perhaps via changes in dopaminergic transmission. The nucleus accumbens (via glutamate receptors within the accumbens) may underlie appetitive instrumental learning and may be an important link in translating limbic functions into functional action (e.g., Cardinal et al., 2002; Kelley, 1999; Ikemoto & Panksepp, 1999).

The Concept of Drive: A Brief History

Drive is an ancient concept. Greek thought is replete with the use of this term, and it seems to be a common term in most languages of which we know. Perhaps each usage does not necessarily convey the exact semantic network; after all, that depends on the culture in which one lives (Shweder, Mahapatra, & Miller, 1987; Shweder, Much, Mahapatra, & Park, 1997).

Drives are often treated as something one should tame. Unquenched and out of control drives lead to pathology (e.g., Freud, 1923/1960). Drives are not the same as the emotions, but they intersect profoundly with one another. Motivational systems are diverse and underlie behavior.

In the heyday of learning theory, drive reduction theories predominated (Hull, 1943). Actually, one can also find the dominant stance of this idea in ethology (Lorenz, 1981; Tinbergen, 1951/1969) and in psychoanalysis (Freud, 1922/1961). Behavior represents an underlying drive. Drives are the regulatory power over behavior. Understanding drive was nearly equivalent to understanding behavior. Drives were linked to instinct (Hinde, 1970) and were thought to underlie arousal of behavior (e.g., Hebb, 1949; LeDoux, 2000; Morgan, 1966; Morgan & Stellar, 1950; Pfaff, 1999; Stellar, 1954). Drives gave direction or purpose to behavior (N. E. Miller, 1959; Tolman, 1949). Our psychological lexicon is pregnant with the concept of drive. It is linked to the detection of novel or discrepant events (Hebb, 1946, 1949), and therefore to learning.

But early on, drive reduction proved to be a quite limited concept. Debates often occurred in behaviorism between drive reduction and drive induction (N. E. Miller, 1959). It was also clear that learning certainly was not dependent on drive states; one can learn about salt even when not needing it, and the learning is fast and long lasting (Bregar, Strombakis, Allan, & Schulkin, 1983; Krieckhaus, 1970; Krieckhaus & Wolf, 1968; Wirsig & Grill, 1982). The sensory preconditioning experiment (described in chapter 2 and depicted in figure 5.3) demonstrated that coming to enjoy an arbitrary taste typically not linked to sodium (quinine) can be expressed as a function of a prior association with sodium (Berridge & Schulkin, 1989; Rescorla, 1981). The rats were not sodium hungry when the quinine was paired with the sodium. When rendered sodium hungry for the first time, they ingested the arbitrary taste that they would normally not ingest, even though it was now not paired with sodium. Recall that a wide variety of animals are prepared to recognize sodium, as it is a primary gustatory signal linked to an innate behavior. Much more generally, incentives (e.g., wanting drugs, a person) are connected to the wide semantic network with which the actual person or object is associated; incentives grow (Bindra, 1968). But the range of as-

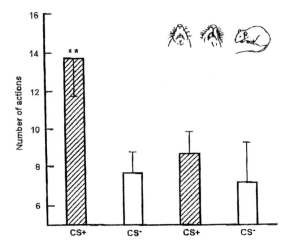

Fig. 5.3. Either citric acid or quinine was infused into the oral cavity with sodium (CS+) or infused without sodium (CS–), then the rats were rendered sodium hungry for the first time in their life, and the arbitrary taste associated with sodium is now ingested in the group for which these were compounded (Berridge & Schulkin, 1989).

sociations that grow[2] consists of a wide array of information-processing systems that organize and make sense of the range of associations, the lexical connections, and so on.

Curiosity and Wanting to Know: A Drive State?

Interestingly, there is a literature that links curiosity to drive states (Berlyne, 1960). The literature emerged several decades ago during the height of drive reduction theory. The more modern variant (Loewenstein, 1994, 1996) placed a curiosity drive in the context of filling in some information: A gap in knowledge is noted, information is needed, and a drive to fill the gap emerges. Variants of this perspective hearken back to Freud and others who construed curiosity as a "thirst for knowledge" (Freud, 1915, p. 153, cited in Loewenstein, 1996; G. A. Miller, Galanter, & Pribram, 1960). Curiosity increases our propensity to acquire new information.

From ordinary everyday activities to the pursuit of scientific knowledge and to aesthetic appreciation, the detection of a discrepant event motivates behavior (Dewey, 1934/1968). The behavior serves in part to quell the sense of discrepancy. Many authors have noted the sense for achieving cognitive equilibrium (e.g., Hebb, 1949; Piaget, 1952).

A "curiosity drive" was invoked to explain why monkeys would press an operant to look at something or to observe an event (R. E. Miller et al.,

1963; Mirsky et al., 1958). Inventing drives was like inventing faculties 100 hundred years earlier. An ethological view, one not shared by earlier drive reduction behaviorists, was that animals are prepared to learn, to notice events, to store that information for later use (Krieckhaus, 1970). There is pleasure in the knowing process, whether related to drives or not (Berlyne, 1971). Moreover, this curiosity drive is less in the shadow of internal processes and more construed in the interaction with environments—not a mind cut off from the world, but one interacting with environmental factors. The behaviors expressed reflect the options available in the environment (Valenstein et al., 1970).

Curiosity drive was related to the exploration of novel objects and was essential for mastering the world, or understanding the world in which one was trying to adapt (James, 1890/1952). The drive to acquire a new habit was shown through behavioral patterns which were aligned to the breakdown of a previous habit (Dewey, 1925/1989). Variants of drive theory and drive reduction grew quite strong in many kinds of behavioral inquiry, but within behaviorism in particular (Hull, 1943).

There can be no doubt that when information is unusual, there is a strong desire to acquire it. But why should all of curiosity be reduced to a thirst? Moreover, why should curiosity be reduced to a thirst that is aversive? No one likes being thirsty, at least under normal conditions. But broad-based response to discrepancy is an important behavioral adaptation (Berlyne, 1954, 1960). Thus, perhaps the most plausible variant of drive theory is the discrepancy model (Dewey, 1925/1989; Hebb, 1949; James, 1890/1952; Peirce, 1877, 1878; Piaget, 1952; Rescorla & Wagner, 1972). In the discrepancy model, disruptions of expected events result in recruiting a greater number of behaviors that might reflect learning. A functionalist and cognitivist view places the behavior patterns that are generated by a central state of the brain in the context of acquiring information (Berlyne, 1960). But for a number of investigators, the state tends to be couched in terms of its being aversive (cf. Dewey, 1925/1989; Hebb, 1949; James, 1890/1952; Loewenstein, 1994, 1996).

Informational acquisition and control is a strong desire. Ambiguity aversiveness, for example, is a real property of our decision making (Baron, 1988/2000; Baron & Schulkin, 1995). Ambiguity can breed indecision, the status quo in action in human decision-making processes (Baron, 1988/2000). Loewenstein (1994) noted a very interesting point that James (1890/1952) made, that we are prepared to recognize discrepancy, and we then search to fill in the gaps. The question is whether or not to construe the desire to seek stability in the knowing process as one of reducing an aversive state. But it remains clear that resolving uncertainty is a major motivator of behavior (Dewey, 1925/1989).

Interestingly, information deprivation is construed as a cognitive deprivation and a hunger to fill this gap. And within the bounds of reason, some forms of curiosity may reflect this search for cognitive equilibrium. Curiosity emerges when one's knowledge and reference points are recognized to be inadequate (Loewenstein, 1994). Human experiences in decision making suggest that human choice is based on informational variables that reduce uncertainty. Based on animal experiments (N. E. Miller, 1957, 1959), motivation increases at the point of resolving uncertainty, of finding a solution. In a number of experimental paradigms, activation of approach and avoidance mechanisms reflects the gradient of conflict and resolution.

For example, in one experiment, subjects were shown parts of a human body (body parts) in a visual array presented so as to evoke curiosity (figure 5.4). Different groups of subjects were shown different numbers of body parts. They were shown hands, feet, a torso, and so on. Subjects were asked to predict the age of the person depicted in the collection of body parts. They were also asked how curious they were to find out the age. Loewenstein (1994) predicted that those subjects shown a greater number of body parts and thus afforded a greater opportunity for visualizing the body as a whole would be more curious about the age of the depicted person. In other words, the greater propensity to fill in the perceived information gap should be stronger in those shown more information about the possible age of the subject, and this should be correlated with their self-reports of curiosity. The experimenters found corroborative evidence for these expectations (figure 5.5).

The suggestion is that curiosity is directly related to our knowledge base or reference point. It is a theoretical advance to put curiosity in the context of one's knowledge base, decision making, or gambles. But why argue that it is only an aversive reaction? One need not. The emphasis on *visceral input* is something vital to curiosity, learning, and inquiry. Interestingly, in

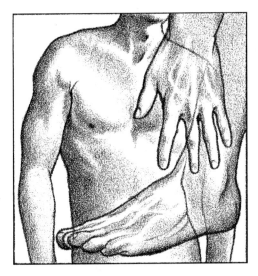

Fig. 5.4. Kinds of bodily parts used in the Loewenstein experiment (Schulkin & Yansen, 2004).

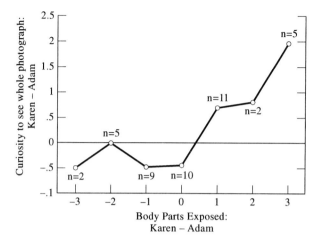

Fig. 5.5. Subjects were shown 0–3 pictures each of parts of a man (Adam) and a woman (Karen). They were then asked to rate how curious they were to see a picture of the whole person on a scale of 0–5. The vertical scale is the difference in rated curiosity between seeing the picture of Karen and the picture of Adam. The horizontal axis is the difference in the number of pictures of body parts the subject saw between Karen and Adam. In general, a subject was more curious to see the picture of the whole person if they saw more pictures of their body parts (Loewenstein et al., 1999, unpublished).

the common phrase "to pique one's curiosity," the word pique (originally, animosity) means "to arouse, provoke," but the word can also mean "to cause to feel vexation or resentment."

The gap of information, both relative and absolute, leads to a possible understanding of curiosity and the joys that one might find in the search for and attainment of information. The relationship of the information gap with curiosity has been articulated through the use of information theory's entropy coefficient:

$$-\sum_{i=1}^{n} p_i \, log_2 \, p_i$$

In this equation, n represents the total possible choices or outcomes of information, whereas p_i is the assessed probability that a particular choice (Loewenstein, 1994) will occur. As knowledge concerning each choice increases, the probabilities of each become more varied and exact. The equation is useful but not necessarily exact in quantifying multidimensional information in a unidimensional manner. In terms of the information gap and curiosity levels, several entropy measures are necessary: the individual's current situation, the informational goal of the individual, and a situational level of total ignorance. The absolute magnitude would therefore be the informational goal minus the current situation. The relative magnitude would be the absolute magnitude divided by the difference of the informational goal and level of total ignorance. The major point is that people tend to rely on both the relative and absolute magnitudes of the information gap to close the gap (Loewenstein, 1994, 1996; table 5.2).

Research suggests, as I indicated in Chapter 2, that current visceral factors may have varying and minimal impact on predicting future decisions (Kahneman, Fredrickson, Shreiber, & Redelmeier, 1999; Loewenstein, 1996; Loewenstein & Lerner, 2003), that some forms of curiosity are related to visceral factors, and there is no doubt that curiosity is linked to frameworks or to a storehouse of knowledge. The questions we pose reflect our background knowledge and appraisal mechanisms. But the identification of curiosity with aversiveness on the model of hunger, as Loewenstein notes, will not work; it would be like identify eating with stomach pangs. We eat for a lot of reasons. We eat because we like food, because we enjoy diverse gustatory stimulation, because of social context and ambiance, and because of habits (Galef, 1996; Galef & Whiskin, 2000; Rozin & Fallon, 1987). We are curious for a lot of reasons, and there is no doubt that one of these reasons is informational discrepancies in an event, but the feeling of the information discrepancies may not be aversive. Deprivation is aversive by its nature. But cognition withdrawal? As Loewenstein rightly acknowledges, we are motivated for more than appetitive reasons to do what we do (e.g., climbing a mountain; Loewenstein & Lerner, 2003). Moreover, real-world observations, just like earlier ethological observations, suggest that learning and

Table 5.2 Propositions Concerning Actual, Desired, Predicted, and Recollected Influence of Visceral Factors on Behavior

I	Discrepancy between actual and desired value increases with intensity of immediate visceral factor.
II	Future visceral factors create little discrepancy between planned and desirable value.
III	Increased immediate and delayed visceral factor simultaneously enhances actual valuation of immediate in comparison to delayed consumption.
IV	Current visceral factors have mild effect on decisions for future, despite the possibility that they may not occur in the future.
V	People underestimate the impact of visceral factors on future behavior.
VI	People forget degree of influence of visceral factors on past behavior over time. This produces the forgetting of past behavior or perplexity.

Adapted from Loewenstein, 1996.

curiosity can occur without discrepancy between knowledge base and observation.

Now, curiosity can reasonably be recruited to serve the drive to fill in some information in a setting in which the discrepancy is unsettling, viscerally displeasing (Hebb, 1949; James, 1890/1952; Loewenstein, 1996). It is a stretch to identify curiosity only as a drive, and an aversive one at that. Curiosity sounds like it fills in to maintain homeostatic equilibrium; cognitive equilibrium is a real metaphorical extension of bodily notions of homeostasis (e.g., Piaget, 1971).

Moreover, to render curiosity an aversive drive to be eradicated is to give short shrift to something else: Peirce called it "play" or "musement." Some of us really enjoy gently musing about things (figure 5.6). Occasionally, interesting ideas emerge at these times. New ideas are hard to find in any context, so why exclude the playful part of the mind? Does it seem less serious because it is not labored, fought over, or overcoming adversity? The play of ideas is something sweet and precious to us, a luxury to be savored and enjoyed and, where possible, extended. It is no less real or important because an idea is constructed with a sense of play.

Finally, turn back to the lowly rat and consider one kind of problem-solving mechanism: recalling relevant objects that have been learned that were not related to former drive states (Tolman, 1949). A wide variety of animals come prepared to associate tastes, places, times, and events with sodium; when the rat needs sodium, for example, it searches its lexical memory of events (Dickinson, 1986; Krieckhaus, 1970). The animal can evaluate that sodium is important, represent sodium in regions of the brain that underlie regulatory behaviors, and search and then find sodium when it needs to; behavior serves internal physiological regulation in the mainte-

Fig. 5.6. Child musing about animate and inanimate objects (Yansen & Schulkin, 2004).

nance of the internal milieu (Richter, 1942–1943). The motivated search for sodium reflects the degree of drive: The greater the deprivation, the longer and harder the animal will work for the sodium (Denton, 1982; Wolf, 1969) or run down a runway for sodium (Schulkin, Arnell, & Stellar, 1985). But the drive for sodium is not in a vacuum. A wide array of animals like the taste of salt, are motivated to ingest sodium when not in need, and, as we know, we humans sprinkle this stuff over all kinds of food that we should and should not eat (Denton, 1982).

This low-level system is the prepared learning of events linked to a perceptual category (saltiness) that is fundamental in taste-related exploratory behavior. Moreover, the taste of sodium is recognized within milliseconds (Bregar et al. 1983), and there are long- lasting effects of tasting sodium, with minimal gustatory input (one lick) necessary for remembering how and where sodium is to be found when it is needed (Schulkin, 1991) and how it can be acquired (Wirsig & Grill, 1982). Problem solving is rooted in object relatedness and perceptual/conceptual orientation (Prinz, 2002) for how to understand the objects that one encounters. Cephalic orchestration in the organization of action draws on the rich source of *visceral/autonomic information* in drawing causal connections and utilizing adaptive mechanisms to restore body fluid balance. Moreover, the recognition of sodium and its importance is not related to the need for sodium. Learning about the terrain one is trying to master, cope with, anticipate, and adapt to necessitates a much larger repertoire than simple drive reduction learning, as we have long known (figure 5.7).

There are countless examples other than the one I have given. Drive reduction was a bad theory of learning, an impoverished theory in which to

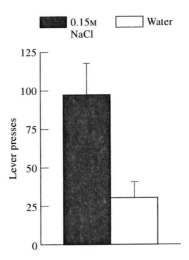

Fig. 5.7. Mean (SEM) number of lever presses of rats during a 1-hr. extinction test. Sodium hungry rats either tasted sodium or water during the training (Bregar et al., 1983).

couch all of animal and human behavior. But the concept of drive, when separated from the hydraulic metaphors to which diverse thinkers from Freud to Tinbergen related it, is a useful category in the explanation of behavior. But let's not tie the concept in a narrow sense to curiosity and learning.

We are the species driven to offer explanations of what we encounter; of course, some of us do this, and do it better than others. As one colleague put it, "We are intrinsically curious creatures" (Goldman, 1979, p. 34). But we come prepared to associate and categorize events. Many kinds of information-processing systems generated by the brain are operative, and they reflect lower-level bodily events.

Objects and Understanding

We come prepared to understand something about objects. Recall the discussion from Chapter 1 about basic cognition running through our grasp of objects; bodily metaphors predominate the idioms of understanding (Lakoff & Johnson, 1999). Children have a natural inclination to generate hypotheses—to determine objects and link events (e.g., Carey, 1985, 1995; Carey & Markman, 2000; Carey & Spelke, 1996; Klahr, 2000). Perhaps they are prepared to develop self-corrective inquiry. But it is no easy task.

One primary set of objects that we have had intimate contact with is the concept animals and food (Waxman, 1999; figure 5.8). We come prepared in some contexts to group objects in taxonomic order (Carey, 1985; Keil, 1989; Altran, 1996). Inductive inferences are operative within a problem-solving orientation. Objects are grouped together into coherence. The cognitive response (like the recognition of sodium) appears reflexive and immediate. They are fast appraisals for making sense of events.[3]

A number of heuristics, pretty good problem-solving devices, aid the organization of behavior (Gigerenzer, 1996, 2000; Gigerenzer & Selten, 2001; Simon, 1982). For example, a face that is safe (that is perceived that way) is approached; one that is not is avoided. The heuristic may be quite specific (Rozin, 1976a) or less so. Recognition heuristics (Is this salt? Should I approach

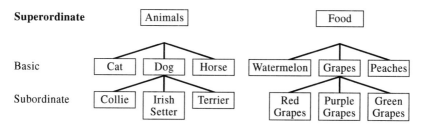

Fig. 5.8. Representation of an object hierarchy (from Waxman, 1999).

that person?) are pervasive and are embodied in environmental adaptations (Rosch, 1973, 1978; Wittgenstein, 1953).

Important sources of problem solving, fast and frugal, to use Gigerenzer's (2000) apt phrase, are persistent. Demythologizing human reason, away from the perfect reasoner to an adaptive reasoner, one who uses diverse resources, allows a more apt way to describe us (Gigerenzer, 2000; Simon, 1982). The range of specific cognitive mechanisms or information-processing systems in the brain is quite outstanding (Duchaine, Cosmides, & Tooby, 2001; Mellers et al., 2001), including spatial mechanisms, diverse mechanisms for the emotions, probability aids, category-specific knowledge, syntax and language acquisition, and theory of mind, to list but a few.

Explanation through Insight (Fast Appraisal)

There is pleasure in gaining insight from a phenomenon. We may call it "insight" or "intuition" but the insight or intuition is embedded in information-processing systems. They are fast, cognitive, and reflexive.

We are driven to explain phenomena. It is a core characteristic of the human problem-solver. Knowledge can be quite pleasurable, as many thinkers have pointed out (Dewey, 1925/1989; Hobbes, 1651/1958). Hitting on the right hypothesis, for those of us who have struggled in science, is rather rare; if we waited for that to govern what we do on a daily basis, we would derive little pleasure (but the anticipation perhaps carries us a bit). Science is a tough racket; there is a lot of disappointment.

Abduction (hitting on the right hypothesis), exciting as it may be, is not common on a large scale, but it is on the mini scale of problems of everyday life. Whether someone is safe or not, abduction (theory formation) does not work independently from inductive and deductive mechanisms, but as Peirce (1878, 1992a) understood, they are separable mechanisms in the reasoning process. Induction, as Peirce noted, "is where we generalize from a number of cases of which something is true and infer the same thing is true of a whole class" (1992a, p. 188). Deduction is the paradigmatic example of axiomatic human reasoning, and inductive reasoning is what we do often in the empirical sciences.

Abduction, in modern terms, is fundamentally linked to hypothesis formation (Hanson, 1958). Put in modern terms, evolution favored mechanisms for hypothesis formation in human decision making. Abduction is part of the information-processing system linked to hypothesis formation, but, as Peirce noted in this regard, "It is impossible to know intuitively that a given cognition is not determined by a previous one" (1992a, p. 25).[4] Again, I suggest that all representations in the brain are part of cognitive systems tied to information processing and problem solving. As I have indicated throughout this book, they are not necessarily detached, because information-processing systems and frameworks are essential to coherent behavioral processes.

James (1890/1952) constantly referred to the bodily sense of causation. And children early on in ontogeny are prepared to look for causal connections (e.g., Gopnik & Metzoff, 1997; Gopnik & Wellman, 1992; see Dickinson & Balleine, 2000; Povinelli, 2000, 2001; Shettleworth, 1998, for some of the thoughts on the animal literature). Drawing causal links is at the heart of problem solving (Gelman, Coley, & Gottfried, 1998). Children, like adults, are not perfect scientists, but they come prepared to search for evidence, to draw connections, to impose order (cf. Carey, 1985, 1995; Koslowski, 1996; Markman, 1989; Piaget, 1932, 1952; Wellman et al., 1997). Aiding this process are mechanisms for hypothesis generation.

The search for explanation is goal-driven (Dewey, 1925/1989; Gopnik, 1993). The search for meaning, semiotic connections of events, coherence, and security is a pervasive activity. And satisfaction is an important element in any explanation. The explanatory content varies with the kinds of issues that are trying to be explained (Aristotle, 1962). Peirce (1868a, 1868b, 1877) noted that the instinct to explain is strongly engraved in our mental architecture and experiences; theories come all too easily (see also Hookway, 2000). The empirical issue is what constrains hypothesis formation. Some of the constraints are built into the architecture itself; others are acquired through maturation and experience. The human mind looks to satisfy its explanatory desires and to feel satisfaction with some sort of closure (Dewey, 1925/1989; Gopnik, 1996; Heelan & Schulkin, 1998; Kroglanski, 1989).

Cephalic representations of faces and food sources, viscerally rich, reflect fast hypotheses, which are constrained, perhaps, in number and are bound to inductive and deductive mechanisms. There is not a special mechanism for the emotions that sets it apart at this level. There is a large body of tools for reasoning (Cherniak, 1986; Gigerenzer, 2000; Simon, 1982), tools that are designed to aid problem solving, emotional or otherwise. In addition, to assert that emotional systems are information systems is not to denigrate the emotions, as some are bound to think.

My goal is, in part, to demythologize our sense of the emotions, as I indicated in Chapter 2, in just the way in which we strive to demythologize our reasoning. We have come to realize that our reasoning, though imperfect, reflects a set of good enough problem-solving mechanisms, and by no means is this a denigration of our experience in problem solving or of the joy and fear that we may feel. Cephalic representations, rich in visceral/autonomic information processing, facilitate these events.

Conclusion

Throughout its organization, the brain is a cognitive organ, entrenched in information processing rich in representations of visceral events. I have suggested in this chapter that understanding curiosity as a positive drive involves more than simply envisioning it as a motivation to fill information gaps, driven by epistemological discomfort. Although this model is based on discrepancy, which the classical pragmatists themselves leaned too heavily on, the characterization is that of the emotions—visceral, bodily, and tending to be understood as noncognitive. I think this view ignores the fact that there is a visceral/autonomic cephalic system distinct from the peripheral system. Thus, like the consideration of the emotions, or aesthetics or morals, cognition is not on one side and the cephalic visceral/autonomic nervous system on the other. From the first-order neurons in the brain, they are not separate; once the events are cephalic, there is no separation. In other words, once the central nervous system is involved, everything is cognitive. There are, however, diverse information-processing systems, some of which reflect appraisal systems, with their respective coded valences and orientations.

We are driven to explain the events that occur in our world, and we take satisfaction when we hit on an idea, when we think we have explained an event. The detection of discrepant events (something that figures in each of the previous chapters) is one facilitator of this drive to explain the world in which we find ourselves. This is not just for the rarified atmosphere of the academic, but is pervasive in our everyday experiences. Along with this matter-of-fact aspect of appetitive and consummatory behaviors that underlie our desires to explain events in reaching cognitive equilibrium is another aspect of this cognitive capacity. Thinking itself, or what Peirce called "musement," is also pleasurable. We are thinking animals, as Descartes (1996) rightfully noted, just not necessarily detached and distant and divorced from the representations that pervade our problem-solving nervous system. And some aspects of our cognitive expression are not painful and aversive, but either neutral or pleasant.

We come prepared to group objects and to draw inferences, abduce ideas. These events are endemic to the information-processing systems in our brain. The appraisal systems that orchestrate human problem solving can be low level or not, conscious or not. Explanation is what we are constantly trying to achieve; explanatory frameworks predominate human reasoning (Kaplan & Murphy, 2000; Keil & Wilson, 2000).

Conclusion: Corporeal Representations

I admire the work of William James, as should be clear from this text. But he is wholly fallible, like the rest of us. A statement such as "Cognition is a function of consciousness" ("The Function of Cognition," 1885/1958) is but one of many wrong-headed statements. He also was essentially a peripheralist with regard to the organization of action, the recognition of our central states. On the other hand, he tended not to reify concepts; he understood something about the body. And he represents a better alternative to Descartes and to classical empiricists.

Finally: Mind in Body–Body in Mind

The traditional view of the mind that has dominated modern inquiry has been Cartesian: The mind is viewed as detached from the body.[1] The rudiments for this separation began as modern science was born. If bodies were predictable, inert, and dumb, then surely minds were something other than this. After all, we are distinguished by our minds. The mind was detached, and divorced representations predominated. This occurred certainly with rationalists (Kant, 1787/1965), but also with classical empiricists (Hume, 1739/1984; Locke, 1690/1959). This view of the body was erroneous, as was the view of the mind. Although most of us today are not dualists and thus do not have this extreme view of the radical separation of body and mind, the separation of the emotional and the cognitive shows its face regularly: The former is tied to the body and the latter is tied to the mind. This way of distinguishing the differences is misleading, and it will not do. It will not do in aesthetic appreciation, moral judgment, or motivation.

121

Who argues against my position? Within the study of the emotions, many still opt for the cognitive-noncognitive distinction; within aesthetics, the separation of judgment from the "chills" of music is commonly made; within moral theory, the separation of intuition from reason is but another way to impose the emotion and cognition split.

Of course, strains of thought can run through our problem solving, such as was demonstrated by Rousseau (1755/1964), who emphasized two key bodily facts about us: (1) the "sentiment about our existence," certainly not detached and divorced thoughts, and (2) the drive for self-preservation and well-being.

During the 19th century, with precursors in the 18th century, an alternative view began to emerge. The mind was seen neither as a conglomerate of sensations nor as merely a faculty for knowing. The mind was part of biological adaptation (Darwin, 1872/1965; James, 1890/1952). One essential feature of this mind was its gathering of information about the environment. This presupposed a coherent world in which successful functioning was an achievement.

There are basic categorical features in the environment that we—and perhaps other animals—come prepared to recognize, such as causal relations, kinds of objects, animate or inanimate, and functions (e.g., Carey, 1985; A. Clark, 1997). All appraisal systems are ways of structuring, characterizing, and understanding events.

Evolutionary constraints on information processing reflect, to some degree, the adaptations achieved: an extension of previous adaptations into novel domains (Rozin, 1976a, 1998). Appraisal systems are ways of orienting to one's world, problem solving (Goldman, 1979), a means of categorizing events (e.g., the link between gustation and visceral illness; Garcia et al., 1974). I suggest that we stick to the description and explanation of the brain as having different kinds of information-processing systems, some subserving low-grade appraisal and others subserving higher, more complicated kinds of information processing.

In addition, we know that understanding a variety of perceived functions of an object (e.g., a hammer), at least at the level of the brain, is represented in premotor and motor areas of the frontal cortex (Martin, 1999). Bodily contact, practice patterns, and habits of action are in part distributed in regions of the brain where they organize thought. Bodies are inhabited by minds; bodies are necessary to form minds. Interestingly, some individuals who have sustained extensive brain damage (in the dorsal frontal cortex and occipital/parietal cortex) respond normally to depictions of emotions in action contexts but are impaired when the emotions are presented as static and isolated (Adolphs, Tranel, et al., 2001).

I have taken liberties, as I indicated at the onset of this book, in my use of language. I do not believe that language is frozen, that the meaning of terms in one context (decision making) cannot be conceptually joined to other contexts (neuronal activation). I just acknowledge that we have a long way to go before achieving the goal of a rich explanation of these sorts of events. We need to be respectful of preserving explanations of ourselves at the level of the "life-world" (Schutz, 1967) in which we experience what we do, our interactions, and coping with the environments in which we find ourselves. We need to emphasize the practices that we participate in, our transactions with each other, our explorations of the world, what we are coping with, enjoying, avoiding.

Biological expression is about adaptation—imperfect and ingenious solutions in problem-solving contexts (cf. Gigerenzer, 2000; Gould, 2002; Marler, 1961; Simon, 1982). Darwin set the stage for understanding that *emotional expressions* manifest in the body are sources of information both as emitted and as received. The body is not an appendage to information gathering; it is at the heart of it. Early intimations of these ideas can be found in James and Dewey. They had incorporated the biological revolution that was occurring at the end of the 19th century into their orientation.

Some of us never held the disembodied view and yet were cognitively oriented. I never understood the mind as disembodied, and I was not alone. Representations of bodily events, pervasive throughout the nervous system, are informative in the organization of action. Representations guide action, but they need not detach one. Representations, when thought of as something that cuts one off from the world, perhaps generated the wrong metaphor. Knowledge is a contact sport: The objects are behind us and in front of us; they are there to be encountered and to be interacted with.

The first part of the cognitive revolution mistakenly omitted or denigrated the importance of the visceral/autonomic system in cognitive systems. The cognitivists tended to commit *Descartes' Error* (Damasio, 1994); they downplayed the importance of bodily or visceral information. Disembodied minds do not act, and certainly not well and over time.

In the organization of action, bodily sensibility is replete with cognitive processing. Most, but not all, cognitive processing is unconscious (e.g., LeDoux, 1996; Rozin, 1976a). The vast cognitive unconsciousness (Rozin, 1976a) underlies the organization of action. Mechanisms for face recognition and motion, rapid determination of what is friendly or not, are typically unaccessible to consciousness. Theater of the mind is the wrong metaphor; I don't think we need more spectators and more degrees of detachment.

Bodily Sensibility, Cognition, and the Brain

We still find in the literature a conception in which the higher function of the mind is interpreting undifferentiated bodily agitation. The S. Schacter and Singer (1962) view of the 1960s is still a dominant conception of the relationship between bodily contact and cognitive processes. This mislead-ing view was that the emotional brainstem emanates undifferentiated exci-tatory or inhibitory states to which the cortex gives structure and coherence. In philosophical terms, the sensory manifold is given form by the catego-ries of understanding (Kant, 1787/1965). It is not as if the ascending activat-ing reticular formation or the catecholaminergic chemical system is not tied to the activation of the brain and therefore behavior. It is just that brainstem regions are actively providing structure and coherence to bodily and exter-nal events. The brainstem, like the forebrain, provides organization for bodily sensibility, intelligent action (Blessing, 1997). And that is an important point: At all levels of the neural axis, the brain is integrative and processing infor-mation. It is not just a *cortical* affair.

It is still very much a part of the neuroscientific literature to see the brain divided in terms of "interpreting" versus "responding" to external events. When it comes to the consideration of older cortical structures, the hippocampus is often construed as performing the interpretative task and the amygdala as responsible for the more reactive task (LeDoux, 1996; McEwen, 2001). Indeed, the hippocampus may process more information related to environmental fear than the amygdala, but both are appraising the environment. In fact, presumably, they are doing the task together, along with a number of other structures that have been laid out in such nice detail (LeDoux, 1996; figure C.1). Interpretation, or appraisal, mecha-

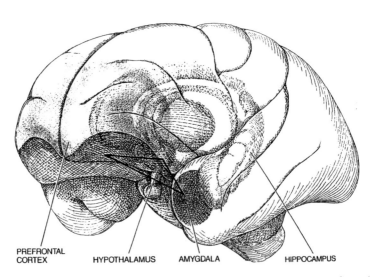

PREFRONTAL
CORTEX   HYPOTHALAMUS   AMYGDALA   HIPPOCAMPUS

Fig. C.1. Key regions of the brain include the amygdala, hippocampus, prefrontal cor-tex, and hypothalamus that underlie emotions and appraisal systems linked to fear, discrepancy, and a rich variety of information-processing systems.

nisms can be reactive and immediate, or revealing and rich in a semantic neural framework.

The point is that feelings, and their diversity, are not detached from cognitive systems in the brain. Surely feeling, or *qualia* in philosophical terms, is essential information for animal life. The idea of denying its scientific reality, as some philosophers would do (Rey, 1997), is patently absurd. Debates about feeling's foundational nature did not yield results of major import to our understanding. But let's not reify the notion of feeling now that it has become legitimate in some scientific circles (Damasio, 1999). Some of us never outlawed or undermined the role of bodily sensibility in our analyses of cognitive and neural function.

Basic Central Visceral Structure and Behavioral Functions

Visceral representations traverse the brain from visceral-topic representations of the systemic physiological end organ systems at the level of the solitary nucleus (Powley et al., 2001; Prechtl & Powley, 1990), through the parabrachial region, including the locus coeruleus, en route to regions such as the ventral thalamus and hypothalamic regions, amygdala, bed nucleus of the stria terminalis and insula cortex, and the prefrontal cortex (Norgren, 1976; Saper, 1995). Specific regions of the visceral neural axis are involved in different aspects of bodily sensibility and problem solving. One critical region of the visceral neural axis is the parabrachial region, which in animal (Flynn et al., 1991; Spector et al., 1992) and human (H. D. Critchley et al., 2001a, 2001b) studies has been linked to the regulation of the internal milieu (sodium hunger, taste aversion learning). Recall that this region of the brain is in the brainstem. In the rat, pathways that underlie viscerally important information that may underlie motivated behaviors project to the central nucleus of the amygdala, lateral bed nucleus of the stria terminalis, and the lateral hypothalamus (Norgren, 1976; Pfaffmann et al., 1977). This parabrachial region contains subnuclei that underlie cardiovascular, gastrointestinal, gustatory representations (Saper, 1995).

The parabrachial region is typically bifurcated in terms of a lateral region that underlies cardiovascular regulation and a medial region that underlies gastrointestinal and gustatory representations and regulation (Norgren, 1995; Saper, 1995). These are core bodily representations in the brain. Depicted in figure C.2 is the parabrachial region.

In functional studies, the gustatory portion may first be identified by electrophysiological recordings following infusions of gustatory stimulation into the oral cavity. Once identified, this region (parabrachial region) is then ablated. Rats, when tested following a recovery period, fail to display normal oral ingestive patterns (switching from ingestion of sucrose to rejection as a function of the malaise generated by the nausea associated with the sweet substance). In subsequent studies using methods that induce cell loss while

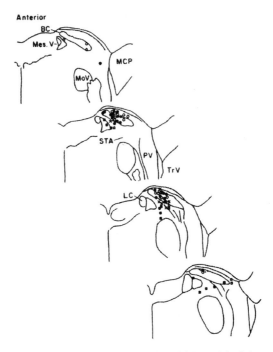

Fig. C.2. Pontine gustatory area in caudal parabrachial nuclei of the rat. Location of single units responding to gustatory and other intra- and perioral stimuli plotted on tracings of projected sections through dorsal pons. Filled circles=neurons that respond best to sapid stimuli applied on anterior tongue. Open circles=units that respond best to sapid stimuli applied in posterior oral cavity and that presumably activate receptors in circumvallate and foliate papillae and on palate. Open squares=response to tongue thermal or tactile stimuli. Filled squares=response to jaw stretch or tooth top. Cross=units that did not respond to any stimulus tested (adapted from Norgren, 1995).

sparing fibers of passage, the parabrachial-damaged rats did not display taste aversion learning (Scalera, Spector, & Norgren, 1995; see Bures, dez-Rattoni, & Yamamoto, 1998, for a general discussion of the neural mechanisms of taste aversion learning). Moreover, this region of the brain is essential for the appraisal of the significance of salt for the sodium-hungry animal and in the learned association of ingestion and visceral discomfort (e.g., Flynn et al., 1991; Spector et al., 1992; figure C.3).

This core brainstem region is vital for core regulation of the internal milieu, for the connection between visceral disruption and the organization of action to ameliorate and restore bodily stability (Damasio et al., 2000). This region, in addition to forebrain visceral structures (e.g., amygdala, bed nucleus of the stria terminalis, regions of the hypothalamus, neocortical regions), contributes to the circuitry for visceral information processing in the brain.

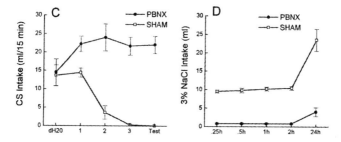

Fig. C.3. Taste aversion learning (C) and sodium appetite (D) are depicted in this figure. Damage to this critical brainstem compromised or abolished both regulatory behaviors (adapted from Scalera et al., 1995).

Changes in the Internal Milieu, Consciousness, and the Organization of Action

Consciousness, as James (1890/1952) suggested at the turn of the 20th century, is not a "thing," but it is an essential piece of who we are (e.g., Sartre, 1943/1973; Searle, 1984a, 1984b; Weiskrantz, 1997). The reticular formation does not equal consciousness; the amygdala does not equal consciousness. But consciousness is not less real because there is no one structure in which it can be located. Of course, one can say that it is the whole of the brain. To be sure, bodily sensibility is most often identified with consciousness (Damasio, 1999; Sartre, 1943/1973; Scheler, 1992). Without brain representations of bodily sensibility, there is no consciousness. Consciousness pervades bodily sensibility and problem solving (Searle, 2001; Wolf, 1981). But mostly, it is erroneous to identify any conscious state with bodily representations. Thirst is not the same as a dry mouth, just as hunger is not the same as stomach contractions (Cannon, 1916/1929).

Detection of discrepant changes has often surfaced as a feature of conscious focus or attention. One form of change is that of homeostatic regulation. Recognition of regulatory needs (broadly conceived) facilitates behavioral options. Bodily representations help inform the central nervous system of important considerations: to drink or eat. They contribute importantly to the organization of action.

It seems that we, as every generation does, have to resurrect something important. In this generation we need to resurrect the mind in body–the body in mind (e.g., Damasio, 1994, 1999; James, 1885/1958, 1890/1952; M. Johnson, 1990; Lakoff & Johnson, 1999). Cognition is essential for problem solving; not all emotions are disorganized forms of expression, but rather are highly evolved forms of expression. The roots are within biology. There is no one knockdown argument about this issue: The major revolt against construing the emotions as sensation or feelings is the realization that sensory systems themselves are specific cognitive devices. If "cognition is the psychological category that covers perception, knowledge, language and reasoning" (Bogden, 2001, p. 14), then indeed, feelings are as cognitive as percepts (Damasio, 2001). There is just a number of appraisal or information-processing systems operative in the nervous system that function quite well through evolutionary selection procedures.

Alterations in the regulation of the internal milieu have long been thought to contribute to conscious mobilization of action (Damasio, 1999; Denton et al., 1999). Consciousness, as Damasio has suggested (see also Berridge, 2000, 2003; Panksepp, 1998), is linked to regulatory systems. But let us resist the temptation to submit "I exist because I'm thirsty due to some alteration of my internal milieu." For the baby, the Cartesian knowing of existence is rather brute and basic (figure C.4). For us adults, it is still pretty basic.

Bodily permutations are represented by neural function throughout the nervous system. These representations of bodily states include the regulation of the internal milieu and visceral and muscular-skeletal control (Damasio, 1999; Denton et al., 1999). Self-preservation is first noted in bodily sensibility: to avoid or approach, to get attached or to quickly ward off. Core changes in basic motivational systems (e.g., thirst) are well represented across

Fig. C.4. Descartes' poop (*Washington Post*, 11 January 2002). By permission of Dave Coverly and Creators Syndicate, Inc.

the brain (Damasio et al., 2000; Denton et al., 1999). But these are central states of the brain, cephalic representations within the visceral/autonomic system.

Visceral Representations and Engagement with the World

As I have said often in this book, representations and appraisal systems need not force one to be detached. Yet the legacy of a view of cognition as detached still lingers. Visceral forms of information highlight affective significance of events. Moreover, there is no loss of the individual's primary sensibility in suggesting that common mechanisms are active when I see you do something and when I do it myself, nor in the fact that my experience is something special. After all, it is my bodily experience, but the range of what we share through our common genetic and cultural background makes all the difference. Without that, there is no conversation, including whether we are having the same bodily sensibility. It is a humbling affair when the issue of consciousness emerges, and of course one should be as empirical as one can in order to not reify or reduce the phenomena out of existence for expedience or for some fantasy of what the cognitive sciences should be like to be legitimate. In the rush to look scientific, some throw out what seems impossible to understand. On the other hand, the reification of this concept has incurred endless confusions and incoherence.

The sense of relatedness in our experience is what James (1890/1952) emphasizes, and he understood it in the context of bodily sensibility. The body was not inert for James. What he had in his intellectual lexicon was the notion of a central state, the profound way in which evolution of the brain resulted in greater connectivity between local circuits and more broadly focused functions.

But again, three concepts are often reflexively linked: cortex, consciousness, and cognition. Representations of gustatory disgust are represented at many levels of the neural axis, from the solitary nucleus to the insular cortex. Gustatory sensibility in many regions overlaps with neuroendocrine and other sensory and autonomic systems (Norgren, 1995; Rolls, 2000). Disgust is certainly a bodily representation, but it is not in the stomach; disgust is cephalic in origin. Decerebrated individuals feel pain and can emit disgust reactions to infusions of tastants into the oral cavity. They do not have the larger motivational abilities to organize behavior, and they look as if they are in a stupor most of the time. However, basic reactions to gustatory stimuli are somewhat intact (Nowlis, 1977). But as one ascends the central nervous system, basic bodily representations (in this case, gustatory) are coded throughout and linked to the larger semantic networks in which this information is of relevance (Downing, Jiang, Shuman, & Kanwisher, 2001). Forebrain visceral regions are essential in regulating the internal demands amid external circumstances (Herbert & Schulkin, 2002; Swanson, 2000a, 2000b, 2003).

Many of the examples that I have given suggest visceral input from end organ systems that are centrally mediated. Bodily sensibility is cephalic, the brain is a cognitive organ; visceral input at the first-order neural sites, whether in the brainstem, olfactory bulb, or retina, are all within coded information-processing systems in the brain. All events have representations in the nervous systems, and the information is processed at various levels of the neural axis. Some emotions, perhaps, are more driven from rich semantic networks that traverse the newly evolved cortical areas (Davidson et al., 2000, 2003). Other emotions (fear, attachment) are more rudimentary and are primarily orchestrated by regions such as the amygdala, bed nucleus of the stria terminalis, and hypothalamic regions, but are also regulated by these same newly evolved sites. Less identifiable as bodily representations for emotions, particularly emotions such as envy, shame, and embarrassment, these are linked to broad-based semantic networks in the brain.

Love and Other Cephalic Matters

James noted correctly that a "purely disembodied human emotion is a nonentity" (1890/1952, p. 452). But love, as we know, is not identical with sexual desire. Moreover, the concept of love captures a variety of meanings in different contexts. Love is not a bodily feeling per se, though at times it certainly contains a wide variety of bodily feelings. To reduce love to a bodily feeling is surely a disservice to this rich concept so essential for the human experience (Nussbaum, 1994, 2001; Solomon, 1990). Love is embodied in a rich lexical network of meanings; love is extended by metaphor and by bodily sensibility in the active and enthusiastic embrace of a person, a place, a subject matter, an object of creation. It may occur via structures of attachment, appraisal mechanisms to approach and to remain in vigorous contact; the emotion of love toward a child, spouse, or friend is theoretically rich. Love, like several other emotions, is also a normative goal; there are better and worse ways of being in love, of being attached, of valuing others (Fromm, 1956/1975). Love, like other emotions, is an orientation to the world, and to particular entities in the world. Love has its biological roots in the primary attachments that we form, with those individuals who provide an initial anchor to the world in which we are to function, make sense of, and survive.

The emotions, through cephalic bodily sensibility, provide an orientation to problem solving (DeSousa, 1987/1997). The emotions are not reduced only to problem solving; they can either aid a particular problem or not. And that is the critical point. Thinkers since Aristotle (see Nussbaum, 1994) have commented on the emotions aiding intelligent functions. Good theory brings one closer to a phenomenon, and yet the view of theory has grown into something that removes one from the phenomenon. Theory varies with the subject matter, as does objectivity and the appraisal mechanisms that underlie it.

And when it comes to understanding bodily sensibility, the emotions, or cognitive competence, one looks to the transactions of individuals coping with an environment (Brandstattr & Eliasz, 2000; Dewey, 1896). Human experience is in the transactions with the world and in the engagements with one another (Dewey, 1925/1989). Individuals are not abstract entities experiencing bodily sensibility, but are concrete existential instances of experiencing emotional joy, fear, loneliness, apathy, and envy. They are enjoying aesthetics and are being revolted by moral transgressions.

There are those of us who have never understood information processing as merely cold and detached, with human experience denied and omitted. Bodily sensibility is rooted in cephalic functions, those diverse cognitive machinations.

Notes

Introduction

1. This is analogous to "good enough parenting."

1. Bodily Representations, Behavior, and the Brain

1. There are many debates on the extent to which information-processing systems are penetrable or not, and the degree to which they are accessible to higher-level systems (Gazzaniga, 2000; Posner, 1990; Pylyshyn, 1999; Scherer et al., 2001). What concerns me in this book is the primary thesis: The sense of the body is orchestrated by the brain; the brain is the cognitive organ. Bodily sensibility cuts across virtually all aspects of human experience. Does that trivialize the thesis? I think not. It will evoke a broad array of things to consider under the rubric of bodily sensibility.

2. We have moved along rapidly, despite some recent protestations (J. A. Fodor, 2000). Now we are in a position to depict the general understanding of cognitive systems. See Harnish's (2002) *Minds, Brains and Computers* for a depiction of the origins of the cognitive sciences.

3. See classical papers presented and translated by von Bonin (1960).

4. Interestingly, Hebb noted in the introduction to Lashley's book on intelligence that "after reading this book one should not equate conscious with cortical." I would add the third layer, namely, not equating cognition, consciousness, and cortex.

5. See the book edited by Scherer et al. (2001) for a broad and insightful discussion of the concept of appraisal systems in emotion research.

6. Consider another issue; Dickinson and Balleine (2000) argue that the gustatory/visceral representation is a noncognitive event, whereas the linking of the devaluation of the food source and the decrease in instrumental responses

is a cognitive/causal event (see also Garcia, 1989). I suggest that we instead consider diverse kinds of representational systems in the brain, some more complicated and extensive than others, rather than one being cognitive and the other not.

7. See Bures et al. (1998) for a nice review of the taste aversion literature and the brain mechanisms that underlie the behavior.

8. Konorski, like Dewey, Tolman, and Miller, was an early cognitive behaviorist (see Schulkin, 2000).

9. The field of study on corticotropin releasing hormone fills volumes of interesting research; see Schulkin (2003).

2. Demythologizing the Emotions

1. See M. Critchley and Critchley (1998) for a nice biography of this great neurologist and for a discussion of the individuals, such as H. Spencer, who influenced the ideas of Jackson. See also Spencer's *First Principles* (1857/1890).

2. Researchers reflexively refer to the cognitive and emotion domains (e.g., Perlstein, Elbert, & Stenger, 2002; regions of the prefrontal cortex), when often, what they are really talking about are different kinds and complexities in information processing.

3. Despite Panskepp's omission of motivation from the emotional-cognitive connection, he does render prescient points about what he calls "deadly sins" in evolutionary psychology. One of these sins is the inability to recognize more broadly conceived systems as all-purpose systems. Other sins include overzealous adaptationist arguments, massive modularity of function, perhaps a disembodied conception of the representational mind (Panksepp & Panksepp, 2000), and the tendency of the cognitive sciences to omit reference to the importance of the emotions. Another mistake, in his view, is the cognitivist view (my view) of the emotions. But top down does not mean disembodied. There is just no extra noncomputational site—no mere givens—no pain without detector systems for pain recognition, and so on.

4. For example, Lane et al. (1998, 1999); see Swanson and Petrovich (1998) for the wide range of definitions of brain regions and the confusion that it engenders.

5. See Swanson and Petrovich (1998); Alheid et al. (1996); Petrovich et al. (2001); Amaral and Price (1984) for discussion and disagreements about what constitutes the amygdala. See also McGinty (1999).

3. Aesthetic Judgment, Discrepancy, and Inquiry

1. Dewey worked hard to naturalize our experience from the detached spectator to the active participator. And experience is replete with cognitive function for pragmatists such as John Dewey (see Kuklick, 2001).

2. Langer was a student of Cassirer and Whitehead. She also resurrected some of the insights of Schopenhauer on music; see Kivy (2001).

3. Statement attributed to Beethoven; see Sullivan (1955).

4. Moral Sensibility and Social Cohesion

1. Of course, this is a disputable characterization. Many investigators would be uncomfortable suggesting that rules underlie bodily sensibility, but not the converse.

2. In Eichenbaum and Cohen's (2001) book on memory (memory is an outcome of the brain's diverse information-processing systems), they make a point similar to the one that I am suggesting about moral behavior, namely, that there is no brain region for morality; instead, there are diverse information-processing systems in the brain that have been recruited and accessed that make possible moral behavior.

3. This is a controversial point. For some, the criteria for something being true or false is that it be cognitive; for others, and I am included, cognitive has to do with the ability to participate in the rules of culture (Wittgenstein, 1953), adapt to our surroundings with effective strategies. Cognition is not simply about what is true or not, but it has everything to do with information-processing systems that are cephalic in nature.

4. This is again controversial. For some, the idea of less than perfect reason, the use of heuristics in everyday reasoning, our cognitive limitations and biases, brought reason to a lower level. That lower level, I suggest, does a fairly good job in problem solving and overall exhibits a form of rationality that is of human and not perfect human proportion.

5. Purists about reason will disagree and want to keep reason elevated and not denigrated. Reasoning for purists is labored, conscious, deliberate, and under self-control. Nonpurists like myself eschew respectfully this characterization of reason.

6. One wonders the extent to which this event is culturally bound. Ask people in less-developed cultures what their response might be, also what the response might be when the consequences matter—when there is someone monitoring the choices and keeping track of them.

7. The empathy literature is filled with the sense that empathy inhibits bestial expression (e.g., Davis, 1996; Eisenberg & Strayer, 1987; R. L. Katz, 1963; Omdahl, 1995; Rousseau, 1755/1964). But bad theories and narrow-minded, short-sighted people can certainly distance themselves from the pain of others, if they are perceived as vermin and the legitimation mechanism is in place (Arendt, 1963; Sabini & Silver, 1982).

8. My use of "disgust" is meant as a metaphorical extension. See M. Johnson (1990) and Lakoff and Johnson (1999) for a nice discussion of metaphor; see also Rozin (1999).

5. Drives and Explanations

1. There are volumes of research on this topic, but see a nice review by Eliot Valenstein (1973).

2. See Berridge (2000) and Dickinson and Balleine (2000).

3. Our idea of understanding ranges from what I would call "small theory" to the notion of theory as abstract, general, and quite large for what it can account for—degrees of representations (Quine, 1961) in organized behavioral

systems (Cherniak, 1986; Dewey, 1925/1989; Gigerenzer, 2000; Gopnik, 1996; Heelan & Schulkin, 1998; Kroglanski, 1989; Simon, 1982). See M. Johnson (1990) for problem solving (see also A. Clark, 2000a).

4. "Questions Concerning Certain Faculties Claimed for Man" (Peirce 1868a).

Conclusion. Corporeal Representations

1. M. Johnson (1990). See David Weissman's (1996, 2003) interesting analysis tracing the Cartesian view back to Plato; both mistrusted the sensory experience as informative from the body and its legacy on contemporary thought.

References

Adolphs, R. (1999). Social cognition and the human brain. *Trends in Cognitive Sciences, 3*, 469–479.

Adolphs, R., Damasio, H., Tranel, D., Cooper, G., & Damasio, A. R. (2000). A role for somatosensory cortices in the visual recognition of emotion as revealed by three-dimensional lesion mapping. *Journal of Neuroscience, 20*, 2683–2690.

Adolphs, R., Denburg, N. L., & Tranel, D. (2001). The amygdala's role in long-term declarative memory for gist and detail. *Behavioral Neuroscience, 112*, 983–992.

Adolphs, R., Tranel, D., & Damasio, A. R. (2003). Dissociable neural systems for recognizing emotions. *Brain and Cognition, 52*, 61–69.

Adolphs, R., Tranel, D., Damasio, H., & Damasio, A. (1994). Impaired recognition of emotion in facial expressions following bilateral damage to the human amygdala. *Nature, 372*, 669–672.

Aggleton, J. P. (2000). *The Amygdala.* Oxford: Oxford University Press.

Aggleton, J. P., & Mishkin, M. (1986). The amygdala: Sensory gateway to the emotions. In R. Plutchik & H. Kellerman (Eds.), *Emotion: Theory and experience.* New York: Academic Press.

Alheid, G. F., Shammah-Lagnado, S., & Beltramino, C. A. (1999). The interstitial nucleus of the posterior limb of the anterior commissure: A novel layer of the central division of the extended amygdala. *Annals of the New York Academy of Science, 877*, 645–654.

Allen, C., & Bekoff, M. (1997). *Species of mind.* Cambridge, MA: MIT Press.

Allison, T. (2001). Neuroscience and morality. *Neuroscientist, 7*, 360–364.

Allison, T., Puce, A., & McCarthy, G. (2000). Social perception from visual cues: Role of the STS region. *Trends in Cognitive Science, 4*, 267–278.

Altran, S. (1996) *Cognitive foundations of natural history.* Cambridge, UK: Cambridge University Press.

Amaral, D. G., & Price, J. L. (1984). Amygdalo-cortical projections in the monkey (Macaca fascicularis). *Journal of Comparative Neurolology, 230,* 465–496.

Anderson, A. R., Christoff, K., Panitz, D., Rosa, E. D. A., & Gabrieli, J. D. E. (2003). Neural correlates of the automatic processing of threat facial signals. *Journal of Neuroscience, 23,* 5627–5633.

Anderson, S. W., Bechara, A., Damasio, H., Tranel, D., & Damasio, A. R. (1999). Impairment of social and moral behavior related to early damage in human prefrontal cortex. *Nature Neuroscience, 2,* 1032–1037.

Angyal, A. (1941). Disgust and related aversions. *Journal of Abnormal and Social Psychology, 36,* 393–412.

Arendt, H. (1963). *Eichman in Jerusalem.* New York: Viking Press.

Aristotle. (1962). *The Nicomachean ethics.* New York: Macmillan.

Arnold, M. B. (1960) *Emotion and personality.* New York: Columbia University Press.

Baier, A. C. (1991). *A progress of sentiments.* Cambridge, MA: Harvard University Press.

Baldwin, D. A., & Moses, L. J. (1994). Early understanding of referential intent and attentional focus: Evidence from language and emotion. In C. Lewis & P. Mitchell (Eds.), *Children's early understanding of mind* (pp. 133–156). Hillsdale, NJ: Erlbaum.

Baron, J. (1998). *Judgment misguided: Intuition and error in public decision making.* Oxford: Oxford University Press.

Baron, J. (2000). *Thinking and deciding.* Cambridge, UK: Cambridge University Press. (Original work published 1988)

Baron, J., & Schulkin, J. (1995). The problem of global warming from a decision-theoretic perspective. *Social Epistemology, 9,* 353–368.

Baron-Cohen, S. (1995). *Mindblindness: An essay on autism and theory of mind.* Cambridge, MA: MIT Press.

Baron-Cohen, S., Flusberg, H. T., & Cohen, D. J. (2000) *Understanding other minds.* Oxford: Oxford University Press.

Bartoshuk, L. M. (1991). Taste, smell, and pleasure. In R. C. Bolles (Ed.), *The hedonics of taste* (pp. 15–28). Hillsdale, NJ: Erlbaum.

Bassili, N. J. (1979). Emotion recognition: The role of facial movement and the relative importance of upper and lower areas of the face. *Journal of Personality and Social Psychology, 37,* 2049–2058.

Bechara, A., Damasio, H., & Damasio, A. R. (2000). Emotion, decision making and the orbitofrontal cortex. *Cerebral Cortex, 10*(3), 295–307.

Bechara, A., Damasio, A. R., Damasio, H., & Anderson, S. W. (1994). Insensitivity to future consequences following damage to human prefrontal cortex. *Cognition, 50,* 7–15.

Bechara, A., Damasio, H., Damasio, A. R., & Lee, G. P. (1999). Differential contributions of the human amygdala and ventromedial prefrontal cortex to decision-making. *Journal of Neuroscience, 19,* 5473–5481.

Bechara, A., Damasio, H., Tranel, D., & Damasio, A. R. (1997). Deciding advantageously before knowing the advantageous strategy. *Science, 275,* 1293–1295.

Bentham, J. (1948). *Principles of morals and legislation.* New York: Hafner. (Original work published 1789)

Ben-Zeev, R. (2000). The subtlety of emotions. Cambridge, MA: MIT Press.

Berlyne, D. E. (1954). A theory of human curiosity. *British Journal of Psychology, 45,* 180–191.

Berlyne, D. E. (1960). *Conflict, arousal and curiosity.* New York: McGraw-Hill.

Berlyne, D. E. (1971). *Aesthetics and psychobiology.* New York: Appleton-Century-Crofts.

Bernard, C. (1859). *Lecons sur les proprietes physiologiques et les alterations pathologiques de l'organisme.* Paris: Balliers.

Berns, G. S., McClure, S. M., Pagnoni, G., & Montague, P. R. (2001). Predictability modulates human brain response to reward. *Journal of Neuroscience, 21,* 2793–2798.

Berridge, K. C. (1996). Food reward: Brain substrates of wanting and liking. *Neuroscience and Biobehavioral Reviews, 20*(1), 1–25.

Berridge, K. C. (2000). Measuring hedonic impact in animals and infants: Microstructure of affective taste reactivity patterns. *Neuroscience and Biobehavioral Reviews, 24*(2), 173–198.

Berridge, K. C. (2003). Comparing the emotional brains of humans and other animals. In R. J. Davidson et al. (Eds.), *Handbook of affective sciences.* New York: Oxford University Press.

Berridge, K. C., Flynn, F. W., Schulkin, J., & Grill, H. J. (1984). Sodium depletion enhances salt palatability in rats. *Behavioral Neuroscience, 98,* 652–660.

Berridge, K. C., & Grill, H. J. (1983). Alternating ingestive and aversive consummatory responses suggest a two-dimensional analysis of palatability in rats. *Behavioral Neuroscience, 97,* 563–573.

Berridge, K. C., & Schulkin, J. (1989). Palatability shift of salt-associated incentive drive during sodium depletion. *Quarterly Journal of Experimental Psychology, 41B,* 121–138.

Berridge, K. C., & Winkielman, P. (2003). What is an unconscious emotion? The case for unconscious "liking." *Cognition and Emotion, 17,* 181–211.

Berthoz, A. (2000). *The brain's sense of movement.* Cambridge, MA: Harvard University Press.

Bharucha, J., & Krumhansl, C. (1983). The representation of harmonic structure in music: Hierarchies of stability as a function of context. *Cognition, 13,* 63–102.

Bindra, D. (1968). Neuropsychological interpretation of the effects of drive and incentive-motivation on general and instrumental behavior. *Psychological Review, 75,* 1–22.

Biringen, Z. C. (1987). Infant attention to facial expressions and facial motion. *Journal of Genetic Psychology, 148,* 127–133.

Bjorklund, A., & Lindvall, O. (1984). Dopamine-containing systems in the CNS. In A. Bjorklund & T. Hokfelt (Eds.), *Handbook of chemical neuroanatomy, classical transmitters in the CNS* (Part 1, Vol. 2, pp. 55–122). Amsterdam: Elsevier.

Blackbun, S. (1998). *Ruling passion.* Oxford: Clarendon.

Blair, R. J., Morris, J. S., Perrett, D. I., & Dolan, R. J. (1999). Dissociable neural responses to facial expression of sadness and anger. *Brain, 122,* 883–893.

Blakemore, S. J., & Decety, J. (2001). From the perception of action to the understanding of intention. *Nature, Neuroscience, 2*, 661–667.

Blasi, A. (1980). Bridging moral cognition and moral action: A critical review of the literature. *Psychological Bulletin, 88*, 1–45.

Blessing, W. W. (1997). *The lower brainstem and bodily homeostasis.* Oxford: Oxford Univeristy Press.

Blonder, L. X., Burns, A. F., Bowers, D., Moore, R. W., & Heilman, K. M. (1993). Right hemisphere facial expressivity during natural conversation. *Brain and Cognition, 21*, 44–56.

Blood, A. J., & Zatorre, R. J. (2001). Intensely pleasurable responses to music correlate with activity in brain regions implicated in reward and emotion. *Proceedings of the National Academy of Science, 98*, 11818–11823.

Blood, A. J., Zatorre, R. J., Bermudez, P., & Evans, A. C. (1999). Emotional responses to pleasant and unpleasant music correlate with activity in paralimbic brain regions. *Nature Neuroscience, 2*, 383–387.

Bogden, M. (2001). Life and cognition. In E. J. Branquinko (Ed.), *The foundations of cognitive science.* Oxford: Oxford University Press.

Boroditsky, L., & Ramscar, M. (2002). The roles of body and mind in abstract thought. *Psychological Science, 13*, 185–189.

Bowlby, J. (1988). *A secure base.* New York: Basic Books.

Boyd, R. (1999). Homeostasis, species, and higher taxa. In R. A. Wilson (Ed.), *Species: New interdisciplinary essays.* Cambridge, MA: MIT Press.

Brandstatter, H., & Eliasz, A. (2000). *Persons, situations and emotions.* New York: Oxford University Press.

Bregar, R. E., Strombakis, N., Allan, R. W., & Schulkin, J. (1983). Brief exposure to a saline stimulus promotes latent learning in the salt hunger system. *Neuroscience Abstracts.*

Breiter, H. C., Aharon, I., Kahneman, D., Dale, A., & Shizgal, P. (2001). Functional imaging of neural responses to expectancy and experience of monetary gains and losses. *Neuron, 30*, 619–639.

Breiter, H. C., Etcoff, N. L., Whalen, P. J., Kennedy, W. A., Rauch, S. L., Buckner, R. L., Strauss, M. M., Hyman, S. E., & Rosen, B. R. (1996). Response and habituation of the human amygdala during visual processing of facial expression. *Neuron, 17*, 875–887.

Broca, P. (1878). Anatomic comparee des ciconvolutions: Le grad lbe limbique et la scissure limbique dans la serie des mammiferes. *Review of Anthropology, 1*, 385–498.

Brodal, A. (1981). *Neurological anatomy.* Oxford: Oxford University Press.

Brothers, L. (1997). *Friday's footprint.* Oxford: Oxford University Press.

Brothers, L., & Ring, B. (1993). Medial temporal neurons in the macaque monkey with responses selective for aspects of social stimuli. *Behavior and Brain Research, 57*, 53–61.

Bruner, J. S. (1973). *Beyond the information given.* New York: Norton.

Bruner, J. S., Goodnow, J., & Austin, G. A. (1956). *A study of thinking.* New York: New York Science Editions.

Bruno, N., & Cutting, J. E. (1988). Minimodularity and the perception of layout. *Journal of Experimental Psychology: General, 117*, 161–170.

Brunswik, D. (1943). Organismic achievement and environmental probability. *Psychological Review, 50*, 255–272.

Brunswik, D. (1955). Representative design and probabilistic theory in a functional psychology. *Psychological Review, 62,* 193–217.

Buck, R., Loslow, J. I., Murphy, M. M., & Costanzo, P. (1992). Social facilitation and inhibition of emotional expression and communication. *Journal of Personality and Social Psychology, 63,* 962–968.

Bures, J., dez-Rattoni, F., & Yamamoto, T. (1998). *Conditioned taste aversion.* Oxford: Oxford University Press.

Buss, D. M. (2001). Cognitive biases and emotional wisdom in the evolution of conflict between the sexes. *Psychological Sciences,* 219–223.

Byrne, R. W., & Whiten, A. (1988). *Machiavellian intelligence: Social expertise and the evolution of intellect in monkeys, apes and humans.* Oxford: Oxford University Press.

Cabanac, M., & LaFrance, L. (1990). Post-ingestive alliesthesia: The rat tells the same story. *Physiology and Behavior, 47,* 539–543.

Cacioppo, J., & Bernston, G. G. (1999). The affect system: Architecture and operating characteristics. *Current Directions in Psychological Science, 8,* 133–137.

Calder, A. J., Keane, J., Manes, F., Antoun, N., & Young, A. W. (2000). Impaired recognition and experience of disgust following brain injury. *Nature Neuroscience, 3,* 1077–1078.

Calder, A. J., Lawrence, A. D., & Young, A. W. (2001). Neuropsychology of fear and loathing. *Nature Neuroscience, 2,* 352–363.

Cameron, O. G. (2002). *Visceral sensory neuroscience.* Oxford: Oxford University Press.

Camras, L. A., Campos, J., Campos, R., Miyake, K., Oster, H., Ujiie, T., Wang, L., & Meng, Z. (1998). Production of emotional facial expressions in European American, Japanese, and Chinese infants. *Developmental Psychology, 34,* 616–628.

Cancelliere, A. E., & Kertesz, A. (1990). Lesion localization in acquired deficits of emotional expression and comprehension. *Brain and Cognition, 13,* 133–147.

Canli, T., Silvers, H., Whitfield, S. L., Gotlib, I. H., & Gabrieli, J. (2002). Amygdala response to happy faces as a function of extraversion. *Science, 296,* 2191.

Cannon, W. B. (1927). The James-Lange theory of emotions: A critical examination and an alternative theory. *American Journal of Psychology, 39,* 106–124.

Cannon, W. B. (1929). *Bodily changes in pain, hunger, fear and rage.* New York: Appleton. (Original work published 1916)

Cardinal, R. N., Parkinson, J. A., Hall, J., & Everitt, B. J. (2002). Emotion and motivation: The role of the amygdala, ventral striatum and prefrontal cortex. *Neuroscience and Biobehavioral Reviews, 26,* 321–352.

Carey, S. (1985). *Conceptual change in childhood.* Cambridge, MA: MIT Press.

Carey, S. (1995). Continuity and discontinuity in cognitive development. In E. E. Smith & D. N. Osherson (Eds.), *Thinking: An invitation to cognitive science.* Cambridge, MA: MIT Press.

Carey, S., & Markman, E. M. (2000). Cognitive development. In B. M. Bly et al. (Eds.), *Cognitive science: Handbook of perception and cognition* (2nd ed.). San Diego, CA: Academic Press.

Carey, S., & Spelke, E. (1996). Science and core knowledge. *Philosophy of Science, 63,* 515–533.

Caron, A. J., Caron, R., Roberts, J., & Brooks, R. (1997). Infant sensitivity to deviations in dynamic facial-vocal displays: The role of the eye regard. *Developmental Psychology, 33,* 802–813.

Carroll, J. M., & Russell, J. A. (1996). Do facial expressions signal specific emotions? Judging emotion from the face in context. *Journal of Personality and Social Psychology, 70,* 205–218.

Carruthers, P. (1996). Simulation and self-knowledge: A defence of theory-theory. In P. Carruthers & P. Smith (Eds.), *Theories of theories of mind.* Cambridge, UK: Cambridge University Press.

Carruthers, P., & Smith, P. (Eds.). (1996). *Theories of theories of mind.* Cambridge, UK: Cambridge University Press.

Carter, C. S. (1998). Neuroendocrine perspectives on social attachment and love. *Psychoneuroendocrinology, 23,* 779–818.

Cassell, J., Sullivan, J., Prevost, S., & Churchill, E. (2000). *Embodied conversational agents.* Cambridge, MA: MIT Press.

Cassidy, J., Parke, R. D., Butkovsky, L., & Braungart, J. M. (1992). Family-peer connections: The role of emotional expressiveness within the family and children's understanding of emotions. *Child Development, 63,* 603–618.

Cassirer, E. (1985). *The philosophy of symbolic forms, Volume 3: The phenomenology of knowledge.* New Haven: Yale University Press. (Original work published 1957)

Chaminade, T., Meltzoff, A. N., & Decety, J. (2002). Does the end justify the means? A PET exploration of the mechanisms involved in human imitation. *Neuroimage, 15,* 318–328.

Chao, L. L., Martin, A., & Haxby, J. V. (1999). Are face-responsive regions selective only for faces? *Neuroreport, 10,* 2945–2950.

Cherniak, C. (1986). *Minimal rationality.* Cambridge, MA: MIT Press.

Chevialier-Skolnikoff, D. (1973). Facial expression of emotion in nonhuman primates. In P. Ekman (Ed.), *Darwin and facial expression: A century of research in review* (pp. 11–89). New York: Academic Press.

Churchland, P. M. (2002). Toward a cognitive neurobiology of the moral virtues. In E. J. Branquinho (Ed.), *The foundations of cognitive science.* Oxford: Oxford University Press.

Clark, A. (1997). *Being there: Putting brain, body, and world together again.* Cambridge, MA: MIT Press.

Clark, A. (2000a). *A theory of sentience.* Oxford: Oxford University Press.

Clark, A. (2000b). Twisted tales: Causal complexity and cognitive scientific explanation. In F. C. Keil & R. A. Wilson (Eds.), *Explanation and cognition.* Cambridge, MA: MIT Press.

Clore, G. L. (1992). Cognitive phenomenology: Feelings and the construction of judgment. In L. L. Martin & A. Tesser (Eds.), *The construction of social judgments* (pp. 133–163). Hillsdale, NJ: Erlbaum.

Clore, G. L., Wyer, R. S., Jr., Dienes, B., Gasper, K., Gohm, C., & Isbell, L. (2001). Affective feelings as feedback: Some cognitive consequences. In L. L. Martin & G. L. Clore (Eds.), *Theories of mood and cognition: A user's guidebook* (pp. 27–62). Mahwah, NJ: Erlbaum.

Coons, E., & Kraechenbuehl, D. (1958). Information as a measure of structure of music. *Journal of Music Theory, 2,* 127–161.

Cosmides, L., & Tooby, J. (1994). Beyond intuition and instinct blindness: Towards an evolutionary rigorous cognitive science. *Cognition, 50,* 41–77.

Cossette, L., Pomerleau, A., Malcuit, G., & Kaczorowski, J. (1996). Emotional expressions of female and male infants in a social and a nonsocial context. *Sex Roles, 35,* 693–710.

Craig, W. (1918). Appetites and aversions as constituents of instinct. *Biological Bulletin, 34,* 91–107.

Critchley, H. D., Cortfield, D. R., Chandler, D. R., Mathias, C. J., & Dolan, R. J. (2000). Cerebral correlates of autonomic cardiovascular arousal: A functional neuroimaging investigation. *Journal of Physiology, 523,* 259–270.

Critchley, H. D., Mathias, C. J., & Dolan, R. J. (2001a). Neural activity in the human brain relating to uncertainty and arousal during anticipation. *Neuron, 29,* 537–545.

Critchley, H. D., Mathias, C. J., & Dolan, R. J. (2001b). Neuroanatomical basis for first and second-order representations of bodily states. *Nature Neuroscience, 4,* 207–212.

Critchley, M., & Critchley, E. A. (1998). *John Hughlings Jackson: Father of English neurology.* Oxford: Oxford University Press.

Croce, B. (1983). *Aesthetic.* Boston: Nonpareil Books. (Original work published 1909)

Cross, I. (2001). Music, cognition, culture and evolution. In R. J. Zatorre & I. Peretz (Eds.), *The biological foundations of music.* New York: New York Academy of Sciences.

Daffner, K. R. Mesulam, M. M., Holcomb, P. J., Calvo, V., Acar, D., Chabrerie, A., Kikinis, R., Jolesc, F. A., Rentz, D. M., & Scinto, L. F. (2000). Disruption of attention to novel events after frontal lobe injury in humans. *Journal of Neurology, Neurosurgery and Psychiatry, 68,* 18–24.

Daffner, K. R., Mesulam, M. M., Scinto, L. F., Acar, D., Calvo, V., Faust, R., Chabrerie, A., Kennedy, B., & Holcomb, P. (2000). The central role of prefrontal cortex in directing attention to novel events. *Brain, 123,* 927–939.

Damasio, A. R. (1994). *Descartes' error: Emotion, reason, and the human brain.* New York: Putnam.

Damasio, A. R. (1996). The somatic marker hypothesis and the possible functions of the prefrontal cortex. *Philosophical Transactions of the Royal Society of London, 354,* 1413–1420.

Damasio, A. R. (1999). *The feeling of what happens.* New York: Harcourt.

Damasio, A. R. (2001) Neurobiology of emotion and feeling. In E. J. Branquinho (Ed.), *The foundations of cognitive science.* Oxford: Oxford University Press.

Damasio, A. R., Grabowski, T. J., Bechara, A., Damasio, H., Ponto, L. L. B., Parvizi, J., & Hichwa, R. D. (2000). Subcortical and cortical brain activity during the feeling of self-generated emotions. *Nature Neuroscience, 3,* 1049–1105.

Damasio, A. R., Tranel, D., & Damasio, A. R. (1990). Individuals with sociopathic behavior caused by frontal damage fail to respond autonomically to social stimuli. *Behavioral Brain Research, 41,* 81–94.

Darwin, C. (1965). *The expression of emotions in man and animals.* Chicago: University of Chicago Press. (Original work published 1872)

Darwin, C. (1982). *The descent of man and selection in relation to sex.* Princeton: Princeton University Press. (Original work published 1871)

Dasser, V., Ulbaek, I., & Premack, D. (1989). The perception of intention. *Science, 243,* 365–367.

Davidson, R. J., Ekman, P., Saron, C. D., Senulis, J. A., & Friesnen, W. V. (1990). Approach-withdrawal and cerebral symmetry: Emotional expression and brain physiology. *International Journal of Personality and Social Psychology, 58,* 330–341.

Davidson, R. J., & Harrington, A. (2002). *Visions of compassion.* Oxford: Oxford University Press.

Davidson, R. J., Putnam, K. M., & Larson, C. L. (2000). Dysfunction in the neural circuitry of emotion regulation: A possible prelude to violence. *Science, 289,* 591–594.

Davidson, R. J., Scherer, K. R., & Goldsmith, H. H. (Eds.). (2003) *Handbook of affective neuroscience.* New York: Oxford University Press.

Davies, M., & Stone, T. (Eds.). (1995a). *Folk psychology: The theory of mind debate.* Oxford: Blackwell.

Davies, M., & Stone, T. (Eds.). (1995b). *Mental simulation: Evaluations and applications.* Oxford: Blackwell.

Davis, H. (1996). *Empathy.* Boulder, CO: Westview.

Davis, M., & Whalen, P. J. (2001). The amygdala: Vigilance and emotion. *Molecular Psychiatry, 6,* 13–34.

Decety, J., & Chaminade, T. (2003). Neural correlates of feeling sympathy. *Neuropsychologia, 41,* 127–138.

Decety, J., Chaminade, T., Grézes, J., & Meltzoff, A. N. (2002). A PET exploration of the neural mechanisms involved in reciprocal imitation. *Neuroimage, 15,* 265–272.

Decety, J., & Grézes, J. (1999). Neural mechanisms subserving the perception of human actions. *Trends in Cognitive Science, 3,* 172–178.

Delza, S. (1996). *The T'ai-Chi Ch'uan experience.* Albany: State University of New York Press.

Dennett, D. C. (1987). *The intentional stance.* Cambridge, MA: MIT Press.

Dennett, D. C. (1996). *Kinds of minds.* New York: Basic Books.

Denton, D. (1982). *The hunger for salt.* Berlin: Springer-Verlag.

Denton, D., McKinley, M. J., & Wessinger, R. S. (1996). Hypothalamic integration of body fluid regulation. *Proceedings of the National Academy of Science USA, 93,* 7397–7404.

Denton, D. A., Shade, R., Zamarippa, F., Egan, G., Blair-West, J., McKinley, M., Lancaster, J., & Fox, P. (1999). Neuroimaging of genesis and satiation of thirst and an interoceptor-driven theory of origins of primary consciousness. *Proceedings of the National Academy of Science, 96,* 5304–5309.

Descartes, R. (1960). *Discourse on method and Mediations.* New York: Bobbs-Merrill. (Original work published 1641)

DeSousa, R. (1980). The rationality of emotions. In A. O. Rorty (Ed.), *Explaining emotions* (pp. 127–151). Berkeley: University of California Press.

DeSousa, R. (1997). *The rationality of emotion.* Cambridge, MA: MIT Press. (Original work published 1987)

Deutch, D. (1989). *The psychology of music*. New York: Academic Press.

Devi, R. (1962). *Dances of India*. Calcutta: Susil Gupta.

Devinsky, O., Morrell, M., & Vogt, B. (1995). Contributions of anterior cingulate cortex to behaviour. *Brain, 118*, 279–306.

De Waal, F. (1982). *Chimpanzee politics*. New York: Harper and Row.

De Waal, F. (1991). The chimpanzee's sense of social regularity and its relation to the human sense of justice. *American Behavioral Scientist, 34*, 335–349.

Dewey, J. (1894a). The theory of emotion. I: Emotional attitudes. *Psychological Review, 1*, 553–569.

Dewey, J. (1894b). The theory of emotion. II: The signifance of emotions. *Psychological Review, 1*, 12–19.

Dewey, J. (1896). The reflex arc concept in psychology. *Psychological Review, 3*, 357–370.

Dewey, J. (1968). *Art as experience*. New York: Putnam. (Original work published 1934)

Dewey, J. (1989). *Experience and nature*. LaSalle, IL: Open Court Press. (Original work published 1925)

Dickinson, A. (1980). *Contemporary animal learning theory*. Cambridge, UK: Cambridge University Press.

Dickinson, A. (1986). Re-examination of the role of the instrumental contingency in the sodium-appetite irrelevent incentive effect. *Quarterly Journal of Experimental Psychology: Comparative and Physiological Psychology, 38*(2), 161–172.

Dickinson, A., & Balleine, B. W. (2000). Causal cognition and goal-directed action. In C. Heyes & L. Huber (Eds.), *The evolution of cognition* (pp. 185–204). Cambridge, MA: MIT Press.

Dissanyake, E. (2000). Antecedents of the temporal arts in early mother-infant interaction. In N. L. Wallin, B. Merker, & S. Brown (Eds.), *The origins of music*. Cambridge, MA: MIT Press.

Dolan, R. (2000). Emotional processing in the human brain revealed through functional neuroimaging. In M. S. Gazzaniga (Ed.), *New cognitive neurosciences*. Cambridge, MA: MIT Press.

Downing, P. E., Jiang, Y., Shuman, M., & Kanwisher, N. (2001). A cortical area selective for visual processing of the human body. *Science, 293*, 2470–2473.

Duchaine, B., Cosmides, L., & Tooby, J. (2001). Evolutionary psychology and the brain. *Current Opinion in Neurobiology, 11*, 225–230.

Duchenne, B. (1990). *The mechanism of human facial expression of an electro-physiological analysis of the emotions* (A. Cuthbertson, Trans.). Cambridge, UK: Cambridge University Press. (Original work published 1862)

Duncan, J., & Owen, A.M. (2000). Common regions of the human frontal lobe recruited by diverse cognitive demands. *Trends in Neural Science, 23*, 475–482.

Eichenbaum, H., & Cohen, N. J. (2001). *From conditioning to conscious recollection*. Oxford: Oxford University Press.

Eisenberg, N., & Strayer, J. (Eds.). (1987). *Empathy and its development*. New York: Cambridge University Press.

Ekman, P. (1972). Universals and cultural differences in facial expressions of emotion. In J. Cole (Ed.), *Nebraska symposium on motivation, 1971*. Lincoln: University of Nebraska Press.

Ekman, P. (1992). An argument for basic emotions. *Cognition and Emotion, 6*, 169–200.

Ekman, P., & Davidson, R. J. (1994). *The nature of emotion*. New York: Oxford University Press.

Ekman, P., & Friesen, W. V. (1986). A new pan-cultural facial expression of emotion. *Motivation and Emotion, 10*, 159–168.

Ekman, P., Sorenson, E. R., & Friesen, W. V. (1969). Pan-cultural elements in facial displays of emotions. *Science, 164*, 86–88.

Elliott, R., Friston, K. J., & Dolan, R. J. (2000). Dissociable neural responses in human reward systems. *Journal of Neuroscience, 20*, 6159–6165.

Elliott, R., Newman, J. L., Longe, A. A., & Deakin, J. F. W. (2003). Differential response patterns in the striatum and orbitofrontal cortex to financial reward in humans: A parametric functional magnetic resonance imaging study. *Journal of Neuroscience, 23*, 303–307.

Ellsworth, P. C. (1994). William James and emotion: Is a century of fame worth a century of misunderstanding? *Psychological Review, 101*(2), 222–229.

Ellsworth, P. C. (1995). The right way to study emotion. *Psychological Inquiry, 6*, 213–216.

Elster, J. (1999). *Strong feelings*. Cambridge, MA: MIT Press.

Elster, J. (2000a) *Alchemist of mind*. Cambridge, UK: Cambridge University Press.

Elster, J. (2000b). *Ulysses unbound*. Cambridge, UK: Cambridge University Press.

Emery, N. J. (2000). The eyes have it: The neuroethology, function and evolution of social gaze. *Neuroscience and Biobehavioral Reviews, 24*, 581–604.

Emery, N. J., & Amaral, D. G. (2000). The role of the amygdala in primate social cognition. In R. D. Lane & L. Nadel (Eds.), *Cognitive neuroscience of emotion*. New York: Oxford University Press.

Emery, N. J., Capitanio, J. P., Mason, W. A., Machado, C. J., Mendoza, S. P., Amaral, D. G. (2001). The effects of bilateral lesions of the amygdala on dyadic social interactions in rhesus monkeys. *Behavioral Neuroscience, 115*, 315–344.

Emery, N. J., Lorincz, E. N., Perrett, D. I., Oram, M. W., & Baker, C. I. (1997). Gaze following and joint attention in rhesus monkeys. *Journal of Comparative Psychology, 111*, 286–293.

Epstein, A. N., Fitzsimons, J. T., & Simons, B. J. (1968). Drinking caused by the intracranial injection of angiotensin into the rat. *Journal of Physiology, 200*, 98P–100P.

Erickson, K., & Schulkin, J. (2003). Facial expression of emotion: A cognitive neuroscience perspective. *Cognition and Emotion, 15*, 52–60.

Eslinger, P. J. (1998). Neurological and neuropsychological bases of empathy. *European Neurology, 39*, 193–198.

Eslinger, P. J., Parkinson, K., & Shamay, S. G. (2002). Empathy and social emotional factors in recovery from stroke. *Current Opinion in Neurology, 15*, 91–97.

Everitt, B. J., Herbert, J., & Keerne, E. B. (1983). The neuroendocrine anatomy of the limbic system: A discussion with special reference to steroid responsive neurons, neuropeptides and monoaminergic systems. *Anatomy, 3*, 235–260.

Fabes, R. S., Eisenberg, N., Jones, S., Smith, M., Guthrie, I., Poulin, R., Shepard, S., & Friedman, J. (1999). Regulation, emotionality, and preschoolers' socially competent peer interactions. *Child Development, 70*, 432–443.

Falk, D. (2000). Hominid brain evolution and the origins of music. In N. L. Wallin, B. Merker, & S. Brown (Eds.), *The origins of music*. Cambridge, MA: MIT Press.

Farah, M. (1984). The neurological basis of mental imagery: A componential analysis. *Cognition, 18*, 245–272.

Fentress, J. C. (1984). The development of coordination. *Journal of Motor Behavior, 16*, 99–134.

Fentress, J. C. (1999). The organization of behavior: Revisited. *Canadian Journal of Experimental Psychology, 53*, 8–19.

Ferguson, J. N., Aldag, J. M., Insel, T. R., & Young, L. J. (2001). Oxytocin in the medial amygdala is essential for social recognition in the mouse. *Journal of Neuroscience, 21*(20), 8278–8785.

Field, T. M., & Walden, T. A. (1982). Production and discrimination of facial expressions by preschool children. *Child Development, 53*, 1299–1311.

Field, T. M., Woodson, R., Greenberg, R., & Cohen, D. (1982). Discrimination and imitation of facial expression by neonates. *Science, 218*, 179–181.

Fiorillo, C. D., Tobler, P. N., & Schutz, W. (2003). Discrete coding of reward probability and uncertainty by dopamine neurons. *Science, 299*, 1989–1991.

Fisher, P. (2002). *The vehement passions*. Princeton: Princeton University Press.

Fisher, R. A. (1956). *Statistical methods and scientific inference*. Edinburgh: Oliver and Boyd.

Fitzsimons, J. T. (1979). *The physiology of thirst and sodium appetite*. Cambridge, UK: Cambridge University Press.

Fitzsimons, J. T. (1998). Angiotensin, thirst, and sodium appetite. *Physiological Review, 78*, 583–686.

Flanagan, O. (1991). *Varieties of moral psychology*. Cambridge, MA: Harvard University Press.

Flavell, J. H., Lindberg, N. A., Green, F. L., & Flavell, E. R. (1992). The development of children's understanding of the appearance-reality distinction between how people look and what they are really like. *Merrill-Palmer Quarterly, 38*, 513–524.

Flynn, F. W., Grill, H. G., Schulkin, J., & Norgren, R. (1991). Central gustatory lesions. II: Effects on sodium appetite, taste aversion learning and feeding behaviors. *Behavioral Neuroscience, 105*, 944–954.

Fodor, J. A. (2000). *The mind doesn't work that way*. Cambridge, MA: MIT Press.

Fonberg, E. (1974). Amygdala function within the alimentary system. *Acta Neurobiologiae Experimentalis, 22*, 51–57.

Fox, N. A., & Davidson, R. J. (1986). Taste-elicited changes in facial signs of emotion and the asymmetry of brain electrical activity in human newborns. *Neuropsychologia, 14*(3), 417–422.

Fox, N. A., & Davidson, R. J. (1989). Frontal brain asymmetry predicts infant's response to maternal separation. *Journal of Abnormal Psychology, 98,* 127–131.

Frank, R. H. (1988). *Passions within reason.* New York: Norton.

Frederick, S., & Loewenstein, G. (1999). Hedonic adaptation. In D, Kahneman, E. Diener, & N. Scharz (Eds.), *The foundations of hedonic psychology.* New York: Russell Sage Foundation.

Freud, S. (1960). *The ego and the id.* New York: Norton. (Original work published 1923)

Freud, S. (1961). *Beyond the pleasure principle.* New York: Norton. (Original work published 1922)

Fridlund, A. J. (1991). Evolution and facial action in reflex, social motive and paralanguage. *Biological Psychology, 32,* 3–100.

Fridlund, A. J. (1994). *Human facial expression.* San Diego, CA: Academic Press.

Fridlund, A. J., Sabini, J. P., Hedlund, L. E., Schaut, J. A., Shenker, J. I., & Knauer, M. J. (1990). Social determinants of facial expressions during affective imagery: Displaying to the people in your head. *Journal of Nonverbal Behavior, 14,* 113–137.

Fried, I., Wilson, C. L., Morrow, J. W., Camerone, K. A., Behnke, E. D., Ackerson, L. C., & Maidment, N. T. (2001). Increased dopamine release in the human amygdala during performance of cognitive tasks. *Nature Neuroscience, 4,* 201–206.

Friederici, A. D., Wang, Y., Herrmann, C. S., Maess, B., & Oertel, U. (2000). Localization of early syntactic processes in frontal and temporal cortical areas: A magnetoencephalographic study. *Human Brain Mapping, 11,* 1–11.

Friedman, S. L., & Stevenson, M. B. (1975). Developmental changes in the understanding of implied motion in two-dimensional pictures. *Child Development, 46,* 773–778.

Frijda, N. H. (1986). *The emotions.* Cambridge, UK: Cambridge University Press.

Frijda, N. H. (1989a). Aesthetic emotions and reality. *American Psychologist, 44,* 1546–1547.

Frijda, N. H. (1989b). Relationships among emotions, appraisals, and emotion action readiness. *Journal of Personality and Social Psychology, 57,* 212–278.

Fridja, N. H., Kulpers, P., & ter Schure, E. (1989). Relations among emotion, appraisal and emotional action readiness. *Journal of Personality and Social Psychology, 57,* 212–228.

Fromm, E. (1975). *The art of loving.* New York: Harper and Row. (Original work published 1956)

Fudim, O. K. (1978). Sensory preconditioning of flavors with a formalin-produced sodium need. *Journal of Experimental Psychology: Animal Behavior Processes, 4*(3), 276–285.

Fuster, J. M. (2001). The prefrontal cortex: An update. Time is of the essence. *Neuron, 30,* 319–333.

Gadamer, H. G. (1986). *The relevance of the beautiful.* Cambridge, UK: Cambridge University Press.

Galef, B. G., Jr. (1986). Social interaction modifies learned aversions, sodium appetite, and both palatability and handling-time induced dietary preference in rats (Rattus norvegicus). *Journal of Comparative Psychology, 100,* 432–439.

Galef, B. G., Jr. (1996). Food selection: Problems in understanding how we choose foods to eat. *Neuroscience and Biobehavioral Review, 20,* 67–73.

Galef, B. G., & Whiskin, E. E. (2000). Social influences on the amount of food eaten by Norway rats. *Appetite, 34,* 327–332.

Gallagher, M., & Holland, F. C. (1994). The amygdala complex: Multiple roles in associative learning and emotion. *Proceedings of the National Academy of Science, 91,* 11771–11776.

Gallagher, S. (2001). The practice of mind: Theory, simulation or primary interaction? *Journal of Consciousness Studies, 8*(5–7), 83–108.

Gallagher, S., & Meltzoff, A. N. (1996). The earliest sense of self and others: Merleau-Ponty and recent developmental studies. *Philosophical Psychology, 9*(2), 211–233.

Gallese, V. (2001). The "shared manifold" hypothesis: From mirror neurons to empathy. *Journal of Consciousness Studies, 8*(5–7), 33–50.

Gallese, V., & Goldman, A. (1999). Mirror neurons and the simulation theory of mind reading. *Cognitive Science, 12,* 493–501.

Gallistel, C. R. (1992). *The organization of learning.* Cambridge, MA: MIT Press.

Gallistel, C. R. (2000). The replacement of general-purpose learning models with adaptively specialized learning modules. In M. S. Gazzaniga (Ed.), *The new cognitive neurosciences.* Cambridge, MA: MIT Press.

Garcia, J. (1989). Food for Tolman: Cognition and cathexis in concert. In T. Archer & L. Nilsson (Eds.), *Aversion, avoidance and anxiety.* Hillsdale, NJ: Erlbaum.

Garcia, J., Hankins, W. G., & Rusiniak, K. W. (1974). Behavioral regulation of the milieu interne in man and rat. *Science, 185,* 824–831.

Garcia, J., & Koelling, R. A. (1966). The relation of cue to consequence in avoidance learning. *Psychonomic Science, 4,* 123–124.

Gazzaniga, M. S. (2000). *The new cognitive neurosciences.* Cambridge, MA: MIT Press.

Gelman, S. A., Coley, J. D., & Gottfried, G. M. (1998). Essentialist beliefs in children: The acquisition of concepts and theories. In L. A. Hirschfeld & S. A. Gelman (Eds.), *Mapping the mind.* Cambridge, UK: Cambridge University Press.

Gelssmann, T. (2000). Gibbon songs and human music from an evolutionary persepctive. In N. L. Wallin, B. Merker, & S. Brown (Eds.), *The origins of music.* Cambridge, MA: MIT Press.

Gibson, J. J. (1966). *The senses considered as perceptual systems.* Boston: Houghton Mifflin.

Gibson, J. J. (1979). *The ecological approach to visual perception.* Boston: Houghton Mifflin.

Gigerenzer, G. (1991). From tools to theories: A heuristic of discovery in cognitive psychology. *Psychological Review, 98,* 254–267.

Gigerenzer. G. (1996). On narrow norms and vague heuristics: A reply to Kahneman and Tversky. *Psychological Review, 103,* 592–696.

Gigerenzer, G. (2000). *Adaptive thinking: Rationality in the real world.* New York: Oxford University Press.

Gigerenzer, G., & Selten, R. (Eds.). (2001). *Bounded rationality: The adaptive toolbox.* Cambridge, MA: MIT Press.

Gilbert, A. N., Fridlund, A. J., & Sabini, J. (1987). Hedonic and social determinants of facial displays to odors. *Chemical Senses, 12,* 355–363.

Gilbert, P., & Andrews, B. (1998). *Shame.* New York: Oxford University Press.

Gilligan, C. (1997). *In a different voice.* Cambridge, MA: Harvard University Press. (Original work published 1982)

Gloor, P. (1978). *Inputs and outputs of the amygdala: What the amygdala is trying to tell the rest of the brain.* New York: Wiley.

Gloor, P. (1997). *The temporal lobe and limbic system.* New York: Oxford University Press.

Gnepp, J., & Hess, D. (1986). Children's understanding of verbal and facial display rules. *Developmental Psychology, 22,* 103–109.

Goldberg, E. (2001). *The executive brain.* Oxford: Oxford University Press.

Goldie, P. (2002). *The emotions.* Oxford: Oxford University Press.

Goldman, A. (1979). Varieties of cognitive appraisal. *Nous, 13,* 23–38.

Goldman, A. (1992). Empathy, mind, and morals. *Proceedings and Addresses of the American Philosophical Association, 66*(3), 17–41.

Goldman, A. (2000). The mentalizing folk. In D. Sperber (Ed.), *Metarepresentations: A multidisciplinary perspective* (pp. 171–196). Oxford: Oxford University Press.

Goldman-Rakic, P. S. (1996). The prefrontal landscape: Implications of functional architecture for understanding human mentation and the central executive. *Philosophical Transactions of the Royal Society of London, 351,* 1445–1453.

Gombrich, E. H. (1978). *Meditations on a hobby horse.* New York: Dutton. (Original work published 1963)

Gopnik, A. (1993). How we know our minds: The illusion of first-person knowledge of intentionality. *Behavioral and Brain Sciences, 16,* 1–14.

Gopnik, A. (1996). The scientist as child. *Philosophy of Science, 63,* 485–514.

Gopnik, A. (2000). Explanation as organism and drive for causal knowledge: The function and evolution and phenomenology of the theory formation system. In F. C. Keil & R. Wilson (Eds.), *Explanation and cognition.* Cambridge, MA: MIT Press.

Gopnik, A., & Meltzoff, A. N. (1997). *Words, thoughts and theories.* Cambridge, MA: MIT Press.

Gopnik, A., & Wellman, H. (1992). Why the child's theory of mind really is a theory. *Mind and Language, 7,* 145–171. (Reprinted in M. Davies & T. Stone, Eds., *Folk psychology,* Oxford: Blackwell, 1995)

Gordon, R. (1992). The simulation theory: Objections and misconceptions. *Mind and Language, 7,* 11–34.

Gould, S. J. (2002). *The structure of evolutionary theory.* Cambridge, MA: Harvard University Press.

Grattan, L. M., Bloomer, R. H., Archambault, F. X., & Eslinger, P. J. (1994). Cognitive flexibility and empathy after frontal lobe lesions. *Neuropsychiatry, Neurology and Behavioral Neurology, 7,* 251–259.

Grattan, L. M., & Eslinger, P. J. (1989). Higher cognition and social behavior: Changes in cognitive flexibility and empathy after cerebral lesions. *Neuropsychology, 3,* 175–185.

Gray, J. A. (1987). *The psychology of fear and stress.* Cambridge, UK: Cambridge University Press. (Original work published 1971)

Gray, P. M., Krauss, B., Atema, J., Payne, R., Krumhanst, C., & Baptista, L. (2001). The music of nature and the nature of music. *Science, 291,* 52–56.

Gray, T. S. (1999). Functional and anatomical relationships among the amygdala, basal forebrain, central striatum and cortex. *Annals of the New York Academy of Sciences, 877,* 439–444.

Graybiel, A. M., Aosaki, T., Flaherty, A. W., & Kimura, M. (1994). The basal ganglia and adaptive motor control. *Science, 265,* 1826–1831.

Greene, J. D., & Haidt, J. (2002). How (and where) does moral judgment work? *Trends in Cognitive Science, 6,* 517–523.

Greene, J. D., Sommerville, R. B., Nystrom, L. E., Darley, J. M., & Cohen, J. D. (2001). An fMRI investigation of emotional engagement in moral judgment. *Science, 293,* 2105–2108.

Greenspan, P. S. (1995). *Practical guilt: Moral dilemmas, emotions and social norms.* New York: Oxford University Press.

Gregory, R. L. (1973). *Eye and brain: The psychology of seeing.* New York: McGraw-Hill.

Grill, H. J., & Norgren, R. (1978a). Neurological tests and behavioral deficits in chronic thalamic and chronic decerebrate rats. *Brain Research, 143,* 299–312.

Grill, H. J., & Norgren, R. (1978b). The taste reactivity test. 1. Mimetic responses to gustatory stimuli in neurologically normal rats. *Brain Research, 143*(2), 263–279.

Groenewegen, H. J., Berendse, H. W., Meredith, G. E., Haber, S. N., Voorn, P., Wolters, J. G., & Lohman, A. H. M. (1991). Functional anatomy of the ventral, limbic system-innervated striatum. In P. W. Scheel-Kruger (Ed.), *The mesolimbic dopamine system: From motivation to action* (pp. 19–59). Chichester, UK: Wiley.

Gurney, M., & Konishi, M. (1980). Hormone-induced sexual differentiation of brain and behavior in Zebra Finches. *Science, 208,* 380–384.

Hacking, I. (1979). *Logic of statistical inference.* Cambridge, UK: Cambridge University Press. (Original work published 1965)

Haidt, J. (2001). The emotional dog and its rational tail: A social intutionist approach to moral judgment. *Psychological Review, 108,* 814–834.

Haines, S. M., & Muir, D. W. (1996). Infant sensitivity to adult eye direction. *Child Development, 67,* 1940–1951.

Hajnal, A., & Norgren, R. (2001). Accumbens dopamine mechanisms in sucrose intake. *Brain Research, 904,* 76–84.

Hamann, S. B., Ely, T. D., Hoffman, J. M., & Kilts, C. D. (2002). Ecstasy and agony: Activation of the human amygdala in positive and negative emotion. *Psychological Science, 13,* 135–141.

Hanson, N. R. (1958). *Patterns of discovery.* Cambridge, UK: Cambridge University Press.

Harlow, J. M. (1993). Recovery from the passage of an ironbar through the brain. *History of Psychology, 4,* 274–281. (Original work published 1868)

Harnish, R. M. (2002). *Minds, brains and computers.* Oxford: Blackwell.

Harris, P. L. (1989). *Children and emotion: The development of psychological understanding.* Oxford: Blackwell.

Harris, P. L. (1992). From simulation to folk psychology. *Mind and Language, 7,* 120–144.

Harwood, K., Hall, L. J., & Shinkfield, A. J. (1999). Recognition of facial emotional expressions from moving and static displays by individuals with mental retardation. *American Journal of Mental Retardation, 104,* 270–278.

Hasselmo, M. E., Rolls, E. T., & Baylis, G. C. (1989). The role of expression and identity in the face-selective responses of neurons in the temporal visual cortex of the monkey. *Behavior and Brain Research, 32,* 203–219.

Hatfield, E., Cacioppo, J. T., & Rapson, R. L. (1994). *Emotional contagion.* New York: Cambridge University Press.

Hauser, M. D. (1993). Right hemisphere dominance for the production of facial expression in monkeys. *Science, 261,* 475–477.

Hauser, M. D., & Konishi, M. (2000). *The design of animal communication.* Cambridge, MA: MIT Press.

Hauser, M. D., & McDermott, J. (2003). The evolution of the music faculty. *Nature Neuroscience, 6,* 663–668.

Haxby, J. V., Gobbini, M. I., Furey, M. L., Ishai, A., Schouten, J. L., & Pietrini, P. (2001). Distributed and overlapping representations of faces and objects in ventral temporal cortex. *Science, 293,* 2473–2477.

Hebb, D. O. (1946). Emotion in the man and animal: An analysis of the intuitive processes of recognition. *Psychological Review, 53,* 88–106.

Hebb, D. O. (1949). *The organization of behavior.* New York: Wiley.

Heelan, P. A., & Schulkin, J. (1998). Hermeneutical philosophy and pragmatism: A philosophy of science. SYNTHESE, 115: 269–302.

Heider, F., & Simmel, M. (1944). An experimental study of apparent behavior. *American Journal of Psychology, 57,* 243–259.

Helmholtz, H. (1963). *Handbook of physiological optics.* New York: Dover. (Original work published 1867)

Herbert, J. (1993). Peptides in the limbic system: Neurochemical codes for co-ordinated adaptive responses to behavioral and physiological demand. *Progress in Neurobiology, 41,* 723–791.

Herbert, J., & Schulkin J. (2002). Neurochemical coding of adaptive responses in the limbic system. In D. Pfaff (Ed.), *Hormones, brain and behavior.* New York: Elsevier.

Herrick, C. J. (1905). The central gustatory pathway in the brain of body fishes. *Journal of Comparative Neurology, 15,* 375–486.

Herrick, C. J. (1929). Anatomical patterns and behavior patterns. *Physiological Zoology, 11,* 439–448.

Herrick, C. J. (1948). *The brain of the tiger salamander.* Chicago: University of Chicago Press.

Herrick, C. J. (1963). *Brain in rats and men.* New York: Hafner. (Original work published 1926)

Hess, W. R. (1957). *The functional organization of the diencephalon.* New York: Grune and Stratton.

Heywood, C. A., & Cowey, A. (1992). The role of the "face-cell" area in the discrimination and recognition of faces by monkeys. *Philosophical Transactions of the Royal Society of London, B: Biological Science, 335,* 31–37.

Hietanen, J. K., & Perrett, D. I. (1996). Motion sensitive cells in the macaque superior temporal polysensory area: Response discrimination between self-generated and externally generated pattern motion. *Behavioral Brain Research, 76,* 155–167.

Hinde, R. A. (1970). *Animal behavior: A synthesis of ethology and comparative psychology* (2nd ed.). New York: McGraw-Hill.

Hobbes, T. (1958). *Leviathan.* New York: Bobbs-Merrill. (Original work published 1651)

Hochschild, A. R. (1979). Emotion work, feeling rules, and social structure. *American Journal of Sociology, 85,* 551–575.

Hoffman, M. L. (1978). Empathy, its development and prosocial implications. In C. B. Keasey (Ed.), *Nebraska symposium on motivation* (Vol. 25). Lincoln: University of Nebraska Press.

Hoffman, M. L. (1984). Interaction of affect and cognition in empathy. In C. E. Izard, J. Kagan, & R. B. Zajonc (Eds.), *Emotions, cognition and behavior* (pp. 103–131). Cambridge, UK: Cambridge University Press.

Hoffman, M. L. (2002). *Empathy and moral development.* Cambridge, UK: Cambridge University Press.

Hoffner, C., & Badzinski, D. M. (1989). Children's integration of facial and situational cues to emotion. *Child Development, 60,* 411–422.

Holland, P. C., Chik, Y., & Zhang, Q. (2001). Inhibitory learning tests of conditioned stimulus associability in rats with lesions of the amygdala central nucleus. *Behavioral Neuroscience, 113,* 1154–1158.

Hollerman, J. R., Tremblay, L., & Schultz, W. (1998). Influence of reward expectation on behavior-related neuronal activity in primate striatum. *Journal Neurophysiology, 80,* 947–963.

Holt, D. J., Graybiel, A. M., & Saper, C. B. (1997). Neurochemical architecture of the human striatum. *Journal of Comparative Neurology, 384,* 1–25.

Hookway, C. (2000). *Truth, rationality and pragmatism.* Oxford: Oxford University Press.

Houser, N., & Kloesel, C. (1992). *The Essential Peirce Vol. 1.* Bloomington: Indiana University Press.

Houser, N., & Kloesel, C. (1998). *The Essential Peirce, Vol. 2.* Bloomington: Indiana University Press.

Hugo, V. (1986). *The hunchback of Notre Dame.* New York: Bantam. (Original work published 1831)

Hull, C. L. (1943). *Principles of behavior.* New York: Appleton.

Hume, D. (1984). *A treatise of human nature.* New York: Penguin Classics. (Original work published 1739)

Humphrey, D. (1959). *The art of making dances.* New York: Grove.

Humphrey, N. K. (1973). The illusion of beauty. *Perception, 2,* 429–439.

Humphrey, N. K. (1976). The social function of the intellect. In P. P. G. Bateson & R. A. Hinde (Eds.), *Growing points in ethology* (pp. 303–317). Cambridge, UK: Cambridge University Press.

Humphrey, N. K. (1999). Cave art, autism, and the evolution of mind. *Journal of Consciousness Studies, 6,* 12–20.

Humphreys, G. W., Donnelly, N., & Riddoch, M. J. (1993). Expression is computed separately from facial identity, and it is computed separately for moving and static faces: Neuropsychological evidence. *Neuropsychologia, 31,* 173–181.

Huron, D. (2001). Is music an evolutionary adaptation? In R. J. Zatorre & I. Peretz (Eds.), *The biological foundations of music.* New York: New York Academy of Sciences.

Iacoboni, M., Woods, R. P., Brass, M., Bekkering, H., Mazziotta, J. C., & Rizzolatti, G. (1999). Cortical mechanisms of imitation. *Science, 286,* 2526–2528.

Ikemoto, S., & Panksepp, J. (1999). The role of nucleus accumbens dopamine in motivated behavior: A unifying interpretation with special reference to reward seeking. *Brain Research Reviews, 31,* 1–41.

Ito, J. (1997). Relationship between inference of feeling and prosocial behavior in preschool children. *Japanese Journal of Developmental Psychology, 8,* 111–120.

Izard, C. E. (1971). *The face of emotion.* New York: Appleton-Century-Crofts.

Izard, C. E. (1993). Four systems of emotion. *Psychological Review, 100,* 68–90.

Izard, C. E., Fine, S., Schultz, D., Mostow, A., Ackerman, B., & Youngstrom, E. (2001). Emotion knowledge as a predictor of social behavior and academic competence in children at risk. *Psychological Sciences, 12,* 18–23.

Jackson, J. H. (1958a). Evolution and disollution of the nervous system; In *Selected Writings of John Hughlings Jackson.* London: Staples Press. (Original work published 1884)

Jackson, J. H. (1958b). *Selected writings of John Hughlings Jackson* (Vol. 1 and 2). London: Staples Press. (Original work published 1897)

James, W. (1952). *The principles of psychology.* New York: Dover. (Original work published 1890)

James, W. (1958). The function of cognition. In *Pragmatism.* New York: Meridian. (Original work published 1885)

Janzen, D. (1977). Why fruits rot, seeds mold and meat spoils. *American Naturalist, 111,* 691–713.

Jaspers, K. (1997). *General psychopathology.* Baltimore: Johns Hopkins University Press. (Original work published 1913)

Jeannerod, M. (1997). *The cognitive neuroscience of action.* Oxford: Blackwell.

Jeannerod, M. (1999). To act or not to act: Perspectives on the representation of action. *Quarterly Journal of Experimental Psychology, 52,* 1–29.

Johnson, M. (1990). *The body in the mind.* Chicago: University of Chicago Press.

Johnson, M. (1993). *Moral imagination.* Chicago: University of Chicago Press.

Johnson-Laird, P., & Oatley, K. (1992). Basic emotions, rationality and folk theory. *Cognition and Emotion, 6,* 201–223.

Jones, M. R. (1981). Music as a stimulus for psychological motion, part 1. *Psychomusicology, 1,* 34–51.

Jones, M. R. (1982). Music as a stimulus for psychological motion, part 2. *Psychomusicology, 2,* 1–13.

Jones, S. S., & Raag, T. (1989). Smile production in older infants: The importance of a social recipient for the facial signal. *Child Development, 60,* 811–818.

Juslin, P. N., & Sloboda, J. I. (2001). *Music and emotion.* Oxford: Oxford University Press.

Kagan, J. (1984). *The nature of the child.* New York: Basic Books.

Kagan, J. (1998). *Three seductive ideas.* Cambridge, MA: Harvard University Press.

Kagan, J. (2002). *Surprise, uncertainty and mental structure.* Cambridge, MA: Harvard University Press.

Kahneman, D., Diener, E., & Schwarz, N. (Eds.). (1999). *Well-being: The foundations of hedonic psychology.* New York: Russell Sage Foundation.

Kahneman, D., Fredrickson, B. L., Shreiber, C. A., & Redelmeier, D. A. (1994). When more pain is preferred to less: Adding to a better end. *Psychological Science, 4*(6), 401–405.

Kahneman, D., & Snell, J. S. (1992). Predicting a changing taste: Do people know what they will like? *Journal of Behavioral Decision Making, 5*(3), 187–200.

Kahneman, D., & Tversky, A. (1982). On the study of statistical intuitions. *Cognition, 11,* 123–141.

Kahneman, D., & Tversky, A. (1984). Choices, values, and frames. *American Psychologist, 39*(4), 341–350.

Kahneman, D., & Tversky, A. (1996). On the reality of cognitive illusions. *Psychological Review, 103,* 582–591.

Kamm, F. M. (1996). *Morality, morality. Vol. 2.* New York: Oxford University Press.

Kant, I. (1951). *Critique of judgement.* New York: Hafner. (Original work published 1792)

Kant, I. (1956). *Critique of practical reason.* New York: Bobbs Merrill. (Original work published 1788)

Kant, I. (1965). *Critique of pure reason.* New York: St. Martin's. (Original work published 1787)

Kaplan, A. S., & Murphy, G. L. (2000). Category learning with minimal prior knowledge. *Journal of Experimental Psychology: Learning, Memory, and Cognition, 26*(4), 829–846.

Kapp, B. S., Schwaber, J. S., & Driscoll, P. A. (1985). The organization of insular cortex projections to the amygdaloid central nucleus and autonomic regulatory nuclei of the dorsal medulla. *Brain Research, 360,* 355–360.

Katz, R. L. (1963). *Empathy.* New York: Free Press.

Kawashima, R., Sugiura, M., Kato, T., Nakamura, A., Hatan, K., Ito, K., Fukuda, H., Kojima, S., & Nakamura, K. (1999). The human amygdala plays an important role in gaze monitoring: A PET study. *Brain, 122,* 779–783.

Keil, F. C. (1989). *Concepts, kinds and cognitive development.* Cambridge, MA: MIT Press.

Keil, F. C., & Wilson, R. A. (Eds.). (2000). *Explanation and cognition.* Cambridge, MA: MIT Press.

Kelley, A. E. (1999). Neural integrative activities of nucleus accumbens subregions in relation to learning and motivation. *Psychobiology, 27*(2), 198–213.

Kihlstrom, J. F. (1987). The cognitive unconscious. *Science, 237*(4821), 1445–1452.

Kihlstrom, J. F., Mulvaney, S., Tobias, B. A., & Tobis, I. P. (2000). The emotional unconscious. In E. Eich (Ed.), *Cognition and emotion.* New York: Oxford University Press.

Kisilevsky, B., Hains, S., Lee, K., Muir, D., Xu, F., Fu, G., Zhao, Z., & Yang, R. (1997). *The still-face paradigm in Chinese infants interacting with their mother, father, and a stranger.* Paper presented at the biennial meeting of the Society for Research in Child Development, Washington, DC.

Kitcher, P. (1990). *Kant's transcendental psychology.* New York: Oxford University Press.

Kivy, P. (2001). *New essays on musical understanding.* Oxford: Oxford University Press.

Klahr, D. (2000). *Exploring science: The cognition and development of discovery processes.* Cambridge, MA: MIT Press.

Kling, A., & Cornell, R. (1971). Amygdalaectomy and social behavior in the caged stump-tailed macaque. *Folia Primatologica, 14,* 91–103.

Kluver, H. M., & Bucy, P. C. (1939). Preliminary analysis of functions of the temporal lobes in monkeys. *Archives of Neurology and Psychiatry, 42,* 979–1000.

Knoesche, T. R., Maess, B., & Friederici, A. D. (1999). Processing of syntactic information monitored by brain surface current density mapping based on MEG. *Brain Topography, 12*(2), 75–87.

Knowlton, B., Mangels, J., & Squire, L. (1996). A neostriatal habit learning system in humans. *Science, 273,* 1399–1402.

Koelsch, S. Gunter, T. C., Cramon, D. Y., Zysset, S., Lohmann, G., & Friederici, A. D. (2002). Bach speaks: A cortical "language-network" serves the processing of music. *Neuroimage, 17,* 956–966.

Koelsch, S., Gunter, T., Friederici, A. D., & Schröeger, E. (2000). Brain indices of music processing: "Non-musicians" are musical. *Journal of Cognitive Neuroscience, 12,* 520–541.

Koelsch, S., Maess, B., Gunter, T. C., & Friederici, A. D. (2001). Neapolitan chords activate the area of Broca: A magnetoencephalographic study. *Annals of the New York Academy of Sciences, 931,* 420–421.

Koelsch, S., Schroger, E., & Gunter, T. C. (2002). Music matters: Preattentive musicality of the human brain. *Psychophysiology, 39,* 38–48.

Konorski, J. (1967). *Integrative activity of the brain,* Chicago: University of Chicago Press.

Koob, G. F., & LeMoal, M. (2001). Drug addiction, dysregulation of reward and allostasis. *Neuropsychopharmacology, 24,* 94–129.

Kornblith, H. (1993). *Inductive inference and its natural ground.* Cambridge, MA: MIT Press.

Koslowski, B. (1996). *Theory and evidence*. Cambridge, MA: MIT Press.

Kosslyn, S. (1994). *Image and brain: The resolution of the imagery debate.* Cambridge, MA: MIT Press.

Kosslyn, S., Alpert, N., Thompson, W., Maljkovic, V., Weise, S., Chabris, C., Hamilton, S., Rauch, S., & Buannano, F. (1993). Visual mental imagery activates topographically organized visual cortex: PET investigations. *Cognitive Neuroscience, 5,* 263–287.

Krieckhaus, E. E. (1970). Innate recognition aids rats in sodium regulation. *Journal of Comparative and Physiological Psychology, 73,* 117–122.

Krieckhaus, E. E., & Wolf, G. (1968). Interaction of innate mechanisms and latent learning. *Journal of Comparative and Physiological Psychology, 65,* 197–201.

Kroglanski, A. (1989). *Lay epistemics and human knowledge: Cognitive and motivational biases.* New York: Plenum.

Krumhansl, C. L. (2002). Music: A link between cognition and emotion. *Psychological Science, 11,* 45–48.

Kuklick, B. (2001). *A history of philosophy in America.* Oxford: Oxford University Press.

LaBarbera, J. D., Izard, C. E., Vietze, P., & Parisi, S. A. (1976). Four- and six-month-old infants' visual responses to joy, anger, and neutral expressions. *Child Development, 47,* 535–438.

Ladygina-Kohts, N. N. (2002). *Infant chimpanzee and human child.* New York: Oxford University Press. (Original work published in 1935)

Lakoff, G., & Johnson, M. (1999). *Philosophy in the flesh.* New York: Basic Books.

Lakoff, G., & Nunez, R. E. (2000). *Where mathematics comes from.* New York: Basic Books.

Lane, R. D., Chau, P. M-L, & Dolan, R. J. (1999). Common effects of emotional valence, arousal and attention on neural activation during visual processing of pictures. *Neuropsychologia, 37,* 989–997.

Lane, R. D., & Nadel, L. (Eds.). (2000). *Cognitive neuroscience of emotion.* New York: Oxford University Press.

Lane, R. D., Reiman, E. M., Ahern, G. I., Schwartz, G. F. & Davidson, R. J. (1997). Neuroanatomical correlates of happiness, sadness, and disgust. *American Journal of Psychiatry, 154,* 7.

Lane, R. D., Reiman, E. M., Axelrod, B., Yun, L-S., Holmes, A., & Schwartz, G. E. (1998). Neural correlates of levels of emotional awareness: Evidence of an interaction between emotion and attention in the anterior cingulate cortex. *Journal of Cognitive Neuroscience, 10*(4), 525–535.

Lane, R. D., Reiman, E. M., Bradley, M. M., Lang, P. J., et al. (1997). Neuroanatomical correlates of pleasant and unpleasant emotion. *Neuropsychologia, 15*(11), 1437–1444.

Lang, P. J. (1995). The emotion probe. *American Psychologist, 56,* 372–385.

Langer, S. K. (1957). *Problems of art.* New York: Scribner.

Langer, S. K. (1972). *Mind: An essay on human feeling.* Baltimore: Johns Hopkins University Press.

Lashley, K. S. (1938). An experimental analysis of instinctive behavior. *Psychological Review, 45,* 445–471.

Lashley, K. S. (1951). The problem of serial order in behavior. In L. A. Jeffres (Ed.), *Cerebral mechanisms in behavior.* New York: Wiley.

Lashley, K. S. (1963). *Brain mechanisms and intelligence.* New York: Dover. (Original work published 1929)

Lazarus, R. S. (1984). On the primacy of cognition. *American Psychologist, 39,* 124–129.

Lazarus, R. S. (1991a). Cognition and motivation in emotion. *American Psychologist, 46,* 352–367.

Lazarus, R. S. (1991b). *Emotion and adaptation.* Oxford: Oxford University Press.

LeBon, G. (1896). *The crowd.* London: Ernest Benn.

LeDoux, J. E. (1993). Cognition vs. emotion again—this time in the brain: A response to Parrott and Schulkin. *Cognition and Emotion, 7,* 61–64.

LeDoux, J. E. (1996). *The emotional brain.* New York: Simon and Schuster.

LeDoux, J. E. (2000). Emotion circuits in the brain. *Annual Review of Neuroscience, 23,* 155–184.

LeDoux, J. E. (2001). The synaptic brain. New York: Random House.

Lee, K., Eskritt, M., Symons, L. A., & Muir, D. (1998). Children's use of triadic eye gaze information for "mind reading." *Developmental Psychology, 34,* 525–539.

Leibniz, G. W. (1982). *New essays on human understanding.* Cambridge, UK: Cambridge University Press. (Original work published 1765)

Lerdahl, F., & Jackendoff, R. (1999). *A generative theory of music.* Cambridge, MA: MIT Press.

Leslie, A. M. (1987). Pretense and representation: The origins of "theory of mind." *Psychological Review, 99,* 412–426.

Leventhal, J. (1982). The integration of emotion and cognition. In S. T. Fiske & S. Clarke (Eds.), *Affect and cognition.* Hillsdale, NJ: Erlbaum.

Lieberman, M. D. (2000). Intuition: A social cognitive neuroscience approach. *Psychological Bulletin, 126,* 109–137.

Lieberman, P. (2000). *Human language and our reptilian brain.* Cambridge, MA: Harvard University Press.

Linas, R. R. (2001). *I of the vortex.* Cambridge, MA: MIT Press.

Lind, R. W., Swanson, I. W., & Ganten, D. (1984a). Angiotensin 11 immunoreactivity in the neural afferents and efferents of the subfornical organ of the rat. *Brain Research, 321,* 209–215.

Lind, R. W., Swanson, L. W., & Ganten, D. (1984b). Organization of angiotensin immunoreactive cells and fibers in the rat central nervous system: An immunohistochemical study. *Neuroendocrinology, 40,* 2–24.

Liu, L., Ioannides A. A., & Streit, M. (1999). Single trial analysis of neurophysiological correlates of the recognition of complex objects and facial expressions of emotion. *Brain Topography, 11,* 291–303.

Locke, J. (1959). *An essay concerning human understanding* (A. C. Fraser, Ed.). New York: Dover. (Original work published 1690)

Loewenstein, G. (1994). The psychology of curiosity: A review and reinterpretation. *Psychological Bulletin, 116,* 75–98.

Loewenstein, G. (1996). Out of control: Visceral influences on behavior. *Organizational Behavior and Human Decision Making, 65,* 272–292.

Loewenstein, G., & Lerner, J. S. (2003). The role of affect in decision making. In R. J. Davidson et al. (Eds.), *Handbook of affective science.* New York: Oxford University Press.

Loewenstein, G., & Schkade, D. (1999). Wouldn't it be nice? Predicting future feelings. In D. Kahneman, E. Diener, & N. Scharwz (Eds.), *Foundations of hedonic psychology.* New York: Russell Sage Foundation.

Lorenz, K. Z. (1981). *The foundations of ethology.* New York: Springer-Verlag.

Lundy, R. F., & Norgren, R. (2001). Pontine gustatory activity is altered by electrical stimulation in the central nucleus of the amygdala. *American Journal of Physiology, 85,* 770–783.

Luyendijk, W., & Treffers, P. D. (1992). The smile in anencephalic infants. *Clinical Neurology and Neurosurgery, 94,* S113–S117.

MacIntosh, N. C. J. (1975). A theory of attention: Variations of associations of stimulus and reinforcment. *Psychological Review, 82,* 276–298.

MacLean, P. D. (1952). Some psychiatric implications of physiological studies on frontotemporal portion of limbic system (visceral brain). *Electroencephalography and Clinical Neurophysiology, 4,* 407–418.

MacLean, P. D. (1970). The triune brain, emotion and scientific bias. In F. O. Schmidt (Ed.), *The neurosciences study program.* New York: Rockefeller University Press.

MacLean, P. D. (1990). *The triune brain in evolution: Role in paleocerebral functions.* New York: Plenum.

MacMillan, M. (2000). *An odd kind of fame.* Cambridge, MA: MIT Press.

Maess, B., Koelsch, S., Gunter, T. C., & Friederici, A. D. (2001). Musical syntax is processed in Broca's area: An MEG study. *Nature Neuroscience, 4*(5), 540–545.

Maier, R. R. M., & Schnierla, T. C. (1964). *Principles of animal behavior.* New York: Dover. (Original work published in 1935)

Majzoub, J. A., McGregor, J. A., Lockwood, C. J., Smith, R., Taggart, M. A., & Schulkin, J. (1999). A central theory of term and preterm labor: Putative role of corticotrophin releasing hormone. *American Journal of Obstetrics and Gynecology, 180,* S232–S241.

Malle, B. F., Moses, L. J., & Baldwin, D. A. (2001). *Intentions and intentionality: Foundations of social cognition.* Cambridge, MA: MIT Press.

Mandler, G. (1999). Emotion. In D. E. Rumelhart (Ed.), *Cognitive science: Handbook on perception and cognition.* San Diego: Academic Press.

Manes, F., Sahakian, B., Clark, L., Rogers, R., Antoun, N., Aitken, M., & Robbins, T. (2002). Decision making processes following damage to the prefrontal cortex. *Brain, 125,* 624–639.

Markman, E. M. (1989). *Categorization and naming in children: Problems of induction.* Cambridge, MA: MIT Press.

Marler, P. (1961). The logical analysis of animal communication. *Journal of Theoretical Biology, 1,* 295–317.

Marler, P. (2000a). On innateness: Are sparrow songs learned or innate? In M. D. Hauser & M. Konishi (Eds.), *The design of animal communication.* Cambridge, MA: MIT Press.

Marler, P. (2000b). Origins of music and speech: Insights from animals. In N. L. Wallin, B. Merker & S. Brown (Eds.), *The origins of music.* Cambridge, MA: MIT Press.

Marler, P., & Hamilton, W. J. (1966). *Mechanisms of animal behavior*. New York: Wiley.

Marler, P., Peters, S., Ball, G. F., Duffy, A. M. Jr., & Wingfield, J. C. (1988). The role of sex steroids in the acquisition and production of birdsong. *Nature, 336*, 770–772.

Marsden, C. D. (1984), The pathophysiology of movement disorders. *Neurological Clinics, 2*, 435–459.

Martin, A. (1999). Organization and origins of semantic knowledge in the brain. In *The origins of language*. San Francisco: California Academy of Sciences.

Martin, A., & Caramazza, A. (2003). Neuropsychological and neuroimaging perspectives on conceptual knowledge. *Cognitive Neuropsychology, 3*, 195–212.

Mayr, E. (1960). The emergence of evolutionary novelties. In S. Tax (Ed.), *Evolution after Darwin, 1: The evolution of life* (pp. 349–382). Chicago: University of Chicago Press.

McCabe, K., House, D., Ryan, L., Smith, R., & Trouard, T. (2001). A functional imaging study of cooperation in two-person reciprocal exchange. *Proceedings of the National Academy of Science, 98*, 11832–11835.

McClelland, J. L., & Rumelhart, D. E. (1986). *Parallel distributed processing: Explorations in the microstructure of cognition. 2: Psychological and biological models*. Cambridge, MA: MIT Press.

McCulloch, W. S. (1988). *Embodiments of mind*. Cambridge, MA: MIT Press. (Original work published 1965)

McEwen, B. S. (2001). Neurobiology of interpreting and responding to stressful events: Paradigmatic role of the hippocampus. In *Coping with the Environment*. Oxford: Oxford University Press.

McGaugh, J. L., Cahill, L., & Rozzendaal, B. (1996). Involvement of the amygdala in memory strorage: Interactions with other brain systems. *Proceedings of the National Academy of Science, 93*, 13508–13514.

McGinn, C. (1999). *Ethics, evil and fiction*. Oxford: Clarendon.

McGinty, J. F. (1999). Advancing from the ventral striatum to the extended amygdala. *Annals of the New York Academy of Sciences, 87*, 129–139.

Mecklinger, A., Opitz, B., & Friederici, A. D. (1997). Semantic aspects of novelty detection in humans. *Neuroscience Letters, 235*(1–2), 65–68.

Mellers, B. A., Rapporteur, I. E., Fessler, D. M. T., Hemelrijk, C. K., Herwig, R., Laland, K. N., Scherer, K. R., Seeley, T. D., Selten, R., & Tetlock, P. E. (2001). Group report: Effects of emotions and social processes on bounded rationality. In G. Gigerenzer & R. Selten (Eds.), *Bounded rationality: The adaptive toolbox* (pp. 263–279). Cambridge, MA: MIT Press.

Mellers, B. A., Schwartz, A., & Ritov, I. (1999). Emotion-based choice. *Journal of Experimental Psychology: General, 128*, 332–345.

Meltzoff, A. N., & Brooks, R. (2001). "Like me" as a building block for understanding other minds: Bodily acts, attention and intention. In B. F. Malle, L. J. Moses, & D. A. Baldwin (Eds.), *Intentions and intentionality: Foundations of social cognition*. Cambridge, MA: MIT Press.

Meltzoff, A. N., & Moore, M. K. (1977). Imitation of facial and manual gestures by human neonates. *Science, 198*, 75–78.

Meltzoff, A. N., & Moore, M. K. (1997). Explaining facial imitation: A theoretical model. *Early Development and Parenting, 6,* 179–192.

Meltzoff, A. N., & Moore, M. K. (1999). Infant intersubjectivity: Broadening the dialogue to include imitation, identity and intention. In S. Braten (Ed.), *Intersubjective communication and emotion in early ontogeny.* Cambridge, UK: Cambridge University Press.

Merleau-Ponty, M. (1970). *Phenomenology of perception.* London: Routledge and Kegan Paul. (Original work published 1962)

Mesulam, M. M. (1998). From sensation to cognition. *Brain, 121,* 1013–1052.

Mesulam, M. M. (1999). Spatial attention and neglect: Parietal, frontal and cingulate contributions to the mental representations and attentional targeting of salient extrapersonal events. *Philosophical Transactions of the Royal Society of London, 354,* 1325–1346.

Metcalf, J., & Mischel, W. (1999). A hot/cool-system analysis of delay of gratification: Dynamics of willpower. *Psychological Review, 106,* 3–19.

Meyer, L. B. (1956). *Emotion and meaning in music.* Chicago: University of Chicago Press.

Meyer, L. B. (1967). *Music, the arts and ideas.* Chicago: University of Chicago Press.

Meyer, L. B. (1973). *Explaining music.* Chicago: University of Chicago Press.

Meyer, L. B. (2001). Music and emotion: Distinctions and uncertainities. In P. N. Juslin & J. A. Sloboda (Eds.), *Music and emotion.* Oxford: Oxford University Press.

Mill, J. S. (1861). *Utilitarianism.* London: Parker, Son, and Bourn.

Miller, G. A., Galanter, E., & Pribram, K. H. (1960). *Plans and the structure of behavior.* New York: Holt, Rinehart and Winston.

Miller, N. E. (1957). Experiments of motivation: Studies combining psychological, physiological, and pharmacological techniques. *Science, 126,* 1271–1278.

Miller, N. E. (1959). Liberalization of basic S-R concepts: Extensions to conflict behavior, motivation and social learning. In S. Koch (Ed.), *Psychology: A study of a science* (Vol. 2). New York: McGraw-Hill.

Miller, N. E. (1965). Chemical coding of behavior in the brain. *Science, 148,* 328–338.

Miller, R. E., Banks, J., & Ogawa, N. (1963). Role of facial expression in "cooperative avoidance conditioning" of rhesus monkeys. *Journal of Abnormal and Social Psychology, 67,* 24–30.

Miller, W. I. (1997). *The anatomy of disgust.* Cambridge, MA: Harvard University Press.

Mirsky, I. A., Miller, R. E., & Murphy, J. V. (1958). The communication of affect in rhesus monkeys. *Journal of the American Psycholanalytic Association, 6,* 433–441.

Mishkin, M., & Petri, H. L. (1984). Memories and habits: Some implications for the analysis of learning and retention. In N. Butters & L. R. Squire (Eds.), *Neuropsychology of memory* (pp. 287–296). New York: Guilford.

Mistlberger, R. E. (1992). Anticipatory activity rhythms under daily schedules of water access in the rat. *Journal of Biological Rhythms, 7,* 149–160.

Mithen, S. (1988). Looking and learning: Upper Paleolithic art and information gathering. *World Archaeology, 19,* 297–327.

Mithen, S. (1996). *The prehistory of the mind.* London: Thames and Hudson.

Moga, M. M., Herbert, H., Hurley, K. M., Yasui, Y., Gray, T. S., & Saper, C. B. (1990). Organization of cortical, basal forebrain, and hypothalamic afferents to the parabrachial nucleus in the rat. *Journal of Comparative Neurology, 295,* 624–661.

Moga, M. M., Saper, C. B., & Gray, T. S. (1990). Neuropeptide organization of the hypothalamic projection to the parabrachial nucleus in the rat. *Journal of Comparative Neurology, 295,* 662–682.

Mogenson, G. J., Jones, D. L., & Yim, C. Y. (1980). From motivation to action: Functional interface between the limbic system and the motor system. *Progress in Neurobiology, 14,* 69–97.

Mogenson, G. J., Swanson L. W., & Su, M. (1983). Neural projections from nucleus accumbens to globus pallidus, substantia innominata, and lateral preoptic-lateral hypothalamic area: An anatomical and electrophysiological investigation in the rat. *Journal of Neuroscience, 3,* 189–202.

Mogenson, G. J., Swanson, L. W., & Wu, M. (1985). Evidence that projections from substantia innominata to zona incerta and mesencephalic locomotor region contribute to locomotor activity. *Brain Research, 334,* 65–76.

Moll, J., Eslinger, P. J., & Oliveira-Souza, R. (2001). Frontopolar and anterior temporal cortex activation in a moral judgment: Preliminary functional MRI results in normal subjects. *Arquivos de Neuro-Psiquiatria, 59,* 657–664.

Moll, J., Oliveira-Souza, R., & Eslinger, P. J. (2003). Morals and the human brain: A working model. *Neuroreport, 14,* 299–305.

Moll, J., Oliveira-Souza, R., Eslinger, P. J., Bramati, I., Miradna-Mourao, J., Angelo- Andreiolo P., & Pessoa, L. (2002). The neural correlates of moral sensitivity: A functional magnetic resonance imaging investigation of basic and moral emotions. *Journal of Neuroscience, 22,* 2730–2736.

Monahan, J. L., Murphy, S. T., & Zajonc, R. B. (2000). Subliminal mere exposure. *Psychological Science, 11,* 462–466.

Montgomery, D. E., Bach, L. M., & Moran, C. (1998). Children's use of looking behavior as a cue to detect another's goal. *Child Development, 69,* 692–705.

Moore, G. E. (1968). *Principia ethica.* Cambridge, UK: Cambridge University Press. (Original work published 1903)

Moran, T. H., & Schulkin, J. (2000). Curt Richter and regulatory physiology. *American Journal of Physiology, 279,* R357–R363.

Morgan, C. T. (1966). The central motive state. In D. Bindra & J. Stewart (Eds.), *Motivation.* Baltimore: Penguin.

Morgan, C. T., & Stellar, E. (1950). *Physiological psychology* (2nd ed.). New York: McGraw Hill.

Morris, J. S., Friston, K. J., Buchel, C., Frith, C. D., Young, A. W., Calder, A. J., & Dolan, R. J. (1998). A neuromodulatory role for the human amygdala in processing emotional facial expressions. *Brain, 121,* 47–57.

Morris, J. S., Frith, C. D., Perrett, D. I., Rowland, D., Young, A. W., et al. (1996). A differential neural response in the human amygdala to fearful and happy facial expressions. *Nature, 383,* 812–815.

Morris, J. S., Ohman, A., & Dolan, R. J. (1998). Conscious and unconscious emotional learning in the human amygdala. *Nature, 393*(6684), 467–470.

Morris, J. S., Ohman, A., & Dolan, R. J. (1999). A subcortical pathway to the right amygdala mediating "unseen" fear. *Proceedings of the National Academy of Sciences USA, 96*(4), 1680–1685.

Morris, J. S., Scott, S. K., & Dolan, R. J. (1999). Saying it with feeling: Neural responses to emotional vocalizations. *Neuropsychologia, 37*(10), 1155–1163.

Mumme, D. L., Fernald, A., & Herrera, C. (1996). Infants' responses to facial and vocal emotional signals in a social referencing paradigm. *Child Development, 67,* 3219–3237.

Murphy, G. I. (2000). Explanatory concepts. In F. C. Keil & R. A. Wilson (Eds.), *Explanation and cognition.* Cambridge, MA: MIT Press.

Murphy, G. L. (2003). *The big book of concepts.* Cambridge, MA: MIT Press.

Nakamura, K., Kawashima, R., Ito, K., Sugiura, M., Kato, T., Nakamura, A., Hatano, K., Nagumo, S., Kubota, K., Fukuda, H., & Kojima, S. (1999). Activation of the right inferior frontal cortex during assessment of facial emotion. *Journal of Neurophysiology, 82,* 1610–1614.

Narmour, E. (1991). The top-down and bottom-up systems of musical implication: Building on Meyer's theory of emotional syntax. *Music Perception, 9,* 1–26.

Nauta, W. J. H. (1971). The problem of the frontal lobe: A reinterpretation. *Journal of Psychiatric Research, 8,* 167–187.

Nauta, W. J. H., & Domesick, V. B. (1982). Neural associations of the limbic system. In *The neural basis of behavior.* New York: Spectrum.

Nauta, W. J. H., & Feirtag, M. (1986). *Fundamental neuroanatomy.* San Francisco: Freeman.

Nauta, W. J. H., & Haymaker, W. (1969). Hypothalamic nuclei and fiber connections. In W. Haymaker, E. Anderson, & W. J. H. Nauta (Eds.), *The hypothalamus.* Springfield: Charles C. Thomas.

Neisser, U. (1994). Multiple systems: A new approach to cognitive theory. *European Journal of Cognitive Psychology, 6,* 225–241.

Neville, R. C. (1978). *Soldier, sage, saint.* New York: Fordham University Press.

Newell, A. (1990). *Unified theories of cognition.* Cambridge, MA: Harvard University Press.

Nisbett, R. E., & Wilson, T. D. (1977). Telling more than we can know: Verbal reports on mental processes. *Psychological Review, 84,* 231–259.

Nitabach, M., Schulkin, J., & Epstein, A. N. (1989). The medial amygdala is part of a mineralocorticoid sensitive circuit for NaCl intake. *Behavioral Brain Research, 15,* 197–204.

Norgren, R. (1976). Taste pathways to hypothalamus and amygdala. *Journal of Comparative Neurology, 166,* 17–30.

Norgren, R. (1995). Gustatory system. In *The rat nervous system* (2nd ed., pp. 751–771). San Diego: Academic Press.

Norgren, R., & Wolf, G. (1975). Projections of thalamic gustatory and lingual areas in the rat. *Brain Research, 92,* 123–129.

Norten, R. E. (1995). *The beautiful soul.* Ithaca, NY: Cornell University Press.

Nowicki, S., & Mitchell, J. (1998). Accuracy in identifying affect in child and adult faces and voices and social competence in preschool children. *Genetic, Social, and General Psychology Monographs, 124,* 39–59.

Nowlis, G. H. (1977). From reflex to representation: Taste-elicited tongue movements in the human newborn. In J. M. Weiffenbach (Ed.), *Taste and development.* Washington, DC: U.S. Department of Health, Education and Welfare.

Nussbaum, M. C. (1994). *The therapy of desire.* Princeton: Princeton University Press.

Nussbaum, M. C. (2001). *Upheavals of thought: The intelligence of emotion.* Cambridge, UK: Cambridge University Press.

Oatley, K., & Jenkins, J. M. (1996). *Understanding emotion.* Oxford: Oxford University Press.

O'Connell, S. M. (1995). Empathy in chimpanzees: Evidence for theory of mind? *Primates, 36,* 397–410.

O'Doherty, J., Kringelbach, M. L., Rolls, E. T., Hornak, J., & Andrews, C. (2001). Abstract reward and punishment representations in the human orbitofrontal cortex. *Nature Neuroscience, 4,* 95–102.

Oehman, A. (1997). As fast as the blink of an eye: Evolutionary preparedness for preattentive processing of threat. In P. J. Lang & R. F. Simons (Eds.), *Attention and orienting: Sensory and motivational processes* (pp. 165–184). Mahwah, NJ: Erlbaum.

Olds, J., & Milner, P. (1954). Positive reinforcement produced by electrical stimulation of septal area and other regions of rat brain. *Journal of Comparative and Physiological Psychology, 47,* 419–427.

Olson, K. R., & Camp, C. J. (1984). Curiosity and need for cognition. *Psychological Reports, 34,* 491–497.

Omdahl, B. L. (1995). *Cognitive appraisal, emotion and empathy.* Hillsdale, NJ: Erlbaum.

Opitz, B., Mecklinger, A., Friederici, A. D., & von Cramon, D. Y. (1999). The functional neuroanatomy of novelty processing: Integrating ERP and fMRI results. *Cerebral Cortex, 9,* 379–391.

Ortony, A., Clore, G. L., & Collins, A. (1988). *The cognitive structure of emotions.* Cambridge, UK: Cambridge University Press.

Ortony, A., & Turner, T. J. (1990). What's basic about basic emotions? *Psychological Review, 97,* 315–331.

O'Scalaidhe, S. P., Wilson, F. A., & Goldman-Rakic, P. S. (1997). A real segregation of face-processing neurons in prefrontal cortex. *Science, 278,* 1135–1138.

Osterhout, L., & Holcomb, P. J. (1993). Event-related potential and syntactic anomaly: Evidence of anomaly detection during the perception of continuous speech. *Language and Cognitive Processes, 8,* 413–437.

Panksepp, J. (1982). Toward a general psychobiological theory of emotions. With commentaries. *Behavioral and Brain Sciences, 5,* 407–467.

Panksepp, J. (1990). Gray zones at the emotion/cognition interface: A commentary. *Cognition and Emotion, 4,* 289–302.

Panksepp, J. (1993). The emotional sources of chills induced by music. *Perception, 13,* 171–207.

Panksepp, J. (1998). *Affective neuroscience.* New York: Oxford University Press.

Panksepp, J., & Panksepp, J. B. (2000). The seven sins of evolutionary psychology. *Evolution and Cognition, 6,* 108–131.

Papez, J. W. (1937). A proposed mechanism of emotion. *Archives of Neurological Psychiatry, 38,* 725–743.

Parkinson, J. A., Crofts, H. S., McGuigan, M., Tomic, D. L. Everitt, B. J., & Roberts, A. C. (2001). The role of the amygdala in conditioned reinforcement. *Journal of Neuroscience, 21,* 7770–7780.

Parrott, W. G., & Sabini, J. (1989). On the "emotional" qualities of certain types of cognition: A reply to arguments for the independence of cognition and affect. *Cognitive Therapy and Research, 13,* 49–65.

Parrott, W. G., & Schulkin, J. (1993). Neuropsychology and the cognitive nature of emotions. *Cognition and Emotion, 7,* 43–59.

Parsons, L. M. (2001). Exploring the functional neuroanatomy of music performance, perception and comprehension. In R. J. Zatorre & I. Peretz (Eds.), *The biological foundations of music.* New York: New York Academy of Sciences.

Pascal, B. (1962). *Pensées.* Paris: Editions du Seuil. (Original work published 1669)

Patel, A. D. (2003). Language, music, syntax and the brain. *Nature Neuroscience, 6,* 674–681.

Patel, A. D., Gibson, E., Ratner, J., Besson, M., & Holcomb, P. (1998). Processing syntactic relations in language and music: An event-related potential study. *Journal of Cognitive Neuroscience, 10,* 717–733.

Paus, T. (2001). Primate anterior cingulate cortex: Where motor control, drive and cognition interface. *Nature Neuroscience, 2,* 417–424.

Peirce, C. S. (1868a). Questions concerning certain faculties claimed for man. *Journal of Speculative Philosophy, 2,* 103–114.

Peirce, C, S. (1868b). Some consequences of four incapacaties. *Journal of Speculative Philosophy, 2,* 140–157.

Peirce, C. S. (1877). The fixation of belief. *Popular Science Monthly, 12,* 1–15.

Peirce, C. S. (1878). Deduction, induction and hypothesis. *Popular Science Monthly, 13,* 470–482.

Peirce, C. S. (1992a). *The essential Peirce. Vol. 1: 1867–1893.* Bloomington: Indiana University Press.

Peirce, C. S. (1992b). *Reasoning and the logic of things.* Cambridge, MA: Harvard University Press. (Original work published 1898)

Pelchat, M. L., Grill, H. J., Rozin, P., & Jacobs, J. (1983). Quality of acquired responses to tastes by Rattus Norvegicus depends on type of associated discomfort. *Journal of Comparative Psychology, 97,* 140–153.

Pennebaker, J. W., & Chew, C. H. (1985). Behavioral inhibition and electrodermal activity during deception. *Journal of Personality and Social Psychology, 49,* 1427–1433.

Peretz, I. (2001). Listen to the brain: A biological perspective on musical emotions. In P. N. Juslin & J. A. Sloboda (Eds.), *Music and emotion.* Oxford: Oxford University Press.

Peretz, I., & Zattore, R. (2003). *The cognitive neuroscience of music.* Oxford: Oxford University Press.

Perlstein, W. M., Elbert, T., & Stenger, A. (2002). Dissociation in human prefrontal cortex of affective influences on working memory-related activity. *Proceedings of the National Academy of Science, 99,* 1736–1741.

Perner, J. (1991). *Understanding the representational ,ind.* Cambridge, MA: MIT Press.

Perrett, D. I., Harries, M., Bevan, R., Thomas, S., Benson, P., Mistlin, A., Chitty, A., Hietanen, J., & Ortega, J. (1989). Frameworks of analysis for the neural representation of animate objects and actions. *Journal of Experimental Biology, 146,* 87–113.

Perrett, D. I., & Mistlin, A. (1990). Perception of facial characteristics by monkeys. In W. Stebbins & M. Berkeley (Eds.), *Comparative perception, Vol. 2: Complex signals* (pp. 187–215). New York: Wiley.

Perrett, D. I., Smith, P. A., Potter, D. D., Mistlin, A. J., Head, A. S., Milner, A. D., & Jeeves, M. A. (1984). Neurons responsive to faces in the temporal cortex: Studies of functional organization, sensitivity to identity and relation to perception. *Human Neurobiology, 3,* 197–208.

Perrett, D. I., Smith, P. A., Potter, D. D., Mistlin, A. J., Head, A. S., Milner, A. D., & Jeeves, M. A. (1985). Visual cells in the temporal cortex sensitive to face view and gaze direction. *Proceedings of the Royal Society of London, B. Biological Science, 223,* 293–317.

Petr, J., Birk, J. L., Van Horn, J. D., Marc, L., Tillman, B., & Bharucha, J. J. (2002). The cortical topography of tonal structures underlying Western music. *Science, 298,* 2167–2170.

Petrovich, G. D., Canteras, N. W., & Swanson, L. W. (2001). Combinatoral amygdalar inputs to hippocampal domains and the hypothalamic behavior systems. *Brain Research Reviews, 38,* 247–289.

Pfaff, D. W. (1999). *Drive.* Cambridge, MA: MIT Press.

Pfaffmann, C. (1960). The pleasures of sensation. *Psychological Review, 67,* 253–268.

Pfaffmann, C., Norgren, R., & Grill, H. J. (1977). Sensory affect and motivation. In B. M. Wenzel & H. P. Ziegler (Eds.), *Tonic function of sensory systems.* New York: New York Academy of Sciences.

Phillips, M. L., Bullmore, E. T., Howard, R., Woodruff, P. W., Wright, I. C., Williams, S. C., Simmons, A., Andrew, C., Brammer, M., & David, A. S. (1998). Investigation of facial recognition memory and happy and sad facial expression perception: An fMRI study. *Psychiatry Research, 83,* 127–138.

Phillips, M. L, Young, A. W., Scott, S. K., Calder, A. J., Andrew, C., Giampietro, V., Williams, S. C., Bullmore, E. T., Brammer, M., & Gray, J. A. (1998). Neural responses to facial and vocal expressions of fear and disgust. *Proceedings of the Royal Society, 265,* 1809–1817.

Phillips, M. L., Young, A. W., Senior, B., Brammer, M., Andrew, C., Calder, A. J., Bullmore, E. T., Perrett, D. I., Rowland, D., Williams, S. C. R., Gray, J. A., & David, A. S. (1997). A specific neural substrate for perceiving facial expression of disgust. *Nature, 389,* 495–498.

Piaget, J. (1932). *The moral judgement of the child.* New York: Free Press.

Piaget, J. (1952). *The origins of intelligence in children.* New York: International Universities Press.

Pick, A. D., Gross, D., Heinrichs, M., Love, M., et al. (1994). Development of perception of the unity of musical events. *Cognitive Development, 9*(3), 355–375.

Pinker, S. (1994). *The language instinct.* New York: Morrow.

Pinker, S. (1997). *How the mind works.* New York: Norton.

Pizarro, D. A., & Bloom, P. (2002). The intelligence of the moral intuitions: Comments on Haidt. *Psychological Review, 110,* 193–196.

Popper, K. (1959). *The logic of scientific discovery.* London: Hutchinson.

Porter, S., Woodworth, M., & Birt, A. R. (2000). Truth, lies, and videotape: An investigation of the ability of federal parole officers to detect deception. *Law and Human Behavior, 24,* 643–658.

Posner, M. I. (1990). *Foundations of cognitive science.* Cambridge, MA: MIT Press.

Povinelli, D. J. (2000). *Folk physics for apes.* Oxford: Oxford University Press.

Povinelli, D. J. (2001). On the possibilities of detecting intentions prior to understanding them. In B. F. Malle, L. J. Moses, & D. A. Baldwin (Eds.), *Intentions and intentionality: Foundations of social cognition.* Cambridge, MA: MIT Press.

Powley, T. L., Martinson, F. A., Phillips, R. J., Jones, S., Baronowsky, E. A., & Swithers, S. E. (2001). Gastrointestinal projection maps of the vagus nerve are specified permanently in the perinatal period. *Developmental Brain Research, 129,* 570–572.

Prechtl, J. C., & Powley, T. L. (1990). B-afferents: A fundamental division of the nervous system mediating homeostasis. *Behavioral and Brain Sciences, 13,* 289–331.

Premack, D., & Premack, A. (2003). *Original intelligence.* New York: McGraw-Hill.

Premack, D., & Woodruff, G. (1978). Does the chimpanzee have a theory of mind? *Behavioral and Brain Sciences, 1,* 515–526.

Preston, S. D., & De Waal, F. B. M. (2002). Empathy: Its ultimate and proximate bases. *Behavioral and Brain Research, 25,* 1–72.

Pribam, K. H. (1969). The primate prefrontal cortex. *Neuropsychologia, 7,* 259–266.

Prinz, J. J. (2002). *Furnishing the mind.* Cambridge, MA: MIT Press.

Pritchard, T. C., Hamilton, R. B., & Norgren, R. (2000). Projections of the parabrachial nucleus in the old world monkey. *Experimental Neurology, 165,* 101–117.

Puce, A., Allison, T., Bentin, S., Gore, J. C., & McCarthy, G. (1998). Temporal cortex activation in humans viewing eye and mouth movements. *Journal of Neuroscience, 18,* 2188–2199.

Pylyshyn, Z. W. (1999). Is vision continuous with cognition? The case for cognitive impenetrability of visual perception. *Behavioral and Brain Sciences, 22,* 341–423.

Quine, W. V. O. (1961). Two dogmas of empiricism. In *From a logical point of view* (2nd ed., pp. 20–46). New York: Harper and Row.

Raffmann, D. (1993). *Language, music, and mind.* Cambridge, MA: MIT Press.

Raine, A., Stoddard, J., Bihrle, S., & Buchsbaum, M. (1998). Prefrontal glucose deficits in murderers lacking psychosocial deprivation. *Neuropsychiatry, Neuropsychology and Behavioral Neurology, 11,* 1–7.

Ramachadran, V. S., & Hirstein, W. (1999). The science of art. *Journal of Consciousness Studies, 6,* 15–51.

Rauschecker, J. P. (2001). Cortical plasticity and music. In R. J. Zatorre & I. Peretz (Eds.), The biological foundations of music. *Annals of the New York Academy of Sciences, 930,* 330–336.

Reid, T. (1969). *Essays on the intellectual powers of man.* Cambridge, MA: MIT Press. (Original work published 1785)

Repacholi, B. M. (1998). Infants' use of attentional cues to identify the referent of another person's emotional expression. *Developmental Psychology, 34,* 1917–1925.

Rescorla, R. A. (1981). Simultaneous associations. In P. Harzem & M. D. Zeller (Eds.), *Probability, correlations and contiguity.* New York: Wiley.

Rescorla, R. A. (1988). Pavlovian conditioning. *American Psychologist, 43,* 151–160.

Rescorla, R. A. (1990). The role of information about the response-outcome relation in instrumental discrimination learning. *Journal of Experimental Psychology: Animal Behavior Processes, 16*(3), 262–270.

Rescorla, R. A., & Wagner, A. R. (1972). A theory of Pavlovian conditioning: Variations in the effectiveness of reinforcement and non-reinforcment. In W. J. Baker & W. Prokasy (Eds.), *Classical conditioning: Current research and theory.* New York: Appleton-Century-Crofts.

Rey, G. (1980). Functionalism and the emotions. In A. O. Rorty (Ed.), *Explaining emotions.* Berkeley: University of California Press.

Rey, G. (1997). *Contemporary philosophy of mind.* Oxford: Oxford University Press.

Richter, C. P. (1942–1943). Total self-regulatory functions in animals and human beings. *Harvey Lectures, 38,* 367–371.

Richter, C. P. (1957). Phenomena of sudden death in animals and man. *Psychosomatic Medicine, 19,* 191–198.

Richter, C. P. (1976). *The psychobiology of Curt Richter* (E. M. Blass, Ed.). Baltimore: York Press.

Rolls, E. T. (1996). The orbitofrontal cortex. *Philosophical Transactions of the Royal Society of London, 351,* 1433–1444.

Rolls, E. T. (1999). *The brain and emotion.* New York: Oxford University Press.

Rolls, E. T. (2000). The orbitofrontal cortex and reward. *Cerebral Cortex, 10*(3), 284–294.

Rorty, R. (1999). *Contigency, irony and solidarity.* Cambridge, UK: Cambridge University Press. (Original work published in 1989)

Rosch, E. H. (1973). Natural categories. *Cognitive Psychology, 4,* 328–350.

Rosch, E. H. (1978). Principles of categorization. In E. Rosch & B. B. Lloyd (Eds.), *Cognition and categorization* (pp. 27–48). Hillsdale, NJ: Erlbaum.

Rosen, J. B., & Schulkin, J. (1998). From normal fear to pathological anxiety. *Psychological Review, 104,* 325–350.

Rosenstein, D., & Oster, H. (1988). Differential facial responses to four basic tastes in newborns. *Child Development, 59,* 1555–1568.

Rousseau, J. J. (1964). *First and second discourses.* New York: St. Martin's. (Original work published 1755)

Rowlands, M. (1999). *The body in mind: Understanding cognitive processes.* Cambridge, UK: Cambridge University Press.

Royzman, E. B., & Sabini, J. (2001). Something it takes to be an emotion: The interesting case of disgust. *Journal for the Theory of Social Behavior, 31,* 25–59.

Rozin, P. (1976a). The evolution of intelligence and access to the cognitive unconscious. In J. Sprague & A. N. Epstein (Eds.), *Progress in psychobiology and physiological psychology.* New York: Academic Press.

Rozin, P. (1976b). The selection of foods by rats, humans, and other animals. In J. S. Rosenblatt, R. A. Hinde, E. Shaw, & C. Beer (Eds.), *Advances in the study of behavior* (Vol. 6). New York: Academic Press.

Rozin, P. (1998). Evolution and development of brains and cultures: Some basic principles and interactions. In M. S. Gazzaniga & J. S. Altman (Eds.), *Brain and mind: Evolutionary perspectives.* Strassbourg: Human Frontiers Science Program.

Rozin, P. (1999). The process of moralization. *Psychological Science, 10,* 218–221.

Rozin, P., & Fallon, A. E. (1987). A perspective on disgust. *Psychological Review, 94,* 23–41.

Rozin, P., Haidt, J., & McCauley, C. R. (1993). Disgust. In M. Lewis & J. M. Haviland (Eds.), *Handbook of emotions.* New York: Guilford.

Rozin, P., & Schulkin, J. (1990). Food selection. In E. M. Stricker (Ed.), *Handbook of behavioral neurobiology.* New York: Plenum.

Ruby, P., & Decety, J. (2001). Effects of subjective perspective during simulation of action: A PET investigation of agency. *Nature Neuroscience, 4,* 546–550.

Rzoska, J. (1953). Bait shyness, a study in rat behaviour. *British Journal of Animal Behaviour, 1,* 128–135.

Sabini, J., & Silver, M. (1982). *Moralities of everyday life.* Oxford: Oxford University Press.

Sabini, J., & Silver, M. (1998). *Emotion, character and responsibility.* Oxford: Oxford University Press.

Saper, C. B. (1982a). Convergence of autonomic and limbic connections in the insular cortex of the rat. *Journal of Comparative Neurology, 210,* 163–173.

Saper, C. B. (1982b). Reciprocal parabrachial cortical connections in the rat. *Brain Research, 242,* 33–40.

Saper, C. B. (1995). Central autonomic system. In G. Paxinos (Ed.), *The rat nervous system.* New York: Academic Press.

Saper, C. B. (1996). Role of the cerebral cortex and striatum in emotional motor response. In C. B. Saper (Ed.), *Progress in brain research.* New York: Elsevier.

Saper, C. B., Loewy, A. D., & Cowan, W. M. (1976). Direct hypothalamic-autonomic connections. *Brain Research, 117,* 305–312.

Sartre, J. P. (1973). *Being and nothingness.* New York: Washington Square Press. (Original work published 1943)

Scalera, G., Spector, A. C., & Norgren, R. (1995). Excitotoxic lesions of the parabrachial nuclei prevent conditioned taste aversions and sodium appetite in rats. *Behavioral Neuroscience, 109,* 997–1008.

Scarry, E. (1985). *The body in pain.* Oxford: Oxford University Press.

Schacter, S. (1975). Cognition and peripheralist-centralist controversies in motivation and emotion. In M. S. Gazzaniga & C. Blakemore (Eds.), *Handbook of psychobiology*. New York: Academic Press.

Schachter, S., & Singer, J. E. (1962). Cognitive, social and physiological determinants of emotional state. *Psychological Review, 69,* 379–399.

Scheler, M. (1970). *The nature of sympathy.* Hamden, CT: Archon. (Original work published 1954)

Scheler, M. (1992). *On feeling, knowing and valuing.* Chicago: University of Chicago Press.

Scherer, K. R. (1988). *Facets of emotion.* Hillsdale, NJ: Erlbaum.

Scherer, K. R., Schorr, A., & Johnstone, T. (Eds.). (2001). *Appraisal processes in emotion.* New York: Oxford University Press.

Schiller, F. (1980). *On the aesthetic education of man.* New York: Frederick Ungar. (Original work published 1795)

Schmidt. L. A., & Fox, N. A. (1999). Conceptual, biological and behavioral distinctions among shy children. In L. A. Schmidt & J. Schulkin (Eds.), *Extreme fear, shyness and social phobia.* New York: Oxford University Press.

Schmidt, L. A., & Trainor, L. J. (2001). Frontal brain electrical activity distinguishes valence and intensity of musical emotions. *Cognition and Emotion, 15,* 487–500.

Schnierla, T. C. (1959). An evolutionary and developmental theory of diphasic processes underlying approach and withdrawal. In *The Nebraska Symposium on Motivation.* Lincoln: University of Nebraska Press.

Schopenhauer, A. (1965). *On the basis of morality.* Indianapolis: Bobbs-Merrill. (Original work published 1841)

Schulkin, J. (1991). *Sodium hunger.* New York: Cambridge University Press.

Schulkin, J. (1996a). *The delicate balance.* Lanham, MD: University Press of America.

Schulkin, J. (1996b). Eliot Stellar. *National Academy of Sciences, 69,* 1–10.

Schulkin, J. (1999). *The neuroendocrine regulation of behavior.* New York: Cambridge University Press.

Schulkin, J. (2000). *Roots of social sensibility and neural function.* Cambridge, MA: MIT Press.

Schulkin, J. (2002). Psychobiological basis of empathy. *Behavioral and Brain Sciences, 25,* 46–47.

Schulkin, J. (2003). *Rethinking homeostasis: Allostasis regulation in physiology and patophysiology.* Cambridge, MA: MIT Press.

Schulkin, J., Arnell, P., & Schulkin, J. (1985). Running to the taste of salt in mineralocorticoid treated rats. *Hormones and Behavior, 19,* 413–425.

Schultz, W. (2002). Getting formal with dopamine and reward. *Neuron, 36,* 241–263.

Schultz, W., Dayan, P., & Montague, P. R. (1997). A neural substrate of prediction and reward. *Science, 275,* 1593–1599.

Schutz, A. (1967). *The phenomenology of the social world.* Evanston, IL: Northwestern University Press.

Schwaber, J. S., Kapp, B. S., Higgins, G. A., & Rapp, P. R. (1982). Amygdaloid and basal forebrain direct connections with the nucleus of the solitary tract and the dorsal motor nucleus. *Journal of Neuroscience, 2,* 1424–1438.

Schwartz, D. A., Howe, C. O., & Purves, D. (2003). The statistical structure of human speech sounds predicts musical universals. *Journal of Neuroscience, 21,* 7166–7168.

Schwarz, N. (1990). Feelings as information: Informational and motivational functions of affective states. In *Handbook of motivation and cognition: Foundations of social behavior* (Vol. 2, pp. 527–561). New York: Guilford.

Searle, J. R. (1984a). *Intentionality: An essay in the philosophy of mind.* New York: Cambridge University Press.

Searle, J. R. (1984b). *Minds, brains and science.* Cambridge, MA: Harvard University Press.

Searle, J. R. (2001). *Rationality and action.* Cambridge, MA: MIT Press.

Selfe, L. (1977). *Nadia: A case of extraordinary drawing ability in an autistic child.* London: Academic Press.

Selfe, L. (1983). *Normal and anomalous representational drawing ability in children.* London: Academic Press.

Sellar, W. (1963). *Science, perception and reality.* Altantic Heights, NJ: Humanities Press.

Sellars, W. (1968). *Science and metaphysics.* New York: Humanities Press.

Sellars, W. (1997). *Empiricism and the philosophy of mind.* Cambridge, MA: Harvard University Press. (Original work published 1956)

Sergent, J. (1993). Music, the brain and Ravel. *Trends in Neuroscience, 16,* 168–172.

Sergent, J., Zuck, E., Terriah, S., & MacDonald, B. (1992). Distributed neural network underlying musical-sight reading and keyboard performance. *Science, 257,* 106–109.

Serrano, J. M., Iglesias, J., & Loeches, A. (1992). Visual discrimination and recognition of facial expressions of anger, fear, and surprise in 4- to 6-month-old infants. *Developmental Psychobiology, 25,* 411–425.

Shepard, R. N. (1984). Ecological constraints on internal representation: Resonant kinematics of perceiving, imagining, thinking, and dreaming. *Psychological Review, 91,* 417–444.

Shepard, R. N. (1994). *The mesh between mind and world.* Cambridge, MA: Harvard University Press.

Shettleworth, S. J. (1998). *Cognition, evolution, and behavior.* New York: Oxford University Press.

Shidara, M., & Richmond, B. J. (2002). Anterior cingulate: Single neuronal signals related to degree of reward expectancy. *Science, 296,* 1709–1711.

Shweder, R. A., Mahapatra, M., & Miller, J. G. (1987). *Culture theory: Essay on mind, self and emotion.* Cambridge, UK: Cambridge University Press.

Shweder, R. A., Much, N. C., Mahapatra, M., & Park, L. (1997). The "big three" of morality (autonomy, community, and divinity), and the "big three" explanations of suffering. In A. Brandt & P. Rozin (Eds.), *Morality and health* (pp. 119–169). New York: Routledge.

Sidgwick, H. (1981). *The method of ethics.* Indianapolis: Hackett. (Original work published 1874)

Siegel, S., & Allan, L. G. (1998). Learning and homeostasis: Drug addiction and the McCollough effect. *Psychological Bulletin, 124,* 230–239.

Simon, H. A. (1956). Rational choice and the structure of environments. *Psychological Review, 63,* 129–138.

Simon, H. A. (1967). Motivational and emotional controls of cognition. *Psychological Review, 74*, 29–39.

Simon, H. A. (1979). Information processing models of cognition. *Annual Review of Psychology, 30*, 363–396.

Simon, H. A. (1982). *Models of bounded rationality.* Cambridge, MA: MIT Press.

Simon, H. A. (1983). *Models of bounded rationality* (Vol. 1). Cambridge, MA: MIT Press.

Simon, H. A. (1992). What is an "explanation" of behavior? *Psychological Science, 3*, 150–161.

Sloboda, J. (1985). *The musical mind: The cognitive psychology of music.* New York: Oxford University Press.

Sloboda, J. (2000). *Generative processes in music.* Oxford: Oxford University Press.

Small, D. M., Zatorre, R. J., Dagher, A., Evans, A. C., & Gotman, M. J. (2001). Changes in brain activity related to eating chocolate: From pleasure to aversion. *Brain, 124*, 1720–1733.

Smith, A. (1976). *A theory of moral sentiments.* Oxford: Oxford University Press. (Original work published 1759)

Smith, J. D. (1987). Conflicting aesthetic ideals in a musical culture. *Music Perception, 4*, 373–392.

Smith, J. D. (1997). The place of musical novices in music science. *Music Perception, 54*, 227–262.

Smith, J. D., & Melara, R. J. (1990). Aesthetic preference and syntactic prototypicality in music. *Cognition, 34*, 279–298.

Soken, N. H., & Pick, A. D. (1999). Infants' perception of dynamic affective expressions: Do infants distinguish specific expressions? *Child Development, 70*, 1275–1282.

Sokolov, E. N. M. (1963). *Perception and the conditioned reflex.* Oxford: Pergamon.

Solomon, R. C. (1980). Emotions and choice. In A. O. Rorty (Ed.), *Explaining emotions* (pp. 251–281). Berkeley: University of California Press.

Solomon, R. C. (1990). *Love.* New York: Prometheus.

Solomon, R. C. (Ed.). (1999). *Wicked pleasures.* Oxford: Roman Litteford.

Spanagel, R., & Weiss, R. (1999). The dopamine hypothesis of reward: Past and current status. *Trends in Neuroscience, 22*, 521–527.

Spector, A. C. (1995). Gustatory function in parabrachial nuclei: Implications from lesion studies. *Revolutions in Neuroscience, 6*, 143–175.

Spector, A. C., Norgren, R., & Grill, H. J. (1992). Parabrachial gustatory lesions impair taste aversion learning in rats. *Behavioral Neuroscience, 106*, 147–161.

Spencer, H. (1890). *First principles.* New York: Collier. (Original work published 1857)

Spinoza, B. (1955). *On the improvement of the understanding.* New York: Dover. (Original work published 1668)

Sprengelmeyer, R., Rausch, M., Eysel, U. T., & Przuntek, H. (1998). Neural structures associated with recognition of facial expressions of basic emotions. *Proceedings of the Royal Society of London B, Biological Sciences, 265*, 1927–1931.

Squire, L., Knowlton, B., & Musen, G. (1993). The structure and organization of memory. *Annual Review of Psychology, 44,* 453–495.

Stein, E. (1964). *On the problem of empathy* (W. Stein, Trans.). The Hague: Martinus Nijhoff.

Steiner, J. E. (1973). The gustofacial response: Observation on normal and anencephalic newborn infants. *Symposium on Oral Sensation and Perception, 4,* 254–278.

Steiner, J. E. (1974). Innate, discriminative human facial expressions to taste and smell stimulation. *Annals of the New York Academy of Sciences, 237,* 229–223.

Steiner, J. E., Glaser, D., Hawilo, M. E., & Berridge, K. C. (2001). Comparative expression of hedonic impact: Affective reactions to taste by human infants and other primates. *Neuroscience and Biobehavioral Reviews, 25,* 53–74.

Stellar, E. (1954). The physiology of motivation. *Psychological Review, 61,* 5–22.

Stellar, E. (1974). Brain mechanisms in hunger and other hedonic experiences. *Proceedings of the American Philosophical Society, 118,* 276–282.

Stellar, E., & Stellar, E. (1985). *The neurobiology of reward.* Berlin: Springer-Verlag.

Sterling, P., & Eyer, J. (1988). Allostasis: A new paradigm to explain arousal pathology. In S. Fisher & J. Reason (Eds.), *Handbook of life stress, cognition, and health.* New York: Wiley.

Sternberg, R. J. (1999). *The nature of cognition.* Cambridge, MA: MIT Press.

Stevenson, C. L. (1944). *Ethics and language.* New Haven: Yale University Press.

Stitch, S. P., & Nichols, S. (1995). Second thoughts on simulation. In M. Davies & T. Stone (Eds.), *Mental simulation.* London: Blackwell.

Strand, F. L. (1999). *Neuropeptides.* Cambridge, MA: MIT Press.

Sullivan, J. W. N. (1955). *Beethoven.* New York: Vintage.

Swain, J. (1997). *Musical languages.* London: Norton.

Swanson, L. W. (1999). The neuroanatomy revolution of the 1970s and the hypothalamus. *Brain Research Bulletin, 50,* 397–398.

Swanson, L. W. (2000a). The cerebral hemisphere regulation of motivated behavior. *Brain Research, 836,* 113–164.

Swanson, L. W. (2000b). What is the brain? *Trends in Neural Science, 23,* 519–527.

Swanson, L. W. (2003). *Brain architecture.* Oxford: Oxford University Press.

Swanson, L. W., & Petrovich, G. D. (1998). What is the amygdala? *Trends in Neural Science, 21,* 323–331.

Swanson, L. W., Sawchenko, P. E., Rivier, J., & Vale, W. W. (1983). Organization of ovine corticotropin releasing hormone immunoreactive cells and fibers in the rat brain: An immunohistochemical study. *Neuroendocrinology, 36,* 165–186.

Symonds, M., Hall, G., & Bailey, G. K. (2002). Perceptual learning with a sodium depletion procedure. *Journal of Experimental Psychology, 28,* 190–199.

Thayer, J. F., & Lane, R. D. (2000). A model of neurovisceral integration in emotion regulation and dysregulation. *Journal of Affective Disorders, 61,* 201–216.

Thompson, E. (2001). Empathy and consciousness. *Journal of Consciousness Studies, 8*(5–7), 1–32.

Thompson, E., & Varela, F. J. (2001). Radical embodiment: Neural dynamics and conscious experience. *Trends in Cognitive Science, 5,* 418–425.

Thompson, E., & Varela, F. J. (in press). *Why the mind isn't in the head.*
Cambridge, MA: Harvard University Press.

Thompson, J. (1976). Killing, letting die and the trolley car problem. *The
Monist, 54,* 204–217.

Thorndike, E. L. (1911). *Animal intelligence.* New York: Macmillan.

Thorpe, W. H. (1974). *Animal nature and human nature.* New York:
Anchor.

Tinbergen, N. (1969). *The study of instinct.* Oxford: Oxford University Press.
(Original work published 1951)

Titchner, E. B. (1910). *A textbook of psychology.* New York: Macmillan.

Toates, F. (1986). *Motivational systems.* Cambridge, UK: Cambridge University Press.

Tolman, E. C. (1949). *Purposive behavior in animals and man.* Berkeley:
University of California Press.

Tomasello, M. (1999). *The cultural origins of human cognition.* Cambridge,
MA: Harvard University Press.

Tomasello, M., & Call, J. (1997). *Primate cognition.* New York: Oxford University Press.

Tomkins, S. S. (1962). *Affect, imagery, consciousness: Vol. 1. The positive
affects.* New York: Springer-Verlag.

Tomkins, S. S. (1963). *Affect, imagery, consciousness: Vol. 2. The negative
affects.* New York: Springer-Verlag.

Travers, J. B., Urbanek, K., & Grill, H. J. (1999). Fos-like immunoreactivity
in the brain stem following oral quinine stimulation in decerebrate rats.
American Journal of Physiology, 277, R384–R394.

Tremblay, L., Hollerman, J. R., & Schultz, W. (1998). Modifications of reward expectation-related neuronal activity during learning in primate
striatum. *Journal of Neurophysiology, 80,* 964–977.

Trivers, R. L. (1971). The evolution of reciprocal altruism. *Quarterly Review
of Biology, 46,* 35–57.

Troland, L. T. (1928). *The fundamentals of human motivation.* New York:
Van Nostrand.

Turing, A. M. (1950). Computing machinery and intelligence. *Mind, 59,* 433–
460.

Turner, J. (2000). *On the origins of human emotion.* Stanford: Stanford
University Press.

Ullman, M. T. (2001). A neurocognitive perspective on language: The de-
clarative/procedural model. *Nature Reviews Neuroscience, 2,* 717–726.

Ullman, M. T., Corkin, S., Coppola, M., Hickok, G., Growdon, H., Horoshe,
W. J., & Pinker, S. (1997). A neural dissociation within language: Evidence
that the mental dictionary is part of declarative memory, and that gram-
matical rules are processed by the procedural system. *Journal of Cognitive Neuroscience, 9,* 266–286.

Urmson, J. O. (1968). *The emotive theory of ethics.* Oxford: Oxford University Press.

Valenstein, E. S. (1973). *Brain control*. New York: Wiley.

Valenstein, E. S., Cox, E. S., & Kakolewski, J. K. (1970). Reexamination of the role of the hypothalamus in motivation. *Psychological Review, 77,* 16–31.

Van der Kooy, D. D., Koda, L. Y., McGinty, J. F., Gerfen, C. R., & Bloom, F. E. (1984). The organization of projections from the cortex, amygdala and hypothalamus to the nucleus of the solitary tract in the rat. *Journal of Comparative Neurology, 224,* 1–24.

Varela, F. J., Thompson, E., & Rosch, E. (1991). *The embodied mind*. Cambridge, MA: MIT Press.

von Bonin, G. (1960). *Some papers on the cerebral cortex*. Trans. from French and German. Springfield, IL: Charles C. Thomas.

Von Neuman, J. (2000). *The computer and the brain*. New Haven: Yale University Press. (Original work published 1958)

Wagner, H., & Lee, V. (1999). Facial behavior alone and in the presence of others. In P. Philippot & R. S. Feldman (Eds.), *The social context of nonverbal behavior*. New York: Cambridge University Press.

Walden, T. A., & Field, T. M. (1982). Discrimination of facial expressions by preschool children. *Child Development, 53,* 1312–1320.

Wallin, N. L., Merkre, B., & Brown, S. (2000). *The origins of music*. Cambridge, MA: MIT Press.

Waxman, S. R. (1999). The dubbing ceremony revisited: Object naming and categorization in infancy and early childhood. In D. L. Medin & S. Altran (Eds.), *Folkbiology*. Cambridge, MA: MIT Press.

Weber, C. O. (1931). Esthetics of rectangles and theories of affect. *Journal of Applied Psychology, 15,* 310–318.

Weddell, R. A., Miller, J. D., & Trevarthen, C. (1990). Voluntary emotional facial expressions in patients with focal cerebral lesions. *Neuropsychologia, 28,* 49–60.

Weiskrantz, L. (1956). Behavioral changes associated with ablation of the amygdaloid complex in monkeys. *Journal of Comparative Physiology and Psychology, 49,* 381–389.

Weiskrantz, L. (1997). *Consciousness lost and found*. Oxford: Oxford University Press.

Weissman, D. (1996). Metaphysics. In D. Weissman (Ed.), *Descartes*. New Haven: Yale University Press.

Weissman, D. (2003). *Lost souls*. Albany: State University of New York Press.

Wellman, H. M. (1990). *The child's theory of mind*. Cambridge, MA: MIT Press.

Wellman, H. M., Hickling, A. K., & Schult, C. A. (1997). Young children's psychological, physical and biological explanations. In H. Wellman & K. Inagaki (Eds.), *The emergence of core domains of thought*. San Francisco: Jossey-Bass.

Wellman, H. M., & Phillips, A. T. (2001). Developing intentional understandings. In B. F. Malle, L. J. Moses, & D. A. Baldwin (Eds.), *Intentions and intentionality: Foundations of social cognition*. Cambridge, MA: MIT Press.

Wellman, H. M., Phillips, A. T., & Rodriguez, T. (2000). Young children's understanding of perception, desire, and emotion. *Child Development, 71,* 895–912.

Whaling, C. (2000). What is behind song: The neural basis of song learning in birds. In N. L. Wallin, B. Marker, & S. Brown (Eds.), *The origins of music.* Cambridge, MA: MIT Press.

Whiten, A., & Custance, D. (1996). Studies of imitation in chimpanzees and children. In C. M. Heyes & B. G. Galef Jr. (Eds.), *Social learning in animals: The roots of culture* (pp. 291–318). New York: Academic Press.

Wicker, B., Michel, F., Henaff, M. A., & Decety, J. (1998). Brain regions involved in the perception of gaze: A PET study. *Neuroimage, 8,* 221–227.

Wilson, J. S. (1993). *The moral sense.* New York: Basic Books.

Wilson, J. S. (1995). *On character.* Washington, DC: American Enterprise Institute.

Wilson, R. A., & Keil, F. C. (2000). The shadows and shallows of explanation. In F. C. Keil & R. A. Wilson (Eds.), *Explanation and cognition.* Cambridge, MA: MIT Press.

Wilson, T. D., Lindsey, S., & Schooler, T. Y. (2000). A model of dual attitudes. *Psychological Review, 107*(1), 101–126.

Wilson, T. D., & Schooler, T. Y. (1991). Thinking too much: Introspection can reduce the quality of preferences and decisions. *Journal of Personality and Social Psychology, 60*(2), 181–192.

Winkielman, P., Zajonc, R. B., & Schwartz, N. (1997). Subliminal affective priming resists attributional interventions. *Cognition and Emotion, 11,* 433–465.

Winnerm, G., & Perner, J. (1983). Beliefs about beliefs: Representation and constraining function of wrong beliefs in young children's understanding of deception. *Cognition, 13,* 103–128.

Wirsig, C. R., & Grill, H. J. (1982). Contribution of the rat's neocortex to ingestive control: Latent learning for the taste of NaCl. *Journal of Comparative and Physiological Psychology, 96,* 615–627.

Wise, R. A. (2002). Brain reward circuitry: Insights from unsensed incentives. *Neuron, 36,* 229–240.

Wittgenstein, L. (1953). *Philosophical investigations.* New York: Macmillan.

Wolf, G. (1969). Innate mechanisms for regulation of sodium intake. In C. Pfaffmann (Ed.), *Olfaction and taste.* New York: Rockefeller University Press.

Wolf, G. (1981). Psychological physiology from the standpoint of physiological psychology. *Process Studies, 10,* 274–291.

Wollheim, R. (1999). *On the emotions.* New Haven: Yale University Press.

Woods, S. C. (1991). The eating paradox: How we tolerate food. *Psychological Review, 98,* 488–505.

Wright, C. L., Fischer, H., Whalen, P. J., McInerney, S. C., Shin, L. M., & Rauch, S. L. (2001). Differential prefrontal cortex and amygdala habituation to repeatedly presented emotional stimuli. *Neuroreport, 12,* 378–383.

Wylie, D. R., & Goodale, M. A. (1988). Left-sided oral asymmetries in spontaneous but not posed smiles. *Neuropsychologia, 26,* 823–832.

Yamamoto, T., Shimura, T., Sako, N., Yasoshima, Y., & Sakai, N. (1994). Neural substrates for conditioned taste aversion in the rat. *Behavioural Brain Research, 65,* 123–37.

Yamane, S., Kaji, S., & Kawano, K. (1988). What facial features activate face neurons in the inferotemporal cortex of the monkey? *Experimental Brain Research, 73,* 209–214.

Young, A. W. (1998). *Face and mind.* Oxford: Oxford University Press.

Young, P. T. (1959). The role of affective processes in learning and motivation. *Psychological Review, 66,* 104–125.

Zaid, D. H., Lee, J. T., Fluegel, K. W., & Pardo, J. V. (1998). Aversive gustatory stimulation activates limbic circuits in humans. *Brain, 121,* 1143–1154.

Zajonc, R. B. (1964). Attitudinal effects of mere exposure. *Journal of Personality and Social Psychology, 9* (Monograph Suppl. 2 Pt. 2).

Zajonc, R. B. (1980). Feeling and thinking: Preferences need no inferences. *American Psychologist, 35,* 151–175.

Zajonc, R. B. (1984). On the primacy of affect. *American Psychologist, 39,* 117–123.

Zajonc, R. B. (2000). Feeling and thinking: Closing the debate over the independence of affect. In J. P. Forgas (Ed.), *Feeling and thinking: The role of affect in social cognition* (pp. 31–58). Cambridge, UK: Cambridge University Press.

Zajonc, R. B. (2001). Mere exposure: A gateway to the subliminal. *Psychological Science, 10,* 227–231.

Zatorre, R. J., & Krumbansl, C. L. (2002). Mental models and musical minds. *Science, 298,* 2138–2139.

Zattore, R. J., & Peretz, I. (2001). *The biological foundations of music.* New York: Annals of the New York Academy of Sciences.

Zeki, S. (1999). *Inner vision.* Oxford: Oxford University Press.

Zeki, S. (2001). Artistic creativity and the brain. *Science, 293,* 51–52.

Zeman, J., & Garber, J. (1996). Display rules for anger, sadness and pain: It depends on who is watching. *Child Development, 67,* 957–973.

Index